STRUGGLING WITH
THE DEMON

STRUGGLING WITH THE DEMON

*Perspectives on Individual
and
Organizational Irrationality*

Manfred F. R. Kets de Vries

Psychosocial Press
Madison, Connecticut

Library of Congress Cataloging-in-Publication Data

Kets de Vries, Manfred F. R.
    Struggling with the demon : perspectives on individual and organizational irrationality /
    Manfred F. R. Kets de Vries.
        p. cm.
    Includes bibliographical references and index.
    ISBN 1-887841-42-3
        1. Leadership. 2. Organizational behavior. 3. Psychology, Industrial. I. Title.

BF637.L4.K4 2000
302.3—dc21
                                                                00-046004

Manufactured in the United States of America

To Katharina

An artist in "the topsy turvy." Whatever you did, it taught me a great deal about myself.

Table of Contents

Acknowledgments

If there is one red thread that ties this book together, it is the theme of leadership. It is a topic that has intrigued me since I was quite young. I remember being around 14 years old when I learned my first important lesson in leadership and group psychology. I was with my brother in a youth camp in the center of the Netherlands where we went every summer. While most children were sent to this camp for only three weeks, we were sent there for the whole summer. After a three-week period, there would be a transition—the old group of children would leave and be replaced by a new group. Of course, when the new group arrived my brother and I were the "old timers"—we knew the ropes. The year I was 14, I decided to liven up the changeover. I came up with the idea of introducing an initiation ritual for the new arrivals. To make this a particularly memorable event we placed a bathtub filled with ice cold water in front of the dormitory. All the newcomers were told that it was an old tradition to dunk themselves in the tub. I can still clearly remember more than 60 boys (most of them much bigger than the two of us) lining up, and, one after another, obediently immersing themselves in the cold water. Everything went well until the headmaster of the camp passed by. He was completely dumbfounded. He broke our spell by inciting the newcomers to rebel, pointing out that they were 60 against the two of us, and encouraged them to give us a taste of our own medicine. After a prolonged struggle we got our deserved punishment. The memory has remained, however, of how two small boys with tremendous determination and powers of persuasion were able to get a large group of children to submit themselves to such an unpleasant experience. It is a scene that has become etched in my "inner theater."

Although writing may seem a very individual activity, this incident indicates that an author draws largely upon experiences he relives in his inner world—a richness of inner images that parades before him. The children I described above set me on a quest to understand leadership, but the images of leadership in my inner theater have been refined and clarified in the process of writing this book by specific people to whom I am emotionally and intellectually indebted. Given the "crowd scene," it is difficult to thank everyone who—directly or indirectly—has contributed to this book. If there is one group of people, however, among this considerable cast of characters, that specifically deserves my gratitude, it is the participants in my various programs who helped to further develop my ideas. I am thinking in particular of the executives who shared their life stories in a top management program that I direct every year at INSEAD called "The Challenge of Leadership: Developing your Emotional Intelligence." The etymological root of the word *emotion* is *motere*—meaning "to move." The many questions raised in this seminar moved *me* as well as the participants. Although it sounds paradoxical, nothing is more stimulating than being asked questions to which one has no immediate answers. The life stories of my participants taught me to live with ambiguity and tolerate a lack of closure concerning (in many instances) very puzzling situations. Many of the issues raised and examined in this leadership seminar are echoed in this book.

A special person who "moved" me is Kathy Reigstad, my cheerful "virtual" editor who lives a continent away. I very much appreciate her creativity in reformulating my rather Dutch sentence constructions. To continue singling out specific people, I am very thankful for the contribution of Katharina Balazs to the chapter on downsizing. Her survey of this (at times) rather tedious literature certainly simplified my life. Two other people deserve my special gratitude for facilitating the writing process—my research associate, Elizabeth Florent-Treacy, and my secretary, Sheila Loxham. Both of them shield me from many of the more pedestrian pressures that intrude into academic life. I also want to express my appreciation to the support given to my work by members of the faculty at INSEAD—particularly the past and present associate deans of research and development, Landis Gabel and Luk van Wassenhove, and the former dean of INSEAD, Antonio Borges. In addition, I want to express my gratitude toward Allison James, INSEAD's R & D administrator, who always has been extremely helpful and supportive. I would like to thank my wife and children for their patience and good cheer in dealing with an "eccentric" husband and father. Last, but certainly not least, I would like to thank my brother Florian for being a true supporter not only in my youthful pranks but also in my present endeavors.

Manfred F. R. Kets de Vries

Introduction

What was your vaunted seercraft ever worth?
And where were you, when the Dog-faced Witch was here?
Had you any word of deliverance then for our people?
There *was a riddle too deep for common wits;*
A seer should have answered it; but answer came there none
From you; bird-lore and god-craft all were silent.
Until I came—I, ignorant Oedipus, came—
And stopped the riddler's mouth, guessing the truth
By mother-wit, not bird-lore. This is the man
Whom you would dispossess . . . .
(Sophocles, *Oedipus the King*)

I do not know whether I was then a man dreaming I was a butterfly, or
whether I am now a butterfly dreaming I am a man.
(Chuang Tse)

Man errs as long as he strives.
(Goethe, *Faust*)

Behave as you usually do; that is already crazy enough.
(Dutch proverb)

Is what you see what you get? Is the manifest behavior of people the only dimension that counts? Are we simply black boxes that process inputs and outputs? Some students of human behavior subscribe with conviction to this point of view. Interested only in the obvious, they embrace the premise that what cannot be directly observed does not exist. Unable to accept the possibility that they are not completely aware of everything they do, they hold to the illusion of being in control. Admitting that they lack complete control over their own actions would simply

1

be too great a narcissistic injury, would cause too much emotional discomfort. People who hold to this viewpoint would rather not look at what is inside the black boxes of humanity, apparently afraid that probing within would give rise to too many disturbing thoughts and feelings.

Beyond the Black Box

In hanging on to the illusion of rational human action—the idea that human beings can be "managed" around simple stimulus–response models—people are taking the easy road, as is their aim; but they are also taking the less scenic road. In sticking to the obvious and the banal, they lose out on the richness of human behavior. Their argument, in its most extreme form, is "That which cannot be seen does not exist." In this highly mechanical, two-dimensional view of humanity, the intrapsychic world of the individual—the richness of a person's inner theater or mental map—is oversimplified or totally disregarded. Yet that individuality is there: within each black box there is a highly complex person, one whose ways of dealing with processes such as perception, learning, and memory are highly variable. Reducing human beings to simple calculators of pleasures and pains results in an incomplete explanation of human behavior and action; it leaves a gap between assumed rational decision-making patterns and what actually happens. Not surprisingly, this discrepancy between rational action and reality—the latter characterized by subjectively determined self-interests and individual motivations—has led to an increasing awareness of the oversimplicity of this approach.

To understand what is happening inside the human box, we have to cast beyond that traditional behavioral paradigm. We need to familiarize ourselves with contributions from domains such as dynamic psychiatry, developmental psychology, ethology, neurophysiology, cognitive theory, psychoanalytic psychology, family systems theory, and individual and group psychotherapy. These areas of study, all of which offer great insights into the vicissitudes of human behavior, need to be explored in our attempts to arrive at accurate explanations of what motivates people. Only by distilling the wisdom gleaned by all of these approaches can we capture the richness of human behavior.

By using concepts taken from these fields of research, we can identify a number of motivational need systems that influence human behavior and that capture the complexity of each individual. These motivational systems are the driving forces that make people tick, the determinants of each person's inner script.

Infant observation and research, clinical experience with people of all ages, and neurophysiological findings indicate that human beings go through a number of developmental steps associated with these need systems in developing a sense of self (Lichtenberg, 1989). Each of these need systems is operational starting at infancy and continues throughout the life cycle, altered by the forces of age, learning, and maturation. Each system self-organizes or self-stabilizes as motivational need gratification is moved forward by symbolic events recorded in the episodic memory. System *in*stability, evidenced in emotional reactions (strong feelings of anger, fear, or loneliness, for example), indicates a shift in motivational need dominance. Developmental "resolutions," self-stabilizing responses to emotional reactions based on motivational needs, determine the content of the inner script of the individual. The self develops as an independent center for initiating, integrating, and organizing experiences and motivation based on these needs.

One motivational need system regulates a person's physiological needs for food, water, elimination, sleep, and breathing, while another system handles an individual's needs for sensual enjoyment and (later) sexual excitement. Yet another system deals with the need to respond to certain situations through antagonism and withdrawal. Although these three systems impact the work situation to some extent, two others are of particular interest for life in organizations: the attachment–affiliation system and the exploration–assertion system.

Among humans there exists an innately unfolding experience of human relatedness. Humankind's essential *humanness* is found in seeking relationships with other people, in being part of something. The need for attachment concerns the process of engagement with another human being, the universal experience of wanting to be close to others. It also relates to the pleasure of sharing and affirmation. When this need for intimate engagement is extrapolated to groups, the desire to enjoy intimacy can be described as a need for affiliation. Both attachment and affiliation serve an emotional balancing role by confirming the individual's self-worth and contributing to the person's sense of self-esteem (Bowlby, 1969).

The need for exploration, closely associated with cognition and learning, affects one's ability to play and to work. This need is manifested soon after birth: child observation has shown that novelty, as well as the discovery of the effects of certain actions, causes a prolonged state of attentive arousal in infants (Lichtenberg, 1989). Similar reactions to opportunities for exploration continue into adulthood. Closely tied to the need for exploration is the need for self-assertion, the need to be able to choose what one will do. Playful exploration and manipulation of the environment in response to exploratory–assertive motivation produces a sense of effectiveness and competency (White, 1959), of autonomy, initiative, and industry. Because striving, competing, and seeking mastery are fundamental motivational forces of the human personality, exercising assertiveness—following our preferences, acting in a determined manner—serves as a form of affirmation.

As indicated, each motivational system self-organizes—a function developed in reaction to innate and learned response patterns and the developmental impact of caretakers—and also has the ability to recreate previous emotional states. Through the nature–nurture interface, these highly complex motivational systems eventually determine the unique ''internal theater'' of the individual—the stage on which the major themes that define the person are played out. These motivational systems are the *rational* forces that lie behind behaviors and actions that are perceived to be *irrational*.

Management scientists focus on the organization and how it works, and while many of them talk about rational choices, astute observers of human behavior have come to understand that the "irrational" personality needs of the principal corporate decision makers can seriously affect the management process. Only by decoding the script in the internal theater of each decision maker—an operational code influenced by these motivational systems that may defy conventional logic—can an organization ensure that there be no surprises.

Students of human behavior need to accept the power of such scripts; they need to accept the fact that there are limitations to the rational-action model, that extrarational forces can strongly influence leadership, two-person relationships, group behavior, and the organization at large. Unconscious intrapersonal, interpersonal, and group-related dynamics—based on the above-mentioned motivational systems—account for many decisions and policies in organizational life and are a powerful force in explaining human motivation and action.

As an archaeologist of the mind, Freud believed that neurotic symptoms can be used to decode these inner scripts. As conspicuous signifiers of a person's inner world, they can be seen as "the royal road to an understanding of the unconscious." Just as every neurotic symptom has a history, so has every organizational act. The repetition of certain phenomena in the workplace suggests the existence of specific motivational configurations. Just as symptoms and dreams can be viewed as signs with meaning, so can specific acts, statements, and decisions in the boardroom. The recognition of cognitive and affective distortions helps us identify the extent to which unconscious fantasies and out-of-awareness behavior affect decision making and management practices in organizations. If these factors are not taken into consideration, many management models simply do not work.

The Clinical Paradigm

In studying the behavior of individuals in organizations—in decoding the scripts—I apply concepts of the *clinical paradigm,* a paradigm grounded in not taking for granted what is directly observable. Using the findings of clinical research on human behavior as its conceptual base, this paradigm helps in understanding all forms of behavior, however irrational these may appear to be. Paradoxically, it could be argued that management scientists who rely on the clinical paradigm, with its emphasis on the nonrational, are the ultimate rationalists!

The clinical paradigm is based on a number of premises. First, given what is known about motivational systems, it argues that a rationale can be found within every irrationality. It suggests that all behavior, no matter how strange, has an explanation. To understand the rationale behind irrational behavior, however, one has to be something of a detective; one has to tease out what is going on. Because making sense out of someone's internal theater is such a challenging task, those who choose to do ''detective work'' to understand bizarre behavior may need to remind themselves repeatedly that there *is* a rationale, and that it *will* be revealed. While these detectives must be persistent, it is even more important that they be perceptive. Effective deconstruction can take place only when a detective's perception is acute enough to withstand a barrage of mitigating factors, including resistances, ingrained behavior patterns, transference reactions, and projective mechanisms—factors that will be discussed in greater depth later.

The second premise on which the clinical paradigm is based is unconscious motivation. That premise maintains, in other words, that there are aspects of each person's character that are outside of conscious awareness. Understandably, many people are uncomfortable with this premise. Because most people want to be in complete control of their thoughts and actions, a lack of awareness of aspects of one's personality is disturbing. Indeed, it is often perceived as a weakness. But like it or not, some of the things individuals do are outside their conscious awareness. The resistances they develop over time make them blind not only to their motivation for certain behavior but also to the behavior itself. While others may notice someone's dysfunctional behavior, that person, because of his or her defense mechanisms, may not see it. And people who fail to see their own dysfunctional behavior certainly will not take responsibility for it. On the contrary, in spite of the pain caused to others by their actions, they may feel very good about what they do and how they interact with others.

Psychiatrists and psychoanalysts may diagnose this disparity between perception and reality as a *character disorder*. That label indicates that an individual's character—the totality of objectively observable behavior and subjectively reportable inner experiences—is causing relational problems. The word *character* in that label also reflects the person's psychological defensive system, a range of defenses that vary from the very primitive (as in "splitting," i.e. seeing the world in black and white without the nuance of gray) to the moderately sophisticated (as in projection, i.e., blaming others, or denial, not accepting personal responsibility for certain actions), to the mature (as in rationalization, e.g., "I pad the expense account because everyone else does it," or intellectualization, i.e., going through an elaborate intellectual discourse to deal with a problem).

The third theme in the clinical paradigm has to do with the content of inter- and intrapersonal processes. This theme emphasizes that we are all products of our past, influenced (via our motivational systems) until the day we die by the developmental experiences given by our caretakers. These experiences contribute to specifically preferred response patterns that in turn result in a tendency to repeat certain behavior patterns. As the Danish philosopher Søren Kierkegaard once said, "The tragedy of life is that you can understand it only backward but you have to live it forward.'' Like it or not, there is a continuity between past and present behavior. Scratch a man and you find a child. The fact that we are very much a product of our early environment is nicely articulated in a song called ''Gee, Officer Krupke'' from *West Side Story*. The song goes as follows: ''My father is a bastard, my ma's an SOB, my grandpa's always plastered, my grandma pushes tea, my sister wears a mustache, my brother wears a dress. Goodness gracious, that's why I'm a mess.''

Many of the executives I meet in the course of my own organizational detective work, particularly when they are getting older, are stuck in a psychic prison. They are not simply influenced by the past; they are governed by it. They seem to have only one way of looking at things, the same way that has served them for decades. As a result, they keep on repeating the same dysfunctional behaviors. It is as if they had no choice; they are, or seem to be, stuck. These executives are like the simple mussel, which has to make only one major existential decision in life: where to settle down. After that decision is made, the mollusk spends the rest of its life with its head cemented against a rock. Many people share that approach.

The challenge facing these executives is to launch themselves away from the rock, to get out of their psychic prison, in other words, to find alternative ways of viewing and doing things. After all, mental health is really about making choices. Although the stage set of a person's inner theater stays largely the same throughout life, the script can be modified for future interactions, *if* the person in question is willing to make an effort.

Sources for Sense-Making

The data from which many of the ideas put forward in this book originate are of two sorts. First, I obtained field data in the course of a large number of consultations and action research projects in global companies interested in corporate transformation (mind-set or attitudinal change among executives being one of the desired outcomes). These interventions also gave me opportunities for personal interviews and for observing executives in action. Because INSEAD (the European Institute of Business Administration, a global business school based in Fontainebleau, France and Singapore) is involved in many corporate renewal programs, on many occasions I have been asked to play a role in organizational change processes, and I have been able to make some generalizations from those specific interventions. Abstracting ideas and developing grounded theories from case observations, as I have done in the organizations I have been affiliated with, is a well-established tradition in management (Glaser & Strauss, 1967). The richness of the data, from a behavioral mode of explanation to one of clinical inference of the underlying dynamics, gives credibility to this kind of exploratory presentation by furthering the understanding of the process of transformation and change.

Second, I gathered much of the material for this book from interviews with over 200 senior executives operating mainly in the information-technology, chemical, and banking sectors. Many of the individuals interviewed were presidents or members of the board of their companies (average age being late forties). Most had taken a leadership seminar at INSEAD ("The Challenge of Leadership: Developing Your Emotional Intelligence"), a seminar that had as its objective providing participants with a better understanding of their leadership style and helping them develop their emotional intelligence.

The interviews with the participants in and outside the seminar were structured around a verbalization of each executive's life history, major relationships (be they personal or work based), emotional patterns, key events, and major organizational complaints. During these open-ended interviews, I asked questions based on psychiatric, clinical–psychological, and organizational diagnostic interviewing techniques. To control for countertransference reactions (an interviewer's transferential biases), I held many of the interviews in a group setting or with the help of a second interviewer to enable a reality check of what was happening during the process.

Information received from people participating in the seminar was particularly rich, because the nature of the seminar and the time I spent with these senior executives (usually three five-day sessions) made it possible to engage in a deep analysis of their preoccupations, motives, drives, needs, desires, and fantasies. And because participation in the leadership seminar was voluntary, most of these people were highly motivated to engage in a process of self-inquiry.

Leaders Make a Difference

Leaders of organizations are the focus of this book of essays. Their trials and tribulations are what this book is all about. These people have the responsibility to motivate and inspire their subordinates, enabling these fellow workers to transcend their prescribed roles in the organization and creating in them a willingness to put in the extra effort to make their organization more successful.

From my observation of leaders in action, I have become convinced that they make a difference. Obvious as this proposition may seem, there are many management theorists who do not subscribe to it. On the contrary, taking a more deterministic view of what makes organizations function successfully, they minimize the role that leaders play in organizations. They view leaders as being subjected to a variety of external forces over which they have little or no control, like bus drivers who cannot influence the schedule or the routing of their bus. Their argument is that a leader's impact on organizational performance is minimal; the leader's perceived effectiveness is all an illusion.

These management scholars postulate that there are iron-clad laws in the environment that determine the evolution of business. Some of these theorists postulate a resource–dependency model, asserting that organizations depend on the availability of critical resources to survive; others suggest a population–

ecology model to explain organizational performance, claiming that a natural selection process operates in the world of business, a process dependent on industry and global business variables over which executives have little or no control (Aldrich, 1979; Hanan & Freeman, 1977; Pfeffer & Salancik, 1978; Porter, 1980, 1990).

In contrast, another school of management thought, a school peopled by advocates of strategic choice, argues that leaders do make a difference (Ackoff, 1970; Andrews, 1971; Ansoff, 1965; Chandler, 1962). Unfortunately, most adherents of this school of thought subscribe to an excessively rational approach to managerial decision making, undervaluing nonrational factors. These strategic-choice advocates view leaders as logical human beings engaging in a sequential process of analyzing the environment; e.g., doing a competitive analysis, looking at the key competencies of the company, going through a value-chain analysis, and arriving at a master plan.

There is value in what all these schools of thought propose. Leaders *are* dependent on resources and environmental forces; leaders *do* make conscious decisions after rational analysis, but these propositions cannot adequately explain all kinds of behavior in organizations. Apart from the impact of resource availability, forces in the external environment, and the consequences of rational analytical processes, there are many out-of-awareness factors that affect life in organizations. These factors warrant attention.

All of us have a tendency to externalize the scripts in our inner theater and act these out on a public stage. But for leaders, given the power that they wield, the consequences of reading from inner scripts are formidable indeed. Understanding and dealing with these scripts is crucial, because while leaders can lead their people to unexpected heights, they can also easily lead them astray. Thus sense making out of perceived irrationality is pivotal. In our efforts at sense making, the clinical paradigm serves us well, helping us make the behavior and actions of leaders more comprehensible.

The Outline of the Book

The clinical paradigm as applied to leadership in organizations is the thread connecting the chapters of this book. The chapters were written as stand-alone essays and may therefore, at first glance, appear to be discrete. That thread winds from a discussion of the inner world of the individual, in the early chapters, through later discussions of two-person relationships, group phenomena, and human behavior in an overall organizational context.

The first three chapters focus on the individual. Chapter 1, essentially a case history, takes a close look at the inner world of one entrepreneur. Given its in-depth nature, this chapter offers a rare insight into a businessman's inner theater. It highlights a number of themes salient to entrepreneurial behavior and permits inferences about the entrepreneur–organization interface.

In chapter 2, two types of puzzling personalities are discussed, those who find themselves at extreme positions on the emotional scale. At one end of the scale we find hypomanics—people whose manic episodes contribute not only to their charisma but also to their potential downfall. At the other end of the emotional spectrum we find alexithymics—people whose behavior has a "dead fish" quality, who seem to have difficulty expressing their emotions. The implications of these types of behavior in an organizational setting are highlighted.

Chapter 3 explores the effects of reaching midlife, with a focus on a dysfunctional emotional behavior pattern whereby individuals experience very little pleasure, their reactions taking on a quasi-anhedonic character. This chapter also looks at the related experience of depersonalization and explores some of the factors that contribute to both these phenomena.

Chapters 4 and 5 focus on two-person relationships. Chapter 4 reviews dysfunctional dyadic relationships in organizations. Taking concepts derived from couple therapy, it identifies various collusive superior–subordinate interaction patterns and highlights the consequences of each such dyad in an organizational setting. Chapter 5 then examines the construct of envy, which plays a major role in interpersonal motivation, with an emphasis on ways of dealing with envy in an organizational setting.

Chapter 6 describes best practices for effective work teams. Taking the behavior of the pygmies of the African rain forest as a primary model of human behavior, this chapter offers a number of suggestions for creating successful teams; in addition, it addresses some of the factors that destroy teamwork and explores themes relevant to high-performance organizations.

Chapter 7 moves the focus from the group to the organization at large. It explores the characteristics and dynamics of individual and organizational change, highlighting the overlap between the two change modalities and outlining the process of working through the loss associated with change, a process that, like the process of mourning, is made up of a number of predictable stages. Chapter 8 then takes these change processes one step further, exploring the individual reaction patterns associated with downsizing and emphasizing the reactions of the executives implementing a downsizing operation. The chapter concludes with a number of recommendations about how to facilitate the downsizing process.

The book concludes by looking at the search for meaning in human activity. To clarify this point the values of effective organizations and the metavalues that foster commitment and involvement will be highlighted. These are the values that make organizations places for self-exploration and personal growth; these are also the values that make organizations humane places to work.

As mentioned earlier, the clinical paradigm as applied to executive behavior is the thread that connects the chapters in this book. My expectation is that by following this thread the reader will arrive at a greater understanding of the vicissitudes of organizational life. My hope is that by having a greater awareness of those vicissitudes readers will feel an impetus to make their own organizations not only more effective but also more humane. In this two-stage process, self-understanding is the foundation for understanding others. I hope that the reader, while going through the various chapters of this book, will be prepared to make two journeys: one journey into his or her inner self, the other into the organizational underworld. Seeking an understanding of what goes on inside the organization does not necessitate that we embark on an exotic odyssey, however. On the contrary, much of the material can be found right in front of us. We just have to learn where and how to look.

There is a story told about a pious, hard-working, but poor old woodcutter who lived near Vienna. One night the woodcutter had a dream wherein he was told to go to the Hungarian capital, Budapest, to unearth a treasure that was buried beneath the main bridge connecting Buda and Pest. Because the dreamer was struck by the dream's clarity, he wondered if there was some truth to it. But occupied as he was with work, he told himself that dreams are nonsense and left it at that. However, the same dream repeated itself the next night and the night after. At that point the woodcutter felt that there must be something to these dreams, that someone was trying to tell him something to which he was not listening. So he overcame his inertia and undertook the journey. When he arrived at Budapest and went to the bridge, he saw that it would be difficult to dig for the promised treasure: soldiers were posted at both ends. Not disheartened by the situation, the woodcutter returned to the bridge each day, looking at the ground beneath it for a sign that would tell him where the treasure was buried. Eventually his daily vigil caught the attention of the captain of the guards, who inquired if he had lost something at the bridge or was waiting for someone to arrive. After some hesitation, the woodcutter decided to recount the dream and explain to the captain his reason for being there. When the officer heard the dream, he began to laugh. How stupid the woodcutter was, he exclaimed, for believing in dreams when every right-minded person knows that dreams are mere nonsense! Take himself, he declared—he would be the last person to believe in dreams. To illustrate his point, he told the woodcutter that he had recently had a dream with a similar message: he was to go to Vienna and find the house of an old woodcutter. According to the dream, the guard would find great treasure buried in the cellar of that woodcutter's house. But he was not foolish enough to go on this wild-goose chase. He knew better. He knew what a waste of time that would be. After he had finished talking, the captain of the guards once more started to laugh. The woodcutter, however, simply smiled. Then he rushed home, went to his cellar, and after some digging found the treasure.

As this story tells us, many treasures are close by, though we do not know it. We often fail to see what is right in front of us. Many students of organizational behavior seem blind to all the signs that are provided to them. Because their sense-making capabilities are not well developed, they step right past every marker given. Even when they are actively looking for signs, they may lack the skills to perceive them. They may not know what to look for or how to look. Our challenge here, then, is to make sense out of complexity—to understand the meaning of what at first glance may seem nonsensical with the help of a process that can be carried into the workplace.

Freud once mentioned to the novelist Stefan Zweig that all his life he had "struggled with the demon" of irrationality. I have adopted this struggle with the demon as the title of this book. After all, it is that very struggle that the book is all about. It is during that struggle—that inner journey—that we learn about ourselves and about others. And the learning that takes place during that journey can help us contribute to the creation of organizations that give pleasure, make for a feeling of community, are embedded with meaning, and help all who work there develop and grow.

References

Ackoff, R. L. (1970). *A concept of corporate planning*. New York: Wiley.

Aldrich, H. E. (1979). *Organizations and environments.* Englewood Cliffs, NJ: Prentice-Hall.

Andrews, K. R. (1971). *The concept of corporate strategy.* Homewood, IL: Irwin.

Ansoff, H. I. (1965). *Corporate strategy.* New York: McGraw-Hill.

Bowlby, J. (1969). *Attachment and loss: Vol. 1. Attachment.* New York: Basic Books.

Chandler, A. D. (1962). *Strategy and structure.* Cambridge, MA: MIT Press.

Glaser, B., & Strauss, A. (1967). *Discovery of grounded theory: Strategies for qualitative research.* Chicago: Aldine.

Hannan, M. T., & Freeman, J. (1977). The population ecology of organizations. *American Journal of Sociology, 82,* 929–964.

Lichtenberg, J. (1989). *Psychoanalysis and motivation.* Hillsdale, NJ: Analytic Press.

Pfeffer, J., & Salancik, G. R. (1978). *The external control of organizations.* New York: Harper & Row.

Porter, M. E. (1980). *Competitive advantage: Techniques for analyzing industries and competitors.* New York: Free Press.

Porter, M. (1990). *The competitive advantage of nations.* New York: Free Press.

White, R. (1959). Motivation reconsidered: The concept of competence. *Psychological Review, 66,* 297–333.

1

The Anatomy of the Entrepreneur:
Clinical Observations

*The case histories I write ... read like short stories. They lack the
serious stamp of science. [However,] a detailed description of mental
processes such as we are accustomed to find in the works of imagina-
tive writers enables me . . . to obtain at least some kind of insight
into the . . . intimate connection between the story of the patient's
sufferings and the symptoms of his illness.* (Sigmund Freud, *Studies
in Hysteria*)

*If you start talking about the weather, you end up learning what you
want to learn.* (Hélène Martine, *owner of Folies Bergére*)

A man who goes to a psychiatrist should have his head examined.
(Samuel Goldwyn)

Hell is when you get what you think you want. (Anthony Clare)

This chapter considers the dynamics of entrepreneurship, and
in particular the work behavior of entrepreneurs. Toward
that end, I first offer a brief overview of the role of work in
psychoanalytic theory. I then review a number of factors important to entrepreneurship from the various perspectives of economic, sociological, anthropological, psychological, and
organizational theory. Finally, I present the case history of one
entrepreneur, a man who came to me to be treated through psychoanalysis. This case study offers a unique insight into the complex ''inner theater'' of one particular entrepreneur.

17

The Foundation: Research and Theory

The Psychodynamics of Work

In his *Civilization and Its Discontents* (1929/1961), Freud commented on the importance of work for adaptive functioning. He concluded that participation in work leads to the neutralization of instincts and helps to bind the individual to reality:

> No other technique for the conduct of life attaches the individual so
> firmly to reality as laying emphasis on work; for his work at least gives
> him a secure place in a portion of reality, in the human community. The
> possibility it offers of displacing a large amount of libidinal components,
> whether narcissistic, aggressive or even erotic, on to professional work
> and on to the human relations connected with it lends it a value by
> a means second to what it enjoys as something indispensable to the
> preservation and justification of existence in society. (p. 80)

However, in the years since Freud made his comments about the importance of work, discussion of this topic in the psychoanalytic literature has remained relatively limited. Only a small group of psychoanalytically oriented scholars have followed Freud's lead and looked at the psychodynamics of work, although observations on work have been made from a number of different psychoanalytic perspectives. Karl Menninger (1942), for example, looks at work in the context of drive theory and stresses the role of work as a form of sublimation, seeing work as one of the more effective ways to absorb aggressive energies and direct them constructively. In contrast, Ives Hendrick (1943) suggests that the "work principle" can be seen as an expression of a partial ego function. He calls it "the instinct to master" and examines work in the context of ego psychology. The presence of a "work principle" is further explored by Robert White (1966), who introduced the notion of efficacy motivation, the striving to attain competence in dealing with the forces in our environment. Barbara Lantos (1943, 1952) advocates a more developmental and cognitive point of view, comparing work with play. According to her, the work-related motive is the drive for self-preservation mediated by intelligence and reinforced by the conscience, while play is done for its own sake. In Erik Erikson's (1963) developmental scheme, the latency period is the crucial stage during which individuals resolve their attitudes toward work. Like Lantos, Erikson compares work to play, stating that "to bring a productive situation to completion is an aim which gradually supersedes the whims and wishes of play." Three other scholars working at the interface of psychoanalysis and organizations—Eliott Jaques, Isabel Menzies, and Larry Hirschhorn—take a more object-relational perspective, viewing work both as a form of reality testing and as a way to cope with the inevitable paranoid and depressive anxiety that is part of living (Hirschhorn, 1988; Jaques, 1960; Menzies, 1960).

If we shift from a metapsychological discussion of work in the psychoanalytic literature to case histories, we find a focus on issues of work inhibition and work compulsion. These studies tend to emphasize themes such as unconscious oedipal guilt, fear of retaliation for aggressive and libidinal striving, and the unconscious association between success and oedipal triumph (in the sense that being favored by one parent is seen as being victorious over the other). They make inferences about the impact of excessive demands placed by the mother on the developing child that create a lofty ego ideal (or image of the ideal self) and a punishing conscience. According to many of these studies, work is equated by certain individuals with the obligation to produce, and that obligation is enforced by the fear of loss of love. Some of these writers see work inhibition not only as a passive form of rebellion but also as a reflection of an unconscious wish to lose, to be humiliated. However, Heinz Kohut looks at severe and chronic work disturbances from a somewhat different angle. He argues that these disturbances are "due to the fact that the self is poorly cathected with narcissistic libido and in chronic danger of fragmentation, with a secondary reduction of the efficacy of the ego" (Kohut, 1971, p. 120).

Predictably, given the attraction of psychoanalysis to people working in the arts and letters, many of the case histories dealing with various forms of work disorders center on the problems experienced by creative individuals. But although this kind of person tends to take central stage in these case histories, some case material considers business professionals, students, and the unemployed. In-depth studies of high-level executives, however, are almost nonexistent. Furthermore, when executives are studied, researchers tend to pay very little attention to the role of work in the overall scheme of things. One of the reasons for this sorry state of affairs may well be that work is not a central concern of clinicians. They are trained to put more emphasis on the role of nonwork factors in human functioning.

Entrepreneurship: An Interdisciplinary Perspective

Clinical information is particularly scarce about entrepreneurs. This is unfortunate, given the influence of entrepreneurs on present-day society. Their impact as initiators and creators of new businesses is considerable. They are the lifeblood of new enterprise. An entrepreneur is usually defined as an individual who is instrumental in the conception and implementation of an enterprise. (The term *entrepreneur* is derived from the French word *entreprendre:* "to undertake.") In this process of conception and implementation, the entrepreneur fulfills a number of functions. These can be summarized as the innovating, risk-taking, and managing–coordinating functions. The first two functions in particular characterize the behavior of entrepreneurs. Innovation implies doing things that are out of the ordinary by finding new opportunities, while risk taking draws on the entrepreneur's ability to deal with uncertainty and ambiguity, his or her willingness to take economic and psychological risks. Because of the nature of these functions, entrepreneurs are major creators of employment and catalysts of change. Given their important contribution to the GNP, their modus vivendi warrants further investigation.

The almost complete absence of case material on entrepreneurship in the psychoanalytic literature stands in stark contrast to the contributions on this subject from other disciplines, such as economics, sociology, anthropology, psychology, and organizational theory. Research on entrepreneurship seems to be truly interdisciplinary. Not surprisingly, all these different perspectives contribute to considerable confusion as to what entrepreneurship is all about, explaining the wide diversity of factors generally cited as influencing entrepreneurship.

For example, societal upheaval is seen as having considerable impact on the making of new entrepreneurs: some research suggests that such upheaval, because of the status incongruities it creates and the repercussions on family life it engenders, affects the choice of nontraditional career paths. Other research from a sociological or anthropological perspective indicates that entrepreneurs are more likely to come from ethnic, religious, or other minority groups. The experience of feeling different seems to have an important influence on entrepreneurs: if the family of an entrepreneur does not fit into the established order of things, he or she may have little choice but to create a new niche in society.

Economists, on the other hand, tend to discuss entrepreneurship in terms of a receptive economic climate. They refer to such factors as favorable tax legislation, the availability of risk capital, a well-functioning banking system, and the existence of "incubator" organizations (such as those found in Silicon Valley, Route 128 in Boston, and Sophia Antipolis in the south of France).

From a psychological perspective, the emphasis has been on the assessment of specific entrepreneurial traits using a variety of psychological tests. Unfortunately, because of a lack of consistency among instruments used and other methodological problems, a very confusing and not always consistent psychological picture of the entrepreneur emerges. Among the qualities regularly attributed to the entrepreneurial personality are high achievement motivation and the need for autonomy, power, and independence. Moderate risk taking, anxiety, and an internal locus of control have also been cited by some studies.

A few clinically oriented studies concerned with the entrepreneurial personality also exist. These studies presently mainly referring to male entrepreneurs, which scrutinize the entrepreneur's family background, conclude that the fathers of many entrepreneurs are self-employed. In other words, familiarity with self-employment seems to facilitate the creation of one's own business. These studies also conclude that the fathers of entrepreneurs are frequently absent (whether literally or emotionally) and the mothers tend to be overbearing and controlling. In addition, these studies note, on the basis of clinical interviews, that the themes of illness, separation, and death in the family are common among entrepreneurs (Collins & Moore, 1970; Kets de Vries, 1985).

Moreover, these studies indicate that a considerable number of entrepreneurs lack a secure sense of self-esteem and identity. Although entrepreneurs often come across as confident and self-assured, appearances can be deceptive: entrepreneurial behavior is often more "counterphobic" (reactive) than proactive. Many entrepreneurial individuals counteract feelings of low self-esteem, inferiority, and helplessness through excessive control and activity; they turn the passive into the active. Instead of passively experiencing difficult situations, they address these situations with active mastery. Because many entrepreneurs appear to be allergic to authority, they do not function well in structured situations. They prefer to be in control themselves.

Entrepreneurs with a reactive narcissistic disposition are continually in search of an admiring audience to shore up their fragile sense of self. Consequently, these entrepreneurs tend to surround themselves with yea-sayers, thereby depriving themselves of the function of critical thinking in their organization. Within the sort of corporate culture that results, the stage is set for possible crises in growth and succession.

What we can discern from this interdisciplinary research is that feelings of rejection, dissatisfaction, and failure dog some entrepreneurs relentlessly. As entrepreneurs move through their career—often a roller-coaster ride, with successes and failures alternating wildly—they feel that achievements are undeserved, and they expect repeated failures.

An Entrepreneur on the Couch: Methodological Considerations

Fascinating as these conjectures may be, the conclusions drawn from interdisciplinary research are necessarily rather superficial. This is largely due to the limited and limiting ways in which data are collected: questionnaires and structured interviews are the norm; truly clinical case histories are missing. Because this research typically touches only the surface of the intrapsychic life of the entrepreneur, it does not unravel the intricate fabric of interpersonal relationships that curtains the inner theater of these people.

The paucity of clinical material in psychoanalytic literature about entrepreneurship indicates that entrepreneurs are unlikely to turn to psychoanalysis when they encounter personal difficulties. They are simply not given to the kind of self-reflection and inner orientation called for by psychoanalysis. Only in extreme situations will they choose psychoanalysis as a form of therapy. Although most of my research on entrepreneurship has been of the more traditional management type, I was fortunate enough to have an entrepreneur come to me for psychoanalytic treatment. This gave me the opportunity to study the inner world of one entrepreneur in great depth. In presenting a clinical case study of that executive, I follow a tradition started by a number of other researchers interested in the nature of managerial work (Carlson, 1951; Kotter, 1982; Mintzberg, 1973; Noel, 1984, 1991; Stewart, 1967). In their search for rich description, these students of executive behavior realized that they had to limit their sample size (for pragmatic reasons) if they wanted to really understand managerial behavior. The subject of analysis in these studies, however, has been the general manager, not the entrepreneur.

Apart from this difference in subject, there is another distinction in my approach. Human behavior can be studied in various ways. The orientation of almost all the research into managerial work mentioned above has been of a behavioral ("objective") type. In this form of *extro*spection, the subjects' behavior is seen as data in its own right, without reference to the previous experience of the observer. In the case of empathic, *intro*spective observation, as represented by the psychoanalytic orientation I favor, the subject's behavior is seen in light of how the observer would feel, think, and react in the same situation, using as an additional tool vicarious introspection. The interpretation of transference and countertransference reactions—a process revealing a distortion in time and place whereby the observer is perceived and reacted to as a person from the past (see chapter 7)—also plays a major role here (Freud, 1912/1958). The observer incorporates and utilizes his own countertransference reactions in arriving at conjectures.

An additional comment is warranted. Although the sample size in various other studies of managerial work has been small, in no instance has it been limited to one, as in this present case. However, the individual under investigation here was studied not for merely a few hours, a day, a week, or a month. On the contrary, I worked with him for five 50-minute sessions each week over a period of four years. This kind of continuity gives the analyst an opportunity to observe microscopic changes in mood state and behavior. Thus I hope that rich description will compensate for sample size. In presenting this case, I hope to give the reader insight into the complexity of the human condition and its effects on decision making in organizations.

As an aside, I would like to add that length of treatment is very much a consequence of the process of working through insights acquired during the analytic process and of dealing with resistances. Insights into the origins of many patterns of behavior can be acquired relatively quickly. However, in psychoanalytic treatment the bulk of the time is spent on reporting, experimenting with, and exploring new ways of dealing with present life experiences. In this process, the Chinese saying, ''The eye cannot see its own lashes,'' is all too often true. Changing established behavior patterns (contrary to what we would like to believe) takes a lot of work, because most people tend, particularly in situations of crisis, to fall back on their old way of functioning. In studying human behavior, we must not forget that *the wish to recover is often strongly offset by the desire to cover.*

Abstracting ideas and developing grounded theories from case observations is a well-established tradition in management. The richness of the data, whether from a behavioral mode of explanation or from psychoanalytic inference leading to true saturation and so-called thick description, gives credibility to this kind of exploratory presentation by furthering the understanding of entrepreneurship.

In evaluating the material presented in the case study, readers should bear in mind the distinction between narrative and historical truth (Edelson, 1993; Spence, 1982). What is important in a person's story is the former; that is, truth as that individual remembers it. It is this version of the truth, flawed though it may be, that creates the psychological impact that shapes personality and leads to dramatization and enactment of the story. From a psychological perspective, the historical truth, what actually happened, is of less importance than the recounted version. Every individual's sense of identity is very much the heir of the personal myth by which he or she lives, a myth that connects the past with the present.

In working with the entrepreneur profiled in this chapter, it was my job as a psychoanalyst to help piece together his story from the different fragments shared in sessions. The result was an integrated whole. Now we will reverse that process: by deconstructing some of the key issues of his personal myth, by identifying a number of the salient themes that emerged during the years of analysis, we may be able to arrive at some conjectures about the entrepreneurial personality structure and the vicissitudes of entrepreneurship.

I would also like to add that this exploratory study has been enhanced by knowledge derived from a considerable number of structured and unstructured interviews with entrepreneurs, as well as a large questionnaire-driven research database. Although these other studies have helped me to understand better the dynamics of entrepreneurship, none has provided me with the kind of insight that I derived from clinical dialogues with my client. This case history permits a rare look at the inner world of an entrepreneur, providing a rich store of information through which the interplay of personality and environment, and the process of personal change, can be observed in great detail. The case material gives the opportunity to test some of the conjectures made about the entrepreneurial personality. It gives the reader a sense of the complex set of psychological interrelationships behind behavioral observations, gives us a better understanding of the person-organization interface, and shows us that many of the management theories that attempt to explain how people make decisions in organizations are oversimplified and grossly inadequate. As this case history reveals, in many instances the apparently rational explanations for certain decisions turn out to be fiction, rationalizations made after the fact.

Finally, readers need to understand that it is impossible to summarize in a short article what happens in the large number of sessions that make up the psychoanalytic treatment process. For the sake of brevity, I have limited myself in this case history to a number of salient themes, those that, in my opinion, affected my client's relationship to work and his organization.

The Presenting Picture

Mr. X, a 44-year-old entrepreneur, the father of four children, sought psychoanalytic treatment following separation from his wife after 21 years of marriage. In the initial interview he explained that he had thrown his wife out of the house about six months earlier. Apparently, her increasing need for independence—a desire to do things on her own and a willingness to make decisions without consulting him—had become a bone of contention. She had been employed in his business until the separation, and her newly found assertiveness had troubled him at the office too; in fact, he had asked her to resign. He complained about her lack of caring and voiced suspicions that she was emotionally involved with a younger man at the office. In addition, he expressed strong annoyance over the fact that his children had taken the side of his wife.

Mr. X's other complaints were rather vague at first. After considerable prompting, he mentioned symptoms that seemed to be of a depressive nature. He felt completely worthless, he said, and believed that life had no prospects. He feared that he was losing his mind. His sorry state constantly reminded him of the fact that his father had died in a mental hospital, a memory that still haunted him. He acknowledged that he had suffered from depression before but said that to the best of his knowledge it had never been so serious.

According to Mr. X, the cause for his present condition was the separation from his wife. Her departure had also had serious repercussions at work, since her role in the company had been quite important. (As a matter of fact, her leaving had meant the loss of two valuable employees, because the younger man Mr. X had been concerned about had also left.) Mr. X was now extremely worried about the future of the company; he wondered whether it would survive all the upheaval. He had been an active person until the separation but now felt paralyzed, especially in the office. He felt disoriented, unable to give direction or make decisions. He admitted, with considerable embarrassment, that he had taken up reading horoscopes, using the information gained as a major input in strategic decision making. This really troubled him, because he had always felt proud of his action orientation and decisiveness. Now he would sit for hours behind his desk simply staring into space. He feared bankruptcy.

Going to work had become increasingly painful. At the office he had only negative thoughts: how he would be humiliated by his bankers, creditors, and customers, how they would gloat about his failure; and how his mother and other family members would react. Many times he had been completely unable to go to work. Instead, he would spend the day in bed. Even taking care of the everyday household chores had become more difficult.

Mr. X also listed a number of somatic complaints. Although he had been an excellent sleeper in the past, he was now troubled by nightmares and suffered from insomnia. Sores in his mouth and throat caused him great discomfort. He suffered from severe headaches that on occasion temporarily obscured the vision in one eye. He also complained of diarrhea and nausea. After the separation from his wife he had had relationships with other women but had been troubled by impotence. Physical checkups had shown nothing wrong with him. The doctors he had consulted suggested that his problems might be of a psychological nature. He knew he needed help, and so, despite initial reluctance, he decided to try psychoanalytic treatment.

Background

Mr. X, the youngest in a family of six, had two brothers and three sisters. His father had been a salesman who also dabbled in a few entrepreneurial ventures. Because of his work schedule, his father had not often been at home. Mr. X remembered him as a boisterous man who had laughed a lot and had brought him presents from his frequent business trips. Mr. X had always felt that he was his father's favorite.

When Mr. X was 7 years old, his father became bedridden. Having his father in the house gave the boy an opportunity to spend more time with him, and he began to feel close to his father. Eventually, though, his mother and older sister had his father transferred to a mental hospital, where he soon died. Mr. X was only 8 years old at the time. Later, he wondered whether the hospitalization had really been necessary. The true nature of his father's illness, however, had been shrouded in secrecy. He had tried a number of times to find out what had really happened, but had not been able to uncover the truth. The whole incident seemed to have been suppressed as a dangerous family secret. Mr. X suspected that his father had committed suicide. Given his family's religious orientation, that would explain the secrecy around the incident.

He described his mother as a very controlling, overprecise, critical woman who constantly worried about money and the future. After the death of his father, she had to bring up the children alone, not an easy task, especially given that his father's death had resulted in a considerable drop in the family's income and standard of living. According to Mr. X, this heavy responsibility affected his mother's entire outlook on life. He felt that she saw everything in a negative light. She would never make a positive comment; nothing he did was ever good enough. He also described her as a perfectionist, adding that he had never been able to live up to her standards. Despite that, he described his childhood, apart from the death of his father, as uneventful and quite happy. He felt proud of the fact that he had been something of a rebel as an adolescent.

Major Issues

The themes that emerged during the course of analysis centered around Mr. X's relationships with women and his attitude toward work. The tone of a large number of sessions in the first phase of the analysis was pessimistic: Mr. X saw life as an ordeal. He also had a terrible fear of being alone. With his wife gone, he felt completely deserted. According to Mr. X, he used to have everything and now had nothing: his health had been ruined; his life was in shambles; he felt worthless. He wondered what had kept him so occupied at work in the past. Thoughts of financial catastrophe preoccupied him.

Mr. X's inner world seemed to be characterized by fragmentation. Because there was no cohesion, and had been none since long before the separation, it took very little to cause some form of disequilibrium. As a defensive reaction, in an effort to arrive at some kind of inner cohesion, he worked hard to be in control. He revealed that even in childhood he had been scared of losing control. He had been reluctant, for example, to fight with other children for fear he would lose control and kill someone. Denial of inner reality and flight into external reality through work had become a way of life. His defensive structure was falling apart, however; his strategy of escaping into action (the so-called manic defense) no longer seemed to work (Klein, 1948).

Falling into Extremes

Initially, in analysis, Mr. X resorted to the defense of ''splitting,'' viewing everything as being either very good or very bad. As symptomized by that defense and by his mood swings, behavior that can be described as having cyclothymiclike overtones (see chapter 2), an all-or-nothing attitude prevailed. Very little was needed to push him in one direction or the other. For example, after having had an extremely intense, positive relationship with his company for over a decade, a period during which he was eager to tell anyone who would listen about his wonderful vision of the future, he now claimed to detest the company and everything associated with it. Running a company was much too complex, he said; there were too many things to think about. He often felt like just giving the company away. He expressed similar feelings about his car and his house. Possessions came with too many complications. So too with people; he saw his relationships with others as expendable in all areas of life. This attitude affected the way he ran the business, influenced his relationships with customers and suppliers, and soured his relationships with his children and friends. At times it even led to extreme and disastrous action.

La Vie en Rose

It soon became obvious that a denial of feelings of depression through unrealistic optimism, forced laughter and humor, frantic activity, and excessive control had always played an important role in maintaining Mr. X's psychic equilibrium. He had attempted to fight his depressive state, with the guidance of self-help books, by eliminating negative thoughts. In fact, for many years this had been one of his strategies for dealing with life. It ultimately proved ineffective, not least because he was not clear about why he needed help.

As analysis progressed, Mr. X began to see his early relations with others in a different light. He was willing to admit to himself that his childhood had not been as happy as he had made out when we first met. He realized that he had always preferred recalling only happy memories. In reality, it had been difficult to be the youngest in the family. The other members of the family treated him like a baby, assuming that he was spoiled and incapable and therefore ignoring his needs. Looking back, he felt that he had had a rough deal. Moreover, he now realized that growing up under these circumstances had not helped him to develop a secure sense of self-esteem.

Mr. X recalled how he would panic when his father and mother went out in the evening. He would scream not to be left without an adult. He was afraid of being tormented by his brothers and sisters, who were envious of him as his father's favorite. Mr. X's anger in our sessions was specifically directed toward his oldest brother, whom he detested. A major reason for his resentment was that this brother had tried to take the place of their father after his death. He also felt that this brother had never treated him fairly, had always made fun of him.

Mr. X remembered how, apart from screaming, he used to complain about physical symptoms to get attention and sympathy, but to no avail. Only one of his sisters seemed to be willing to lend a friendly ear. Many times during therapy he would mention that the saddest thing he could imagine was to see a young child cry, an ill-disguised reference to his own earlier situation.

Mr. X had conflicting memories of his father. While he was a powerful, flamboyant man who brought presents and favored the youngest son, he also had a darker side. The image gradually emerged of a father who at times beat his children. Mr. X recalled that his father would stifle the behavior of his offspring, forbidding them to speak at the dinner table: "Children should be like flies on the wall; they should not be heard." He had also an oedipal memory of sitting in the car between his father and mother and pulling at the gearshift to bring the car to a halt. When that happened, his father had not been angry, as one might have expected; instead, he had shown an understanding of his son's budding assertiveness.

A more realistic picture of his father began to form. After describing a kind, powerful man who catered to his son's needs, Mr. X would ask himself whether, in fact, his father had not been a very shallow person, a fake, all posturing masked by laughter. These reflections made him realize how much he was like his father. He acknowledged that he behaved in a very similar manner; he too would cover up his feelings by making lots of noise.

When he thought about his father during our sessions, he said he usually felt like crying. He interpreted this as a belated process of grieving. Apparently, because of the secrecy around his father's death, true mourning had not been permitted at the time. Now, as the adult Mr. X mourned his father, he saw a stark image of an abandoned child crying into his handkerchief.

The Medusa Women

During childhood Mr. X's anger toward his mother was reflected in his fear of becoming an orphan. He used to pray every night that his mother would not die. But he was also afraid that he would sleepwalk and kill his mother in his sleep. At the same time he had the irrational thought of hanging himself. Obviously, anxiety and guilt about his aggressive desires were regular companions. It took some time, however, before he recognized the origin and meaning of these feelings.

Gradually, in the course of analysis, he began to admit his anger toward his mother. He remembered that his mother had often said she should not have had six children, a statement that still troubled him. Because he was the last child, it had made him feel unwanted. His arrival must have been an "accident," he assumed. His mother had always seemed busy, never available. Because of her seeming indifference, proving to her that he was worth having had become a major theme in his life. He wanted her to be proud of him, to admire him. But no matter what he achieved in the business world, it was never good enough. She never gave him any praise. He blamed his mother for driving his father crazy (as he felt she was driving him crazy). He actually questioned whether his father had been crazy at all, and wondered whether his mother had just wanted to get rid of him when he became bedridden, choosing commitment to a mental hospital as the handiest solution.

Given the kind of relationship Mr. X had with his mother, it is not surprising that he treated women very circumspectly. He perceived them as dangerous, overcontrolling, not to be readily trusted. Here the splitting defense mechanism was also evident. Mr. X would divide women into the categories of "easy" and "proper." He had always been fascinated by prostitutes (and still was), but the fascination was accompanied by fear. Prostitutes were tempting, but they could also carry diseases. He told of visiting a prostitute and mentioned that he felt he had not treated her as he was sure other men did. He had not taken advantage of her, he said; rather, he had gained her admiration. Paradoxically, he also remembered that as a young adult he had had many brief relationships with women, treating them rather callously, usually dropping them when they became too clingy. He disliked feeling "choked," he explained.

It was clear that Mr. X felt threatened by women. His dreams illustrated the role women played in his inner life. In many of his dreams, ''phallic'' women, portrayed as women with guns, would appear and lie on top of him, having intercourse while putting him in a passive position. He would wake up frightened, feeling smothered. In other dreams, however, women would admire him from a distance. He described one dream in which he was persecuted by a number of large bees who kept sticking to him. They were almost impossible to brush off. He associated this imagery with all the women he had dealt with in his life. Women could cling and sting, but they also could give honey. They could repel but also give pleasure. Gradually, however, after some months of analysis, he began to have dreams in which he became more assertive with women. In these later dreams the degree of anxiety was much diminished.

The Importance of Work

The Need for Control

Starting and managing an enterprise had multiple meanings for Mr. X. It signified much more than merely a means of making a living. Though he had started his worklife as an employee, he soon found working for others stifling. When he got a job with a German company, he discovered that being controlled by Germans was more than he could handle, particularly in light of his associations about their behavior in World War II. When he let his fantasies run wild during analysis, he sometimes associated Germans with baby killers. He also complained that they wanted everything done by the book; they were perfectionists like his mother and did not permit individual initiative. While he was associating in this way, the irrational thought came to him one day that the Germans may have had some responsibility for taking his father away from him. Obviously, in Mr. X's inner world there was some kind of connection between his mother and Germans. (He had previously compared his mother to a Prussian general who exerted totalitarian control.) To be independent, to be in control, meant to be free from mother. His inability to work for other people—people who told him what to do—made him decide to start out on his own, as his father had done before him. That was the only way to get some power, to get out from under subjection to the whims of others.

The importance of control became very clear in the transference process during analysis. During the sessions, Mr. X's perception of me as the analyst oscillated. At times I was perceived as the benevolent father figure. At other times, however, analysis meant domination and I turned from an idealized, benign, all-powerful father into a nagging, controlling, never-satisfied mother. During these latter times, Mr. X sometimes experienced physical sensations of choking. At times he wanted to be considered the favorite patient; at other times he wanted to quit, demanding to know how much longer it would take before he was "cured," before he would be able to function on his own again. Obviously, "cure" in this context meant liberation from the "controlling" analyst.

Mr. X recalled how, as a child after his father's death, he had been troubled by the family's poverty, by his mother's financial preoccupations, by his inability to obtain certain things, and by his envy of wealthier schoolmates. To these frustrations was added his insecurity about his position in the family. Home had never seemed like a safe environment. He had always had to be on his guard. He recalled vividly an incident in which his oldest brother had cheated him of the little money he had. As a child he had vowed to change all that. He was going to have money, serious money. He was going to be a smarter businessman than everybody else. However, even as an adult—when he did in fact have serious money—he was filled with intense rage whenever someone took advantage of him. This was an indication of the extent of his narcissistic vulnerability.

Setting up his own enterprise seemed to be predetermined. But it also, as a compromise solution in dealing with an injured self, presented a paradox. By starting his own enterprise, Mr. X combined a life of insecurity with the prospect of security. The excitement of dealing with an unpredictable environment became a way of warding off painful underlying feelings of depression. In addition, owning a company meant defying his mother, who had always emphasized security. It was a way of being in control and escaping her clutches. Moreover, starting a business held the possibility of great success. He might become financially independent, might even—who knows?—do better than his father or siblings, forcing his mother to admire him. Finally, he was driven by the thought that he had given his bedridden father an unspoken promise to amount to something. To be successful in an enterprise of his own creation would be his way of fulfilling that covenant.

The Need for Admiration

A central theme for Mr. X was that success in business would provide him with the admiration he sought from colleagues and peers. And deep down it also meant pleasing both his still critical mother and his long deceased father. Success would make him special in his parents' eyes; it would get their attention.

Thus it does not come as a surprise that he threw his wife out of the business when she started to compete and stopped admiring him. In addition, her interest in his younger employee had revived oedipal concerns and sibling rivalry. It had also created a paranoid fear that the two coconspirators were going to steal his money. Since money symbolized success, power, and prestige, without it he would not amount to much. Yet after his wife left him, owning the company had become meaningless. Instead, both work and money had turned into symbols of defeat. Obviously, Mr. X found it difficult to carry on without having a "cheerleader" around.

The trouble with his wife began at a time when he had started to become concerned about growing older. He had reached the age at which his father had become bedridden and been sent by his mother to a mental hospital to die. For some time Mr. X suffered from a "nemesis" feeling, the sense of repeating the life script of others. He wondered whether he would share his father's fate. Symptomatic of this "anniversary reaction" was his hypochondriacal concern that he had cancer and was going to die.

Love and Work

Grandiosity and Depression

As we saw earlier, managing an enterprise was an intense emotional activity for Mr. X. Success in business, and the consequent admiration he received, were very important for his self-esteem. During the course of the analysis, it became increasingly clear that when Mr. X was a child, his emerging narcissistic needs had not been dealt with in an age-appropriate manner. Affection had been a precious and rare commodity during his infancy. With so many siblings, and a negative, overcontrolling mother and an absent (later deceased) father, there had not been much love to go around. Responses to narcissistic striving had been lacking, causing problems in Mr. X's regulation of self-esteem. His mother had never been able to give him the narcissistic reserve he needed. Fortunately, his father's interest in him had helped somewhat to alleviate that lack, but his father's death at an early age had created a vacuum, leaving him more vulnerable than ever. His father's death had also revived oedipal guilt (as reflected in fantasies of being victorious over his father but also feeling responsible for his death), further hampering age-appropriate growth and development. The kind of situation to which he was subjected resulted in the acquisition of many of the qualities listed by Alice Miller in her description of depression and grandiosity (Miller, 1979). A "false" self, fragile self-esteem, perfectionism, fear of loss of love, envy, unneutralized aggression, oversensitivity, a readiness to feel shame and doubt, and

restlessness were all evident. Mr. X's mother, depressed herself
and possessing strong obsessional traits, had fostered the development of extremely high standards and a very severe, even
punishing superego. Mr. X pursued ways to be "grandiose" as
a cover for the ever-lingering threat of depression, which originated in his inability to fulfill the introjected expectations of
his mother (i.e., those expectations that he had unconsciously
adopted). To this was added the loss of the father, whom he had
never properly mourned. This needed self-image of specialness, a
form of narcissism, could be viewed as a compensatory, reactive
refuge against never having felt loved.

Competition and Self-Defeating Behavior

Mr. X's account of his childhood years helped clarify the extent
to which family members had been deficient in creating a supportive climate. His parents (for many different reasons) had
not provided a good enough "holding environment" (Winnicott,
1975). The situation deteriorated even more with the death of
his father, whom Mr. X felt at the time to be his only protector.
This unfortunate incident exacerbated the already intense sibling
rivalry existing in the household. Ungratified narcissistic needs
led to strong, poorly modulated aggression in Mr. X; and compensatory grandiosity led to competitiveness, which became his
preferred way of dealing with the world, both in private life and
later in business.

Mr. X was caught in a bind as a youngster. On the one
hand, the domination and terror that he was subjected to by his
mother and older siblings was a form of attention (albeit painful),
a commodity he craved. But this form of relating was understandably unsatisfactory. In fact, he hated it and wanted to escape
from it. His way of dealing with this psychological bind as an
adult was to do everything possible to avoid getting stuck in
similar situations. He needed to be in control; and if pain was
going to be involved, he would be the one to inflict it. He was
never going to be a helpless victim again.

It is interesting to note that when Mr. X found himself in "triangular" situations (oedipal reactivations of the childhood situation), he experienced an even greater need to compete for attention. The women he desired most, those whose admiration he needed most, were the ones attached to powerful, successful business colleagues. In order to impress these women, he sometimes made impulsive, dramatic business decisions that he later regretted. Yet when on occasion his wife admired another man, his jealousy was so intense that he flew into a rage that burned for weeks or months. In one case he even started a personal campaign to defame the man in question, allowing nothing to deter him. These feelings of jealousy often led to inappropriate actions that endangered his business.

Mr. X's work habits had strong masochistic overtones. His intensive work behavior—his need to keep himself busy, to be involved in everything—was driven by a great need for perfection. Nobody in the company could do things as well as he could, it seemed. He would always find something wrong with the work of others. His unrealistic expectations reflected the despair and rage he felt over his inability to fulfill the archaic, introjected expectations of his mother. Again, his behavior demonstrated the internalization of a very punitive superego and a lofty ego ideal; the standards he set for others were no higher than those he set for himself. Moreover, he externalized his mother's incessant demands and the ever-present criticism of his older siblings, playing a similar role toward his subordinates in his business. Predictably, as a boss, a slave driver, he was very difficult to deal with.

But as we have seen, playing the controlling, powerful businessman was only one of his leadership styles. As he cycled through highs and lows, there were times when he was unable to handle the stress he had imposed on himself. Feelings of despair, of being unable to satisfy these internalized demands originating in childhood, would lead to a state of work paralysis. In fact, Mr. X, even at the best of times, rarely found work pleasurable. Because work symbolized submission to authority, he viewed it as an obligation. He felt assigned to the role of martyr in the larger scheme of things. Success, power, and money were elusive entities that could be taken away at any time.

The Symbolic Nature of the Enterprise

As is the case for many entrepreneurs, for Mr. X the enterprise became an extension of himself, vulnerable to attack and prone to failure. Much more than a business, as I have noted, the enterprise in many ways represented his own feeble self. In that respect, it was like a house of cards, ready to collapse. And the unpredictable way he ran his business, with its negative effects on company performance and his employees, added a dose of reality to this concern.

In one dream that he described to me, his business looked like a bombed-out church; in another it was transformed into a sinking platform. Many dreams also contained an Icarus motif. In those he would fly, trying to soar higher and higher. But this pleasurable interlude of flight would soon be broken by feelings of anxiety; his wings would start to fall off and a crash would seem inevitable.

A considerable amount of the material brought up in analysis concerned machinery. Machines fascinated Mr. X, and many of his dreams centered around them, reviving preoedipal and oedipal memories of preoccupation with his body image, physical functions, and sexual curiosity. In one dream he was hiding behind a machine and looking through the cracks, afraid to be caught; in another he was busy with a mud-throwing machine. His excitement about machinery and preoccupation with primal-scene imagery seemed to be closely interwoven.

The enterprise also symbolized his ability to rebel. When he set up the enterprise, he saw his action as a personalized statement of separation. He anticipated that it would make him a person in his own right. Unfortunately, however, it was only partially successful in doing this. The separation-individuation phase of the developmental process had never fully been resolved

(Mahler, Pine, & Bergman, 1975). The precariousness of individuation was indicated by the ease with which those early developmental conflicts became reactivated.

In addition, the business took on the quality of a "transitional object"—a childhood plaything evoking the illusion of unity with the mother and creating an intermediate area of experience (Winnicott, 1975). Like a transitional object, the business served as a safe place between inner and external reality, a place where Mr. X could reenact his fantasies and master his anxieties. It is interesting to note that the kinds of products made by his various companies can be traced to the playful fantasies he conceived in childhood. The sort of imaginary companions he had as a youngster and the way he magically transformed his toys played a role in the business he chose to run and in the products he chose to make. This lingering imagery colored some of his strategic decisions in the enterprise and determined the selection of his portfolio of companies.

As a symbolic extension of the self, the business became a means of reparation: Mr. X would keep his promise to his dead father and care for the needs of the simultaneously hated and desired mother. Business success also provided Mr. X with the means to acquire confirming and admiring responses, bringing him the applause he needed to fight his sense of worthlessness and low self-esteem. The business became a means to acquire money, prestige, and power, thus warding off feelings of weakness, passivity, and helplessness. It also offered an opportunity for Mr. X to recreate a family situation according to his wishes, or so he hoped. At one point, for example, he planned to reorganize the company in a move toward centralization, putting all his businesses under one roof. This poorly conceived business idea, which was never put into practice, can be traced back to a desire for a unified family over which he had control. As the owner of a business, he could take charge and make the rules. Through hiring and firing, he could create an environment that would correspond to his alternating states of pessimism and grandiosity.

The Process of Change: Redressing the Imbalance

In the course of psychoanalysis, Mr. X's attitude toward the people in his life began to change. His relationship with his wife gradually became more balanced. Feeling more secure after exploring his reactions toward her during the sessions, he asked her out on a date. For the first time in many years they had a meaningful conversation. More of these meetings followed, equally successful. As the almost sadomasochistic quality of their previous interactions disappeared, both parties found it less important to question who was controlling whom. Mr. X began to accept that his wife could be both assertive and affectionate. After several months of these trial encounters, Mrs. X moved back into the house.

Another major change was apparent in Mr. X's attitude toward his mother. He made a strong effort to empathize with her. He tried to understand what it had meant for her to suddenly find herself a widow with limited means and a large family to raise. He wanted to end the psychodrama they had both become stuck in; he wanted to create a new type of relationship. To his great surprise, he discovered that when he began behaving differently toward her, their relationship improved. This changed relationship gave him increased peace of mind.

Changes in his behavior were also noticeable at work. Less driven to be controlling and competitive, he made an effort to create a more relaxed atmosphere around the office. As he became better at neutralizing his aggression, he began to perceive the world as less threatening. As he became less worried about competition, he found himself more at ease with his suppliers and customers—and he discovered that unrestrained aggression was not the only (or the best) way to succeed in business.

Ironically, as a first step toward creating a more pleasant atmosphere at work, he fired an older woman whom he had hired soon after his separation from his wife. She had created a very negative atmosphere at the head office. It dawned on him that he had hired this woman, with her pessimistic outlook on life, because she reminded him of his mother. Now, seeing things more clearly, he wondered what had ever made him hire her. Was it that he needed to have a criticizing woman around, for lack of an admiring one?

Mr. X no longer wanted to sell his business. At times, however, he fantasized about the money he could get for the company. He wondered how his mother would react if he showed her how much his company was worth. Maybe *that* would make her admire him. But he realized that he did not really want to let go of the company. Although it had become less of an emotionally overinvested entity, he found that having his own business was crucial for his psychic equilibrium.

Increased insight into the reasons for his behavior made working more pleasurable. Understanding why he behaved as he did widened his area of choice. He felt less like a prisoner of his past. Previously, he had had a need to create work, to be constantly busy; without activity, he had felt lost. Now, however, he was making an effort to take life easy, to find more effective ways of managing the business. He tried to redress the earlier imbalance between action and reflection. He spent more time thinking about what he was trying to achieve.

Mr. X also tried to be less of a perfectionist. When he became less controlling of others, as noted above, he realized the importance of giving his subordinates space. Because they would learn from mistakes, they needed to be allowed to make them. He realized that some of his best people had left the company because of the way he had treated them. He now tried to change his personnel practices, hiring stronger people, individuals who were willing to stand up to him. He no longer viewed disagreement with the boss as high treason. He also developed the ability to delegate, becoming better at controlling his tendency toward micromanagement. He had less need to be constantly at the center of things. Focusing more on those around him, he became interested in developing his people, taking on the role of mentor.

He broadened the scope of the human resource function at the head office (previously restricted to salary and wage administration) to encompass management training and development. He also began to make plans for leadership succession, having learned that his sons were interested in coming into the business. Together they decided that each son would run a part of the business. To prevent future conflict, each eventually could become majority shareholder of his share of the business.

Mr. X's new way of running the company was reflected in very positive results on the balance sheet. As the corporate climate changed and employees felt increasingly empowered, product innovation took off; consequently, the launching of new product lines accelerated. Employees started to experiment with better ways of satisfying their customers. Not only product innovation was on the rise, however; so was process innovation. Good corporate citizenship became the norm: as team players rather than turf defenders, people went out of their way to help each other be more effective in the organization. Market share increased, and so did profitability.

Mr. X, pulled by constant temptation to speed up the growth of the company, struggled for a long time in psychoanalysis with his need for power and prestige. Yet he realized that this urge was driven by his need to feel powerful and that too rapid growth and overexpansion were dangerous. For a long period in the analysis he oscillated between the grandiose fantasy of building a conglomerate and his fears of the business becoming too big. At times he felt like the mythological King Midas: everything he touched turned into gold. But then he became anxious that growth might endanger his relationship with his wife and ruin his health. Being too conspicuous might also invite disaster: others might grow envious and spoil his success, as had often happened while he was growing up. Or his depression and symptoms of physical illness might return. Gradually, however, he began to see the relationship between his need to expand the company and certain key themes in his inner world. This gave him an increased sense of freedom, liberating him from the past. His actions became more balanced and his strategy making more rational. He stopped reading horoscopes and became less impulsive when making business decisions. He was more able to delegate, to stand back from the actions of his employees, to value constructive dialogue. All these changes improved the quality of decision making in his organization.

Organizational Implications

The Keeper of the Keys

The case of Mr. X highlights a number of themes important to the understanding of entrepreneurial behavior. It corroborates some issues that have emerged in previous studies. Mr. X's history illustrates how the complex set of early object relations, i.e., relations with key caregivers and other figures, influences later attitudes toward work and the enterprise. For the entrepreneur, archaic self and object representations continue to have an influence throughout life; they are not easily given up or modified. The superego can take on an extremely punitive quality; the ego ideal can become excessively lofty. As the case history illustrates, these psychological functions are really introjects derived from parental figures.

Mr. X is typical among a subgroup of entrepreneurs in being prone to mood swings. The mental equilibrium of these entrepreneurs can easily be disturbed, triggering outbursts of rage or bouts of depression. Impaired narcissistic development and a very fragile sense of self-esteem contribute to this tendency, which affects entrepreneurs' decision making and behavior in the workplace.

Among that subgroup of entrepreneurs, narcissistic behavior is characteristically of a "reactive" type; it is not based on a secure sense of self. Although these entrepreneurs generally present a convincing facade, many of them never feel truly confident. To many entrepreneurs, the fear of failure and the fear of success are inseparable companions: success is frequently accompanied by the fear that it will not last.

As a caveat, it should be mentioned that there is such a thing as "constructive" narcissistic development. Entrepreneurs with this sort of narcissistic development in their background do not feel the same need to distort reality as a way to deal with life's frustrations, nor are they as prone to anxiety. As a result, their behavior does not have the cyclothymic quality of reactive entrepreneurs. Because constructive entrepreneurs are characterized by a greater sense of balance, the business is less vital for mental equilibrium. Given their ability to "play," they have access to numerous other outlets. They are lucky in that they acquired a strong sense of self-confidence while growing up, based on the validating encouragement of their parents. Their way of dealing with the world is a continuation of this pattern. These people generate a sense of positive vitality and self-worth.

For entrepreneurs of the reactive type, however, the enterprise becomes a highly emotionally charged entity and can be viewed as an extension of the self. It is not just an enterprise; it is part of the entrepreneur's identity. It can also possess the qualities of a transitional object, as we saw earlier. It allows for play but also becomes an instrument for coping with depressive affect. In addition, as a transitional object the business helps the person take on the challenge of moving from dependence and symbiotic attachment to individuation and autonomy. Moreover, to add to the symbolic nature of the enterprise, the business is also a means of repairing the hurts of childhood. Starting a business enables the entrepreneur to acquire the admiring audience he or she needs to nourish a fragmented self.

As we have seen, in the entrepreneurial theater a need for control, a sense of distrust, a desire for applause, and the use of fairly primitive defensive mechanisms (such as splitting, projection, denial, and the flight into action) are regular themes. We have also seen, and this is valid not only for entrepreneurs, how work can become a way of channeling aggressive feelings. Although in most instances aggression tends to be directed outwardly, at times, because of unresolved guilt, individuals may redirect aggression toward themselves, making for work compulsion and inhibition.

Rationality versus Rationalization

The case of Mr. X illustrates that running a business is not necessarily a rational process. As a matter of fact, it is often the contrary. Real-life decision making is basically a very messy business, far removed from the descriptions found in management textbooks. The way a business is managed is very much influenced by the inner makeup of the key power holders. These key people are rarely dyed-in-the-wool economic men or women, acting according to rational principles. In many instances, top executives do not follow prescribed "rational" processes, arriving logically at a "master plan," as many management scholars suggest they should. On the contrary, as the case history of Mr. X demonstrates, while they may have a master plan, its rationale is strongly influenced by their deeply rooted inner theater.

However, by going below the surface to study an individual's inner theater, as we have done in this case, we can often find a rationale behind specific actions. Because people act according to their core conflictual relationship patterns, deciphering those patterns is always helpful, and never easy! (Luborsky & Crits-Christoph, 1998). Although the case of Mr. X may be an extreme example, it illustrates that a clinical investigative approach to organizational analysis goes a long way toward making sense out of an individual's behavior and the effect that behavior has on the organization.

This case history contradicts the notion that leaders do not make a difference, that they are governed by forces over which they have no control (Kets de Vries & Miller, 1984a, 1984b). The case material about Mr. X shows that CEOs are major actors in the play; CEOs *do* make a difference, for better or worse. Furthermore, the case material indicates that the actions of leaders are a product of both rational and irrational processes. Leaders externalize internal motives and act these out on a public stage. The seemingly irrational behavior of Mr. X—the dysfunctional elements in his leadership style—permeated all levels of the company, influencing its strategy, structure, and organizational culture and laying the groundwork for corporate failure.

The Dramatic Organization

This case study makes clear the extent to which organizational pathology mirrors individual pathology, the latter leading to various problems (particularly poor performance). Mr. X's behavior highlights the dynamics of the person–organization interface, particularly in situations where power is highly centralized. Power holders tend to create companies that are compatible with their inner world and their specific personality makeup. Previous research has described the kind of company created by Mr. X as a "dramatic organization" (Kets de Vries & Miller, 1984a, 1984b).

In dramatic organizations, everything seems to revolve around the leader. Leaders of dramatic companies, because of their great need to impress others and command attention, often attract subordinates with dependent personality structures. This type of follower subordinates his or her own needs to those of the leader. Consequently, at lower management levels there is generally little reflection or analysis; subordinates simply rely on the inspired judgment of their boss. Obviously, independent-minded executives do not last long in this kind of environment.

Leaders of dramatic firms often lack self-discipline. They also tend to have a poor capacity for concentration and a tendency to overreact. When these characteristics are present, they soon permeate the organization, since with dependent subordinates there is nobody powerful enough to counterbalance the leader. Dramatic leaders tend to centralize power and restrict initiative, their attitude alternating between extremes of over-idealization and devaluation. Thus second-tier executives retain too little influence in policy making. The outcome of all this is that dramatic firms tend to be hyperactive, impulsive, dramatically venturesome, and dangerously uninhibited.

As illustrated in the case of Mr. X, dramatic leaders depend on hunches and impressions rather than facts. Seemingly rational actions often turn out to be after-the-fact rationalizations. Hence impulsive leaders such as Mr. X create an idiosyncratic environment—entering new product markets while abandoning others at a whim, for example, putting a sizable portion of the firm's capital at risk. Audacity, risk taking, and new ventures are the corporate themes. Deeper interpretation of Mr. X's behavior has made clear, however, that the basis for many of his decisions had very little to do with a rational analysis of the relevant facts. Many of his actions were based on stark themes in his inner theater.

The structure of dramatic firms is usually far too "primitive" for their broad markets. Frequently, such firms concentrate too much power in the CEO, a micromanager who meddles even in routine operations. They also tend to overcentralize, which in turn reduces the perceived importance of an effective information system. As the case of Mr. X illustrates, leaders of dramatic firms do not carefully analyze the business environment. They react according to a predetermined script in their inner theater rather than dealing with the factual information needed to do a thoughtful analysis.

The case history provided here illustrates the delicate interplay of person and organization. It shows the enormous impact senior executives can have on the design and overall functioning of an organization. The way in which the intrapsychic themes of these people are translated into external reality often determines the success or failure of their enterprise.

In Defense of Craziness

Venture capitalists, investment bankers, people acquiring entrepreneurial businesses, and individuals who work for an entrepreneur—basically anyone who deals with an entrepreneur—are well advised to heed the complex drama playing in the inner world of this sort of business leader; they will profit by looking beyond the surface of things. A grasp of underlying factors will help them understand what otherwise could be brushed aside as irrational behavior and action. They will discover the extent to which many decisions in organizations turn out to be after-the-fact rationalizations. Unfortunately, the complex mosaic of contributing factors that lead to idiosyncratic leadership is all too often neither recognized nor understood in the workplace.

Obviously, the individuals who should be the most concerned with this inner world are the entrepreneurs themselves. Entrepreneurs who resort to the manic defense—who force themselves into constant activity without ever asking themselves why they are running, or where—are in for a shock. The darker side of entrepreneurship can have a devastating effect; all too many entrepreneurial businesses self-destruct because of such behavior patterns. Too many entrepreneurs are self-made prisoners of their past; they get themselves stuck in a vicious circle. To break that circle is difficult without some form of professional help, however, though the recognition of this need is a step in the right direction.

But even the recognition of trouble is hard to come by. For many entrepreneurs, the early-warning signs may not function. These leaders realize that they are in trouble only when it is far too late. They are unable to balance action with reflection and have no sense of the continuity between past, present, and future. Unfortunately, it is true that those who do not understand the past are condemned to repeat it. If more entrepreneurs were aware of the fact that they are the keepers of the keys to their own prison, if they accepted the "craziness" inside them and did not run away from it, they could make more of an effort to understand and work with that "craziness."

On the other hand, it is also important to point out that entrepreneurs do not necessarily have greater personal problems than other people. Entrepreneurs, like all of us, have their own unique ways of dealing with the vicissitudes of life. We should not forget that in personality development there is a continuum between what is considered normal and what is considered pathological, just as there is a continuum between waking and sleeping, between childhood and adulthood. Entrepreneurial individuals occupy their own specific position on this continuum of normality and pathology. They are certainly not excessively conventional "normopaths," however. Indeed, it is their mix of the creative and the irrational that makes many entrepreneurs so successful.

Mr. X is an example of a person who realized in time that something had to be done to prevent both self-destruction and damage to the many people he affected as CEO of his organization. Mr. X managed to take charge of his life; he refused to be a passive bystander and allow himself to be swept away by the power of intrapsychic forces. In providing us with a glimpse of his inner world, Mr. X has enriched our understanding of the dynamics of entrepreneurship.

References

Carlson, S. (1951). *Executive behavior: A study of workload and the working methods of managing directors.* Stockholm: Strömberg.

Collins, O. F., & Moore, D. G. (1970). *The organization makers: A study of independent entrepreneurs.* New York: Meredith.

Edelson, M. (1993). Telling and enacting stories in psychoanalysis. In J. Barron, M. Eagle, & D. Wolitsky (Eds.), *Interface of psychoanalysis and psychology* (pp. 99–134). Washington, DC: American Psychological Association.

Erikson, E. (1963). *Childhood and society* (2nd ed.). New York: W. W. Norton.

Freud, S. (1958). The dynamics of transference. In J. Strachey (Ed. & Trans.), *The standard edition of the complete psychological works of Sigmund Freud* (Vol. 12, pp. 97–108). London: Hogarth Press. (Original work published 1912)

Freud, S. (1961). Civilization and its discontents. In J. Strachey (Ed. & Trans.), *The standard edition of the complete psychological works of Sigmund Freud* (Vol. 21, pp. 57–145). London: Hogarth Press. (Original work published 1929)

Hendrick, I. (1943). Work and the pleasure principle. *Psychoanalytic Quarterly, 12,* 311–329.

Hirschhorn, L. (1988). *The workplace within: Psychodynamics of organizational life.* Cambridge, MA: MIT Press.

Jaques, E. (1960). Disturbances in the capacity to work. *International Journal of Psycho-Analysis, 41,* 357–367.

Kets de Vries, M. F. R. (1985). The dark side of entrepreneurship. *Harvard Business Review, November/December,* 160–167.

Kets de Vries, M. F. R., & Miller, D. (1984a). *The neurotic organization.* San Francisco: Jossey-Bass.

Kets de Vries, M. F. R., & Miller, D. (1984b). Neurotic style and organizational pathology. *Strategic Management Journal, 5,* 35–55.

Klein, M. (1948). *Contributions to psychoanalysis: 1912–1945.* London: Hogarth Press.

Kohut, H. (1971), *The analysis of the self.* New York: International Universities Press.

Kotter, J. P. (1982). *The general managers.* New York: Free Press.

Lantos, B. (1943). Work and the instincts. *International Journal of Psycho-Analysis, 24,* 114–119.

Lantos, B. (1952). Metapsychological considerations on the concept of work. *International Journal of Psycho-Analysis, 33,* 439–443.

Luborsky, L., & Crits-Christoph, P. (1998). *Understanding transference: The core conflictual relationship theme method.* Washington, DC: American Psychological Association.

Mahler, M. S., Pine, F., & Bergman, A. (1975). *The psychological birth of the human infant.* New York: Basic Books.

Menninger, K. (1942). Work as sublimation. *Bulletin of the Menninger Clinic, 6,* 170–182.

Menzies, I. E. P. (1960). A case study in the functioning of social systems as a defense against anxiety. *Human Relations, 13,* 95–121.

Miller, A. (1979). Depression and grandiosity as related forms of narcissistic disturbances. *International Review of Psycho-Analysis, 6,* 61–77.

Mintzberg, H. (1973). *The nature of managerial work.* New York: Harper & Row.

Noel, A. (1984). *Un mois dans la vie de trois présidents: Préoccupations et occupations stratégiques* (A month in the life of three presidents: Strategic preoccupations and occupations). Unpublished doctoral dissertation, McGill University, Faculty of Management.

Noel, A. (1991). Magnificent obsession: The impact of unconscious processes on strategy formation. In M. F. R. Kets de Vries (Ed.), *Organizations on the couch.* San Francisco: Jossey-Bass.

Spence, D. P. (1982). *Narrative truth and historical truth.* New York: W. W. Norton.

Stewart, R. (1967). *Managers and their jobs.* London: Collier Macmillan.

White, R. (1966). *Lives in progress.* New York: Holt, Rinehart and Winston.

Winnicott, D. W. (1975). *Through paediatrics to psycho-analysis.* New York: Basic Books.

2

Managing Puzzling Personalities:
Navigating Between "Live Volcanoes" and "Dead Fish"

I used to say of him [Napoleon] that his presence on the field made the difference of forty thousand men. (Arthur Wellington, 1st Duke of Wellington)

For I have known them all already, known them all—
Have known the evenings, mornings, afternoons,
I have measured out my life with coffee spoons . . . .(T. S. Eliot)

As an experience, madness is terrific, I can assure you, and not to be sniffed at; and in its lava I still find most of the things I write about. (Virginia Woolf)

This chapter looks at two kinds of personalities that can be found at opposite ends of the emotional spectrum: hypomanics and alexithymics. People who are *hypomanic* are high-spirited, self-confident, and exhilarating, but they are also unpredictable; like "live volcanoes," they erupt with little warning. Because of their charm and charisma, such individuals can be highly effective at influencing others. The second group of people, *alexithymics*, present the opposite picture. It is their *lack* of feeling and emotion that sometimes leads to difficulties. Their emotions are flattened; whatever feelings of zest, enthusiasm, and passion they may once have had are now nonexistent. It is as if they were emotionally color-blind. Thus the impression they make on others is that of "dead fish." This chapter identifies the symptoms of hypomania and alexithymia, explores the interpersonal styles related to these character types, highlights possible causes, and suggests methods of intervention. The chapter also examines the effect these types of people can have in an organizational setting and offers examples of both types of behavior.

Introduction

Interpersonal encounters can be extremely perplexing. Interchanges with some people are routinely enigmatic, disconcerting, even bewildering; they leave us with a strange aftertaste. Often after an encounter with such a mystifying person, we ask ourselves, What happened? What did this person do to us? What kind of emotional feelings did he or she elicit, and why?

Making sense out of these feelings is not always easy; indeed, it is a terrain full of traps and minefields. But because the ability to establish and maintain relationships with others is a central part of what *management* means in the workplace, it is a terrain that needs to be explored. To be effective as managers, we need to know the business, yes; but, more important, we need to be able to engage ourselves effectively with our coworkers, subordinates, and superiors, each with his or her own unique personality makeup. We have to understand what makes each person tick. We have to understand the kinds of emotions that are central to each person's being. This understanding and cultivating of emotion and motivation, an endeavor we might call *emotional management*, demands that we be able to know our own emotions, handle our emotions, use our emotions in the service of a purpose, recognize emotions in others, and manage emotions in others. Emotional management is crucial because of emotional "contagion": each person's mood state affects those around him or her. Indeed, the "catching" of other people's emotions is what *esprit de corps*—team spirit—is all about.

Taking the issue of emotional contagion into the organizational setting, we recognize that the emotional style of senior executives influences the prevailing climate of the workplace. It sets the tone for the way people deal with each other; it determines employees' interpersonal styles and ways of interacting. Effective leaders know how to use emotions, how to make emotions cascade down the organization. They understand that emotions can be a great lever for action. Thus they orchestrate emotions for organizational ends to articulate frameworks for organizational experience. They realize that without the acknowledgment of emotions, people feel empty, confused, and fragmented, lacking the impetus to take action. Effective leaders recognize that shared emotions help connect people, make for strong group ties, and provide a focus.

But in contemplating the transfer or contagion of emotions, we must look at the full picture. Although effective emotional management can be a great positive force, injecting an enormous amount of energy into the system, this process can also be destructive. While the ability to inspire others can be used for the good, it also has a dark side, as history has shown. Sometimes people astute in emotional management are like the Pied Piper, entrancing those around them to their doom. We have only to think of such charismatic leaders as Mussolini, Stalin, Hitler, and Saddam Hussein to be convinced of this danger. Many such people seem to engage in self-destructive behavior; and when, because of the power of their personality, they draw in others with them, the consequences can be far-reaching and even deadly.

These sordid examples are extreme, to be sure. Emotional management in a work setting does not need to have disastrous consequences. Yet because of the underlying fear that strong emotions may undermine seemingly rational organizational processes, the management of emotions is usually undertaken with trepidation. The expression of intense emotion, whether negative or positive, tends to be viewed as potentially disruptive. And most executives adhere to this position, being astutely tuned in to what is socially acceptable. In many organizations emotional expressiveness is circumscribed, the expression of emotions by most executives falling well within a middle range. With emotions thus buffered—high highs and low lows being rather rare—their impact is modest.

At times, however, we encounter executives whose ways of behaving and interacting puzzle us, whose emotional style seems to occupy an extreme position on the emotional spectrum. For such people there is no such thing as a middle range. In testing the outer limits of acceptable behavior, they have an enormous effect on the people they deal with, be it for better or for worse.

When we observe such people in action, we find that some seem to be proselytes of the psychology of elation, while others seem to be disciples of the psychology of dissociation. While the first group sweeps us off our feet with their charm and charisma, the other group fills us with a sense of apprehension and dread through the apathy they evoke. While the first group possesses the kind of infectious behavior that sparks enthusiasm and inspires action in the people around them, the other group leaves us ice cold. While we are drawn to the first group as moths to a flame, with the other group we experience only boredom and frustration.

The charismatic types that make up the first group are highly attractive; they are singled out, whether at a social function or in the boardroom, as the objects of admiration. They are the kinds of executives who have the ability to touch and stretch the people they deal with. They have the capacity to transform others by emphasizing concerns that transcend narrow self-interests. As they energize others, they create high commitment and enable efforts beyond the call of duty. Their emotional presence—their enthusiasm—can be a key ingredient in making for peak experiences and highly successful company performance. They are like live volcanoes, roiling with energy. Acting passionately, as they do, they make others feel alive, involved, and motivated. They exemplify, through the tool of contrast, how a lack of passion impedes inspiration and bold action. They demonstrate the extent to which emotional management is a potent force for change and a key ingredient in the creation of high-performance organizations—as long, that is, as their peak experiences remain grounded in reality.

The other group of executives poses a very different quandary. Instead of having a charismatic modus operandi, they have an interpersonal style that tends to be quite factually based. For these people, emotions are something out of place, dangerous, chaos inducing. Such people turn away from emotions, believing that feelings have to be controlled or suppressed. Making sense of the inner world of others, or, for that matter, themselves, is not their cup of tea. They prefer to put their emphasis on external factors, things, objectivity, logic. Their worldview does not have a place for people as individuals. For these executives, abstractions, tasks, set ideas, and inanimate objects are of overriding importance; feelings are simply superfluous. Because what really counts in their eyes is the system, they lack the personal touch. Their contact with others tends to be depersonalized and mechanical; what they feel attached to is procedures, rules, and regulations. And their emotional absence is noted by those they work with. Just as the presence of strong emotions can have a contagious effect, so can the absence. The lack of warmth in this group of executives, what we might call their emotional unavailability, can, if prolonged, be quite infectious, coloring the organizational climate, demotivating people, and contributing to a decline in the organization's performance.

The kinds of mood states represented at these extremes of the spectrum have been recognized by psychiatrists, psychoanalysts, and clinical psychologists. The object of many studies, they have been widely described in the psychological literature. While people who make up the first group—the proselytes of the psychology of elation—have been described in the literature as *hypomanics* (a mild form of bipolar disorder), the second group—the disciples of dissociation—have been called *alexithymics*.

Hypomania and alexithymia are more widespread than one might think, though these behavior patterns have not been systematically identified in the work setting. In postindustrial societies, approximately one person in one hundred suffers from the most extreme form of bipolar illness (affecting both sexes equally) (Weismann, Leaf, & Tischler, 1988). If that figure seems rather low, it should be noted that severe bipolar illness typically represents only the tip of the iceberg; there are many milder variants, including hypomania. The underestimation of the frequency of bipolar disorders may be due to undiagnosed hypomania. If all the variants were counted, the actual number would be much larger. Some studies even suggest that some kind of bipolar illness may affect approximately one out of every eleven individuals at one point in their lives (Goodwin & Jamison, 1990). The prevalence of alexithymic characteristics in the general population is also significant. Although the exact numbers are not out yet—more epidemiological work is needed—some researchers suggest that up to 8.2% of men and 1.8% of women possess these characteristics (Blanchard, Arena, & Pallmeyer, 1981).

Just as these personality styles, these ways of managing mood states, are more common than most of us would expect, their impact is likewise greater than we would anticipate. The objective of this chapter is to highlight these conditions so that we can be better prepared to deal with them. Identifying the symptoms of hypomania and alexithymia, recognizing the origins of both interpersonal styles and the kinds of mood states they represent, and understanding methods of intervention can be of help as we strive to work more successfully with these perplexing people.

The Psychology of Elation

The severity of manic behavior ranges widely, as do the corresponding consequences of that behavior. Hypomania, or "mild" mania, falls within a class of disturbances of mood usually described as *bipolar disorder,* a class that encompasses a wide range of mood disorders and temperaments varying in severity from cyclothymia (noticeable but not debilitating changes in mood, behavior, and thinking) to life-threatening, full-blown manic-depression. What makes the behavior of people suffering from bipolar disorder distinctive is its cyclical nature. Such people are as often depressed and irritable as they are elated.

Mood disorders are listed in the American Psychiatric Association's *Diagnostic and Statistical Manual of Mental Disorders (DSM-IV)* according to their intensity (1994). Broadly speaking, going from more to less extreme, that volume distinguishes between bipolar I disorder, bipolar II disorder, and cyclothymia. Bipolar I disorder, or true manic-depressive illness, the most serious form of affective illness, is not something to be taken lightly. It is a clinical course characterized by episodes of depression alternating with excessive euphoria, increased energy, and poor judgment. This mood disturbance is sufficiently serious to cause a marked impairment in occupational functioning and in relationships and social activities. In some people, especially those who experience psychotic episodes characterized by delusional thinking or hallucinations, hospitalization is required to prevent harm to self or others. The two other forms of mood disorder, bipolar II disorder and cyclothymia, are more commonly found in organizational settings than is classic manic-depression. They are characterized by milder periods of euphoria that alternate with periods of despondency and depression. Instead of engaging in true manic behavior, with its increasingly formidable highs (and potentially suicidal lows), bipolar II's and cyclothymics are prone to *hypomanic* behavior (mildly manic states).

Bipolar disorders cover the extremes of human experience. They represent a strange mixture of feelings: a well-being characterized by sparkle and exhilaration juxtaposed against loneliness and terror. This biphasic quality is the heart of the problem: hyposomnia alternating with a decreased need for sleep, shaky self-esteem alternating with grandiose overconfidence, periods of mental confusion alternating with periods of sharpened creative thinking, uninhibited sociability alternating with introverted self-absorption. During their highs, those with a bipolar disorder have a feeling of unlimited physical and mental energy, the expansiveness in mood state symptomized by grandiose thoughts and feelings. With their sense of exaltation and rapture, they may experience a heightened sense of reality. Hypersexuality is also typical: sexual fantasies are pervasive, colored by the desire to seduce and be seduced. Bipolars on the upswing enjoy feelings of ease, strength, buoyancy, financial omnipotence, and euphoria. There is an underlying instability, however. The threat of an upcoming depression, with its accompanying melancholy, hopelessness, tearfulness, suicidal thoughts, and self-deprecatory and self-accusatory behavior, is always present. Just on the horizon are the angry, explosive outbursts that alienate loved ones, the promiscuity and the marital failure, the resort to alcohol and drug abuse as a form of self-treatment, the financial extravagances that cause disaster. Although hypomanics by definition do not reach the high highs of full-blown manic-depression, their behavior often manifests aspects of such mood states. People who know them well may recognize glimmerings of the melancholic temperament that lies beneath their ebullience.

The Hypomanic Profile

I had had highs before, and also lows. But when I was appointed executive vice president of our largest division, I felt better than I had for years—an unprecedented high. I was walking on water. I was convinced that I was going to build the greatest organization in the world. It was my big chance to make a mark. I know that some people were laughing behind my back, convinced that I was going over the top when I told them what I planned to do, but I really believed in my vision for the future. I would change the very nature of the industry. I was going to right all wrongs and straighten things out. All the problems in the company were going to be corrected by me. I realize now that my schemes may have been somewhat grandiose, unrealistic. But I lived under the illusion that I had powerful friends in the company who would help me implement my plans. Most important, I had the feeling that I could do anything. I felt I was on a roll; nothing could stop me. I was in tremendous high spirits, enjoying an incredible intensity of feelings.

I remember that all my senses were more acute than usual. I had this graphic script; everything that had to be done became so clear to me. How could others fail to see it? I tried to get my colleagues to join me in my feelings, to share my excitement. I tried to convince everybody of the value of my ideas. I took an active interest in everything going on around me. And as I got others moving in my direction, everything seemed rosy. Things appeared to be going according to plan. I wouldn't take no for an answer. Nothing could dampen my enthusiasm. My wife told me later that even my speech changed during this period. I talked louder and faster; I was harder to follow; I was more difficult to interrupt. She felt that I wasn't my usual self.

I remember that thoughts would fly through my mind. I would switch from topic to topic without building connections. My thoughts came so fast that I often couldn't remember the beginning of a sentence by the time I was halfway through it. Fragments of ideas, images, and sentences would race through my mind. I was easily distracted and had trouble concentrating. I was told later that at times I became downright illogical. I'm not very clear about that now.

I was propelled to constant action. I couldn't sit still. When people didn't pay attention to what I was trying to do, I would become irritated and aggressive, showing my anger. I started to drink as well, and I experimented with cocaine. My wife felt that I'd turned into a completely different person. It was like Dr. Jekyll and Mr. Hyde. She never knew which me was going to come through the door. The unpredictability was unnerving to her. She felt it was like living on a knife-edge. She could never relax. When she tried to reason with me, she bore the brunt of my anger. I worked twenty hours a day to make my dream come true. I couldn't calm down. I tried to work out—running, swimming, bicycling—but nothing brought the calm I sought. I slept very little. I needed only a few hours of sleep every night and still seemed to be full of energy.

As a result, I took on too many things. Apart from the commitment to build up the company, I agreed to be the major fund-raiser for the local college, to be the president of the golf club, and to give a course on strategic management at the university. I also spent far too much money. It just slipped through my fingers. I bought things that now seem useless. That overspending caused lots of problems between me and my wife. Of course, she was right: there was no need to buy two sports cars, I needed a Harley-Davidson like a hole in my head, and we didn't need a new house. But money was the least of my worries at the time. I believed it would always be there when needed. And buying all those things was terrific fun. Money flowed; things accumulated. As if I weren't already expending enough energy, I also started an affair with my planning assistant. The sex was great.

Then the whole house of cards crashed. I was accused of spending way over my budget at work. A number of companies I had acquired to get better market penetration turned out to be lemons. I was told that my picture of their viability had been completely unrealistic from the start. Some of my colleagues accused me of being a con artist, said that I'd been deliberately misleading them all along. Within a matter of weeks, all my responsibilities were taken away; I was put on ice. True enough, for a short time they gave me a new job: vice president of communications. But it was just a title really, handed out for cosmetic reasons. It was clear that I had to leave the company.

At about the same time my wife decided to separate from me. She could no longer stand my self-indulgence, my sexual indiscretions, and my abdication of responsibility toward the children. My financial situation was a real mess as well. I had to sell everything to pay off my debts. Now, eight months after the worst of it, I do a little bit of consulting to make ends meet. Recently, things are looking up somewhat. I'm in psychotherapy and I take medication. My mental state has stabilized considerably, and I no longer experience extreme states of euphoria. But to be quite honest, at times I do miss the highs of the past. (From interview with the author.)

Hypomanics are extremely persuasive; they know how to use their own enthusiasm to sway other people. That enthusiasm is their trademark: their mood is usually high-spirited, self-confident, and exalted. When in a euphoric state, they have a genuine sense of well-being, mentally and physically, a feeling of happiness and exhilaration that makes for a world of unlimited ideas and possibilities, a world in which success is assured. There is, however, a volatile and fluctuating undertone to even their elevated mood state. Often characterized by great emotional irritability, hypomanics can easily become dissatisfied, intolerant, and fault-finding when their demands are not met. When confronted with opposition, they can become pretentious, impertinent, and even rough. Trifling incidents can bring about open hostility and violent outbursts. Compounding that emotional irritability is the ever-present threat of depression.

A disorder of thinking (as well as mood) is often part of the hypomanic picture. Expansiveness, grandiosity, and overconfidence, traits that taint reality testing, color the way many hypomanics relate to others. These traits change the rate, quality, and fluency of thought and speech; they alter associational patterns and logical processes; and they impair memory. Manic thought disorder manifests itself in various ways. Ideas come easily to the hypomanic; a peculiar mixture of sense and nonsense, they appear almost involuntarily and are often disorganized. Yet these ideas, often only loosely strung together, are extravagantly combined and elaborated. Even thoughts that are coherent may occur disconnectedly in the hypomanic. Irrelevant intrusions in social conversation become typical, as do jokes that are completely out of place. This intrusive disconnectedness reflects the flightiness of hypomanic thought. With poor concentration and distractibility par for the course, the original focus of a conversation may be lost along the way. As a result, the hypomanic jumps from one subject to another.

Hypomanic behavior is noted for its powerful but potentially confusing influence on others. Hypomanics are active and indefatigable when in an elevated mood state. Engaging, charming, and charismatic, they often aggressively seek out people; they also tend to be firmly opinionated. As a result of this combination, hypomanics can be extremely manipulative and exploitative. Sometimes their charismatic style is targeted at some kind of shared purpose; it helps to achieve a common good. At other times hypomanics pursue an agenda that is both personal and inappropriate.

In pursuing such an agenda, they can be extremely ingenious and not a little underhanded. They have the ability to recognize and exploit areas of covert conflict in others. In interpersonal encounters, they possess—and rarely hesitate to use—a highly refined talent for sensing an individual's vulnerability and exploiting it in a manipulative fashion. They can also intuit a group's area of conflict. They are masters in the manipulation of the self-esteem of others, and they put other people off balance by simultaneously drawing others toward them and pushing them away. They can be extraordinarily perceptive at an unconscious level, exceptionally skillful in evoking and utilizing feelings (especially guilt) in those around them; and they use this ability to increase or lower other people's self-esteem as a way of exerting interpersonal leverage. Talented in projecting fault, they know how to shift responsibility in such a way that others are assigned blame for their actions.

Hypomanics are also prone to sexual and financial indiscretions. Heightened sexuality is characteristic of this group: normal sexual inhibitions seem to disappear, and sexual thoughts, fantasies, and adventures become a preoccupation. In hypomanics who are married, adultery is a common result. No wonder, then, that marriages of hypomanically inclined people tend to be turbulent and often end in divorce. Financial extravagances exacerbate these interrelational problems, as does the violent behavior that sometimes surfaces when hypomanics are in an extremely manic phase. Alcoholism and drug addiction, when they are part of the profile, further endanger relationships. Depressive episodes complete this dysfunctional picture.

In summary, hypomanics are passionately involved in the world around them. Stimulus-seekers, they pursue thrills, drama, and variety. Their sensations and feelings are incredibly intensified. Their ideas are boundless—brilliant, creative, and apparently spontaneous—but they are also flighty. Their behavior is decisive; they seem to be extremely confident in their judgment about what they plan to do.

The Charismatic Component

Hypomanic experience magnifies common human experience to larger-than-life proportions: abundant energy, unbridled enthusiasm, thirsty gregariousness, heightened intensity of emotion, compelling sense of destiny, strong belief in oneself and one's ideas (bordering on the grandiose), forceful persuasiveness in convincing others of one's point of view, eager willingness to go where others dare not go, intuitive grasp of self and others, boundless optimism, heightened alertness and observational ability, formidable courage, unusual willingness to take risks (bordering on the imprudent), unpredictable and subtle changes in mood, recurring impatience, and shortened attention span.

As that description suggests, hypomanics are rarely dull. On the contrary, they tend to be colorful figures. Their lively speech and behavior stimulate the imagination of others. Because hypomanics are seen as capable and energetic, they are often at the center of activities. But their remarks can be so rapid-fire that they confound listeners. As those listeners scramble to apprehend their ideas, hypomanics can be intolerant and unyielding, given to impulsive action. If that action brings success—conviction and purpose triumphing over even adverse conditions—hypomanics attribute the result to their gifts in foresight and decision. If the consequences are less favorable, hypomanics find ready excuses.

The expansive mood enjoyed by hypomanics on good days helps them find new ways of doing things, ways that challenge the status quo. Because their fluency of thinking results in a great variety of ideas, they are sometimes able to come up with unusual but ultimately satisfactory solutions to problems that have confounded their colleagues. Furthermore, they are very astute in assessing environmental discontinuities, having the ability to recognize major changes in the world around them. These qualities make them extremely good at envisioning.

People with the hypomanic mind-set, the ability to dream up new schemes and to pursue them with decisiveness and unbridled enthusiasm, generally have a magnetic effect on others. Hypomanics can get the best out of people. They possess the ability to inspire others to make exceptional efforts, to do things they would not otherwise do; in other words, they "stretch" those with whom they work. In vividly describing a glorious future, given their talent in envisioning, they provide a roadmap for others; they create order out of chaos; they generate excitement about what is to come; they instill confidence and trust in their leadership; and they offer criteria for success. Thus the increased energy, expansiveness, fluency of thought, imagination, and willingness to take risks can be extremely beneficial to any organization.

Hypomanics share many characteristics with historical figures known for their impassioned authority. We can find many political and military leaders in this domain, including the biblical King Saul, Martin Luther, Winston Churchill, and General George Patton. Their unconventional behavior makes these individuals larger than life. The success of such leaders, their charisma, can be attributed to a hypomanic mood state. Such people can be extremely effective in dealing with discontinuous states and turnaround situations; indeed, it is in such conditions that they shine.

As an example, let us look at General Patton, one of the most charismatic, controversial, and mercurial figures ever to set foot on a modern battlefield. "Old Blood and Guts" (so called because of the language he used in addressing his troops) became known as the fastest moving, hardest hitting battle commander in World War II. His heroic behavior was the stuff of which legends are made. Behind the public persona, however, we find an intensely private individual, a man troubled by inner turmoil and mood swings, a surprisingly accomplished poet, a person whose tendencies toward impulsive, bizarre behavior and irrational acts seemed to grow worse with time.

Patton was a man of contrasts. He could be demanding, empathic, and innovative, but he could also be moody, angry, and depressed. He believed in reincarnation and was convinced that in previous lives he had been both a Viking and a Roman legionnaire, but he was also capable of assessing battlefield situations with an accuracy that gave him an enormous advantage over other commanders. He could be calm with the fury of battle storming around him, yet his mercurial temperament got him into trouble time after time. In this day and age, would a "politically incorrect" person such as Patton ever have been given the chance to show his mettle? Although his superiors recognized his emotional instability, his commanding officer, General Dwight Eisenhower, also recognized his leadership qualities and was willing to tolerate the eccentricities, protecting Patton politically when those eccentricities threatened his military career. And Eisenhower seems to have been right: in assessing World War II in hindsight, we can speculate that a victory over the German army would have been an even costlier affair, in terms of human lives, had Patton not been at the helm.

Yet we cannot simply ignore those aspects of Patton's personality that conflict with our image of heroic leadership. It is only against the background of his dark side that his leadership can be clearly defined. And that dark side could be dark indeed. At times Patton's black moods were so bad, and he behaved so tyrannically, that no one wanted to be around him. His womanizing, his inability to handle alcohol, and his bad temper were extremely trying to the people closest to him. His irrational behavior reached a climax with the "Sicilian slapping incident," in which, during his Mediterranean campaign, he slapped two hospitalized soldiers for alleged cowardice. We may speculate that such an outburst was a reaction to his own inner fear of not being able to handle himself in battle. However, that impetuous behavior put the most competent battle commander of that period on ice for some time (only his friendship with Eisenhower preventing total disgrace) and most likely caused a considerable delay in the Allied victory.

Between the two world wars, when destiny was not kind to Patton and he feared that he would die without having achieved fame on the battlefield, his mood grew increasingly somber. In his most difficult moments, he turned to poetry, writing depressive verse such as this:

In the valley of the slaughter where the winged Valkyrie dwell
And the souls of men go naked to their God
I have seen the curtain parted, I have glimpsed the flinty trail

The final road the spirits have all trod. (cited in D'Este, 1995, pp. 314–315).

Poetry was only one of the ways in which Patton attempted to "mend" his mood state. Vigorous activity, playing of polo, was another way he tried to channel his energy. The people around him also played an important role in the management of his emotions. His wife, the most important of these emotional "managers," bore the brunt of his mood swings and depressions, and she made heroic efforts to cheer him up. One of their daughters recalled her once saying, "One or both of you girls go down and talk to your father! He's lying brooding in a hammock about not knowing his children and the fact that no one loves him, and he is very depressed, and I can't do another thing with him" (quoted in D'Este, 1995, p. 364).

This depressive picture was only one side of him, of course. The Patton most people knew, the man we generally call to mind today, was driven by emotions of a more ebullient nature. These usually emerged when he needed to accomplish something, when he was asked to turn around an impossible situation. Patton felt truly alive only in the middle of action. It was then that he shone, then that his impact on others was tremendous. Consider these words of one of his new staff officers after Patton took charge of the Third Army:

> When the drum ruffles and bugles sounded the General's march . . . we stood transfixed—there wasn't one square inch of flesh on 250 officers and 750 enlisted men which was not covered in goose pimples. It was one of the greatest thrills I shall ever know. . . . That towering figure, impeccably attired, froze you in place and electrified the very air. . . . In a somewhat boyish, shrill yet quiet voice he said, "At ease gentlemen. . . . I can assure you that the Third United States Army will be the greatest army in American history. We shall be in Berlin ahead of everyone. To gain that end we must have perfect discipline. I shall drive you until hell won't have it. . . . ." When he had finished, you felt as if you had been given a supercharge from some divine source. Here was a man for whom you *would* go to hell and back. (quoted in D'Este, 1995, pp. 572–573)

This example and the one that follows illustrate the oratory abilities of Patton. His prebattle speeches have become famous, immortalized in the Hollywood blockbuster of 1970 that won an Oscar for George C. Scott, who played Patton:

> Men, this stuff we hear about America wanting to stay out of the war—not wanting to fight—is a lot of bullshit. Americans love to fight—traditional! All real Americans love the sting and clash of battle. When you were kids, you all admired the champion marble player, the fastest runner, the big league ball players, the toughest boxers. Americans love a winner and will not tolerate a loser. Americans play to win all the time. I wouldn't give a hoot in hell for a man who lost and laughs. That's why Americans have never lost and will never lose a war, for the very thought of losing is hateful to an American. (quoted in D'Este, 1995, pp. 602)

As the example of Patton illustrates, the elevated mood state of hypomania, with its increased enthusiasm and emotional intensity, is infectious. It inspires and motivates. It draws other people to it. It helps those who possess it or are possessed by it to reach positions of leadership. The enhanced liveliness of hypomanics, their uninhibited gregariousness, their interpersonal charm, their ability to find vulnerable spots in others and to make use of them, their perceptiveness at the subconscious or unconscious level, and their social ease create a special kind of interpersonal and group dynamic that can positively affect organizational performance, eliciting exceptional efforts from those affected.

But, as I have suggested, leadership driven by hypomania is not always effective. Although hypomania is usually perceived as highly intoxicating, powerful, productive, and desirable—Patton was glorified by the public, after all—the flurry of ideas it generates may result in confusion rather than clarity. As a leader's hypomanic judgment sours in the absence of reality testing, all caution abandoned, absorption on colleagues' faces may be replaced by concern or even fear. Hypomania can also make a leader irritable, angry, frightened, or uncontrollable; it can imprison its victim in the blackest caves of the mind. Moreover, when the intoxication of an elevated mood state has passed, hypomanics may experience an emotional reaction of shame and disgust, an acute feeling of humiliation for their bizarre and inappropriate behavior, their violence, their financial irregularities, and their sexual indiscretions. As Robert Lowell (a manic-depressive himself) wrote in his poem "Since 1939," "If we see a light at the end of a tunnel, it's the light of an oncoming train."

Managing Hypomania

The practical consequences of hypomania usually include alienation, withdrawal from and rejection of friends, lovers, and family members, the inability to move forward in a career, and major financial problems stemming from overspending and catastrophic investment. Unfortunately, people close to a person who suffers from this syndrome tend to engage in a conspiracy of silence, preferring to ignore the symptoms and deny that there is a problem.

This conspiracy of silence applies not only to laypeople but also to physicians, who often either fail to recognize a bipolar disorder or are reluctant to acknowledge its existence. They tend instead to link symptoms to a specific environmental or interpersonal event. Although stressful incidents can certainly aggravate hypomania, to focus on such stressors is to deny the biological origin of the disorder. Adding to the difficulty in diagnosis is the cyclical nature of hypomania. Furthermore, spontaneous remission may occur, creating the illusion that the problem is under control. During remission, the severity and nature of manic episodes are minimized or even forgotten. As a consequence of all these factors, the proportion of bipolar people in treatment—a mere 27%, despite the effectiveness of available therapies—is the lowest of all major psychiatric disorders. This is scandalous, since the illness does not go away on its own. If untreated, it only worsens over time, the highs and lows becoming ever more dramatic. What makes the need for treatment even more urgent is that people with affective disorders are far more likely to commit suicide than individuals in any other psychiatric or medical risk group. The mortality rate for untreated manic–depressive patients is higher than for most types of heart disease and many types of cancer. At least 19% of all deaths among manic–depressive patients are the result of suicide, and 25 to 50% of bipolar patients attempt suicide at least once. (Goodwin & Jamison, 1990).

Recognizing the Danger Signs

As indicated, it is not always easy to discriminate between the hypomanic state and a more normal condition. Many emotions range across several mood states. Irritability and anger, for example, are part of normal human existence; however, they can also be symptoms of hypomania. Feeling good, being productive and enthusiastic, and working hard can likewise be either normal or signs of hypomania. Given this ambiguity, we must learn to unravel what is normal from what can become dysfunctional: the turbulence, impulsiveness, lack of predictability, and looming depression.

What, then, are the major indicators? The questions that need to be addressed in assessing whether a person has hypomanic tendencies include the following: Is the person overtalkative? Does the person aggressively seek out others to the point that those others feel intruded upon? Does the person laugh inappropriately and make inappropriate jokes? Does the person verbalize feelings of excessive well-being? Does the person seem to possess an inflated sense of self-esteem? Does the person have grandiose ideas? Does the person make unrealistic plans? Does the person exercise poor judgment? Is the person unusually distractible, jumping from one subject to the next? Does the person exude a physical restlessness? Is the person quickly irritated when things do not go his or her way? Is the person extremely combative and argumentative? Is the person overactive, trying

to do too many things at once? Does the person seem to have
unlimited energy? Does the person have a markedly diminished
need for sleep? Does the person appear to have diminished impulse control? Is the person sexually preoccupied and inclined
to engage in sexual indiscretions? Is the person engaged in irrational financial activities, including massive overspending and
unwise investment?

Looking for Origins

The origins of hypomanic behavior seem to be physiological.
Epidemiological evidence, particularly the study of twins, indicates that affective disorders are heritable (Goodwin & Jamison,
1990). The onset of the problem is usually in late teens or early
adulthood. Defects in the neurotransmitter system seem to play
a role in these kinds of disorders. Genetic vulnerability of the
nervous system that serves the selective integration of cognitive,
emotional, and motor functions seems to be at its base. In the
case of bipolar illnesses, the nervous system appears to be unable
to dampen unwanted oscillations and provide regulatory stability
while maintaining the necessary flexibility. But in spite of the
genetic underpinning, the nature–nurture question remains. Environmental stressors seem to play a role in the precipitation of
symptoms. It is to be expected, however, that the specific genes
responsible for this kind of illness will be identified in the near
future.

Methods of Intervention

No other form of illness has been more profoundly affected by
advances in neurophysiological research than the bipolar disorders. Lithium, the most specific antimanic drug, remains the
treatment of choice. The development of lithium as an effective
preventative measure against manic–depressive illness has been

one of the most important developments in psychiatry. Lithium helps people suffering from severe bipolar disorders to lead a more normal life. A maintenance level of lithium can lessen the frequency and severity of manic–depressive episodes. In the case of extremely severe symptoms, lithium can be supplemented with neuroleptics and other drugs. In some instances, because of undesirable side effects, substitute drugs may be necessary. All these drugs are highly effective in controlling the devastating effects of dysfunctional mood states.

Before lithium, psychotherapy was the treatment of choice for people suffering from bipolar disorders, but it tended to be a rather heroic exercise. Because of their alienating behavior, they were rarely considered good candidates for that form of treatment. Fortunately, with modern medicine permitting relief from the extremes of despair and chaotic behavior, "talk therapy" interventions that were not previously effective now work. An attitude change on the part of patients—the realization that manic–depressive illness is fundamentally a *medical* disorder—has also helped. Such a conceptualization decreases the stigma of family or individual responsibility for the origin of the disorder. It is a welcome irony that the pharmacological revolution has had a positive effect on the psychotherapy of manic–depressive people, allowing both therapist and patient to focus on psychological issues related to the disorder and confront basic life tasks without the severe disruptions that mood swings bring.

When bipolars are functioning normally, it is not easy to convince them of the need for psychotherapy. They are not always the best of listeners, and in their manic state often have little insight into their condition. Furthermore, because bipolar illness takes a heavy emotional toll due to estrangement of family members and friends, dismissal from jobs, stranded careers, drug abuse, alcoholism, financial chaos, hospitalizations, and suicide attempts, it gives rise to denial (a normal reaction to the unpleasant, the painful, the unpredictable, and the destructive) and anger. Individuals may reject treatment irrationally or direct their wrath at the clinician who treats the disease; in either case, they will not easily admit to the maladaptive nature of their behavior and actions, preferring to remember the euphoria. Fortunately, odd as this may sound, those advocating psychotherapy can use the leverage of the depressed state. In that state, bipolars tend to be more realistic about their abilities and possess more insight; thus they are more easily reachable.

Treatment is complicated in patients who, once lithium is effective, believe that they are able to handle things *without* medication. To get people to take medication who do not want to do so is no easy task. After all, *there are no pills for people not wanting to take pills.* The central theme in treatment for this subgroup is to make them realize the consequences of noncompliance. Psychotherapy can play a critical role with these patients. As difficult as psychotherapy with such people may be, it can help to clarify the ambivalence behind their concerns about the disorder, underscore their personal responsibility in maintaining a medication regime, and emphasize the need to preserve their equilibrium.

Unfortunately, there are realistic losses brought on by medication that may indeed be undesirable to the patient. In restoring emotional equilibrium, medication deprives individuals of the highs that many value, the episodes of unmitigated well-being. It also burdens many with bothersome side effects, such as a decrease in energy level, an increased need for sleep, a decrease in productivity and creativity, and a diminished interest in sexuality. Suddenly the bipolar patient is just like everyone else—a goal that is desirable only when the way is rough. To be middle-of-the-road in mood state is not attractive to one who has been on the mountaintop. Life in the new emotional state seems so much flatter, less colorful, and less fun. Bipolars with this reaction may continually compare their present state with the former in its best moments—those times when they were at their liveliest, most creative, and most outgoing. Missing the highs of hypomania (and the lively people they themselves were under its spell), they may stop taking medication. In other words, there is an addictive quality to the hypomanic state.

Therapists and patients alike hope that medication for the regulation of moods will not also suppress the creative abilities of bipolars. We can ask ourselves how General Patton would have acted if he had been on medication. Would his exceptional accomplishments during World War II have occurred? Similarly, we can ask ourselves whether the Sicilian slapping incident—with its temporary but negative consequences—would have occurred. These questions, interesting as they may be, must remain academic. However, for each patient in the present, similar questions are at the heart of treatment.

Despite the flood of new medications available for bipolar disorders, the word is not yet out to what extent creativity and productivity will be affected, if at all. Present research shows conflicting findings on the effects of medication on creative achievement. However, even if research should prove that the intensity of experience and creativity is lessened by giving pharmacological treatment to people with mood disorders, *not* giving such treatment generally results in far worse consequences. If nothing is done about bipolar illness, it is almost certain that it will progress, the mood swings becoming increasingly more frequent and severe. As mentioned before, there is also the risk of suicide. Furthermore, secondary problems centered around alcohol and drugs may come to the fore.

To ensure that people with bipolar disorders take long-term medication and allow others to help them monitor their mood states, a therapeutic alliance in the treatment process is needed—an alliance between the clinician and the affected person. An active collaboration between these two people is of extreme importance to assure compliance. Here patient education becomes important. Techniques that involve the patient in assessing progress are invaluable in fostering collaboration—techniques such as mood charting, in which the patient grades each day on a continuum from "worst I've ever felt" to "best I've ever felt." Graphing mood states is useful not only in noticing patterns of mood and treatment response but also in giving the patient a sense of control, instilling a feeling of a collaborative effort, and underscoring the importance of systematic observation.

It is important that people with a history of mood swings pace themselves. Indeed, they have a personal responsibility to do so. First and foremost, they should seek the help of both physician and psychotherapist. They should also allow family members and friends to fulfill a balancing function. These associates can take on the "container" role, psychologically "holding" the person while he or she is on a high or low.

Moreover, people with a genetic vulnerability to mood swings should strive to avoid situations that would aggravate mood state. They should likewise be careful about plunging into risky relationships. They would do themselves a service to commit themselves to life partners who have a balancing influence, partners who have a calming effect on them.

Bipolars, along with family members and other intimates, need to be educated about the nature of the disorder so that they can recognize the early signs and symptoms of elevated or depressed episodes. Changes in sleep patterns, unusual sexual or financial behavior, mood expansiveness or undue enthusiasm, involvement in an excessive number of projects, and changes in judgment are all characteristic of impending affective episodes. Given the proximity of family members, these people can be crucially important to the patient with early interventions, such as contacting the clinician. Family counseling and therapy may be called for to encourage this sort of familial collaboration, since early and aggressive treatment goes a long way in stabilizing this condition.

Colleagues can also collaborate effectively with bipolars, helping to ensure both effective treatment and organizational success. Intoxicating as their behavior may be in a work setting, hypomanics live under a sword of Damocles. Disaster is just around the corner. As in the case of life partners, colleagues can play a "container" role. Partnering more sober minds with bipolars results in highly effective teams. Given an organizational role-constellation whereby other executives can exert a balancing influence, colleagues have the power to caution the bipolar before he or she plunges into ill-conceived business ventures. When a hypomanic is the CEO of an organization, the role of board members as a balancing power is critical.

Thus, the treatment of choice for individuals suffering from hypomania is currently psychotherapy in combination with medication and social support. Medication frees the person from the devastation caused by extreme depressive and manic episodes; social support creates containment and serves as an early-warning system; and psychotherapy helps the person understand the psychological implications of mood swings and their aftermath and persuades him or her to take the medication required to prevent recurrence. Psychotherapy can also be seen as a form of preventive maintenance, as a life strategy that the bipolar makes use of to mitigate the expected fluctuations.

If these preventive steps are faithfully followed and the excesses of hypomanic behavior are thereby kept under control (without suppressing creativity and vivacity, it is hoped), people with a hypomanic disposition can make an exceptional contribution to any organization.

Dealing with the Emotionally Illiterate "Dead Fish"

Thus far we have focused on people whose symptomatology is centered around their highs. Other people offer a completely different picture: for them it is the *lack* of feeling rather than the *excess* of feeling that gives rise to difficulties. Some people are unable to relate in depth to others, evidencing instead an emotional detachment. This detachment extends beyond relationships to every area of life. Feelings of zest, enthusiasm, and passion are nonexistent; emotions are flattened; there is very little, if any, pleasure. In the absence of emotion, such people live in a world permeated by tedium and apathy. When this detachment appears in the workplace—especially in those holding leadership roles—it affects morale, creativity, spontaneity, and productivity.

Alexithymia: The Dead-Fish Syndrome

In psychiatry the word *alexithymic* is applied to people who have a dead-fish quality to their behavior—individuals who either struggle, or are unable, to understand their emotions or moods, who are incapable of perceiving the subtleties of mood change. In such people, the normal experience and expression of emotions has been subdued, removed from conscious awareness (Krystal, 1988; McDougall, 1989). These people are, in effect, emotional illiterates. They engage in "operative thinking"; that is, there is a rather concrete, mechanical quality to their speech and expression. There is no color to their description of events, and there is no reflective self-awareness. They express little interest in their inner subjective lives. Instead, they possess a more externally oriented style of thinking.

The term *alexithymia* was coined in the early 1970s. It comes from the Greek and means, literally, "no word for emotions." The concept of alexithymia is rooted in a large body of consistent clinical and phenomenological observation that telescopes a number of features into an easily communicated term. In a nutshell, *alexithymia* refers to a cluster of characteristics that include an inability to verbally describe feelings, an impoverished fantasy life, and a pragmatic thought content. Alexithymics do not seem to experience intrapsychic conflict. They are unable to symbolize their emotions as fantasies, dreams, images, and desires. They have marked difficulty verbally expressing or describing their feelings. They go through considerable effort, however, to mask this deficit. They frequently behave like color-blind patients who have learned to *infer,* from indirect indicators, what they cannot see. Unfortunately, although alexithymics may use the right words to describe certain feelings, that is where the process stops; they cannot develop their personal reactions to emotionally charged issues any further. Their observations remain at a rather vague and general level. They seem to live in a world of concrete operations. Their tendency to externalize—that is, to steer clear of emotion—is reflected in a cognitive style focused on external processes and activities. True alexithymics are individuals who feel and show neither passion nor enthusiasm, individuals who have no fire in their belly.

Alexithymics tend to adopt a rather lifeless, detail-oriented, stilted way of speaking. Rather than developing a language of feelings and symbols, these people tend to communicate through "organ language": with no other emotional outlet, their emotional life (including whatever primitive fantasy and dream life they have) is channeled into physical symptoms. Via a mysterious leap from the mind to the body, they communicate psychic distress by means of physical complaints. While they rarely express sadness, anger, or joy, they can describe in endless detail what ails them physically.

Identification of alexithymics is not difficult. They behave like the Tin Man in *The Wizard of Oz,* the character who could not cry. For the Tin Man, the expression of emotions was dangerous. After all, if he were to cry, the tears would rust the hinges of his face and his joints. If that happened, he would no longer be able to open his mouth, talk, or walk.

Alexithymia is essentially a communication disorder. The following interview between an executive and an organizational coach sheds some light on the modus operandi of the alexithymic:

Consultant: Can you say something about the kind of work you do?
Executive: I'm in charge of the planning department. I've been in this function since September three years ago. I joined the company two and a half years earlier. Before that I worked five years for a large department store chain. I've always done quite similar work. In my role as planning director, I ask for input from the people responsible in other areas. It means a lot of e-mail. I compile the data people submit and try to shape it into an integrated plan. I remind the heads of the various departments and regions of a number of specific deadlines that we have to meet. For example, there's the September date. You can

see that on the flow chart (pointing). Another date important for the planning cycle is in October. Do you notice how the numbers relate to each other? Some consolidation of input takes place in November. Of course, the whole planning process starts much earlier. I remind people by e-mail way back in March and then June that they have to come up with some provisional information by certain preliminary dates.

Consultant: You find that people take an active interest in the plan? They find it useful?

Executive: I don't know. But every company *needs* plans.

Consultant: Do you like the kind of work you do?

Executive: We need a plan. Without a plan many processes in this organization would come to a halt.

Consultant: Does your work imply many personal interchanges with colleagues?

Executive: It could, but I try to minimize such interactions. I'm interested in facts. I find that e-mail and the occasional memo serve me well; they get the job done.

Consultant: Are there certain things in the organization that irritate you, make you less effective?

Executive: Not really. With the plan things work fine.

Consultant: Can you say anything more about that, about how you feel about the organization?

Executive: What else would you like to hear?

Consultant: I heard that you weren't considered for promotion to the board. Instead, a person who used to work for you got promoted. How did you feel about that? Were you very disappointed?

Executive: I don't understand your question.

Consultant: Did you feel hurt? Were you upset that someone else got promoted?

Executive: Not that I can remember. Why would I be upset? Life in organizations is like that.

Consultant: What about your physical well-being?

Executive: I sometimes have asthma attacks. They come and go. I also have stomach problems.

Consultant: Do you have any idea why you get these asthma or stomach problems? Do you feel that they're related to your job?

Executive: Well, I don't know exactly *how* to explain them. They're bothersome, that's for sure. I always get this stomach pain somewhere around here (gesturing). At times, it moves a bit. It comes and goes. I don't feel sorry for myself, though. I can live with it. Pills seem to help somewhat.

Consultant: Do you have any interests outside work?

Executive: Not many. I'm building a garage, though. I like masonry, working with bricks.

Consultant: Are you married?

Executive: I used to be. My wife doesn't live with me anymore. One day she told me that she'd had enough. I still don't understand it. I thought everything was fine. She just started screaming at me one day and then left. I don't know why she did that. I didn't see any grounds for divorce.
Consultant: Do you ever dream or daydream?
Executive: No, I don't remember any dreams.
Consultant: Do you ever have wild fantasies?
Executive: What did you say?
Consultant: Wild fantasies—do you ever have them?
Executive: I don't understand.
Consultant: Fantasies about doing something completely different, for example. Take Gauguin, who decided to become a painter and left his family to live on a Polynesian island after working as a stockbroker for years.
Executive: I still don't know what you mean.
Consultant: How do you feel now?
Executive: I don't know what you expect me to say when you ask me how I feel. I told you I have stomachaches.

Coping with Alexithymia

The preceding interview illustrates how hard it is to establish an effective rapport with alexithymics, who tend to be rigid, say little, and present trivial incidents from everyday life instead of focusing on real issues. Their language is flat and banal, focused on the present and reporting chronologically stated facts. When talking about their experiences, they fail to supply color; everything happens in shades of gray. When drawn against their will into relational conflict, they tend to respond with action—for example, purchasing new computers for a work team experiencing problems in collaboration—rather than really addressing and managing the conflict.

Recognizing the Danger Signs

People who have to deal with alexithymics sense the dullness and boredom quickly, and they become frustrated when their attempts at interaction fail. Winston Churchill's description of the Russian politician Vyacheslav Molotov fits this type of person generally: "I have never seen a human being who more perfectly represented the modern conception of a robot." Alexithymics seem to live out a robotlike existence, going through life mechanically, as suggested by their stiffness of posture and lack of expressive facial movements.

That mechanical quality is the essence of alexithymia; it reaches into every corner of life. As I have noted, alexithymics express emotion in physical terms rather than abstract thoughts. They appear to remain unperturbed by what other people would find emotionally shattering experiences. A death in the family, a partner's infidelity, betrayal, being passed over for a promotion—nothing seems to ruffle them. All experiences slide into a black hole of inexpressiveness and blankness. Superficially, alexithymics often appear to be well adapted and show a high degree of social conformity. Indeed, they seem to be superadjusted to reality. But theirs is a *pseudo*normality; apparently incapable of spontaneous reaction, they are "normopaths" (McDougall, 1985).

The emotional illiteracy of alexithymics is revealed both in their incapacity for empathy and in their mechanical, robotic responses to conflict. That incapacity for empathy is not surprising, certainly, given the difficulty alexithymics have with recognizing and using their own feelings as signals to themselves. Preoccupied with the concrete and objective, alexithymics have no use for metaphors, allusions, and hidden meanings; such verbal tools are a foreign language to them.

What, then, are the major indicators of alexithymia? (Sifneos, 1973; Taylor, 1994). In determining whether a person possesses alexithymic qualities, the following questions should be asked: Does the person have difficulty communicating with other people? Does the person describe endless details rather than feelings? Does the person use action to express emotion? When talking about feelings, does the person use inappropriate words? Does the person appear confused about what emotion he or she is feeling? Does the person find it difficult to tell how he or she feels about others? Does the person describe the circumstances rather than the feelings surrounding an event? Does the person become preoccupied describing physical problems? Does the person suffer from an absence of fantasy and imagination? Do dreams and day-dreams play little role in the person's life? Does the person prefer movies with action rather than psychological dramas? Is the person's thought content associated more with external events than with fantasy or emotion? Does the person find life pretty boring most of the time, rarely exhibiting excitement? When talking with such a person, do you yourself get bored and frustrated, eager to get away from him or her?

Looking for Origins

There are a number of explanations for this kind of disorder—some physiological, some psychological (Taylor, 1994). Researchers who have a physiological answer to the origins of alexithymia see it as a deficit in the connection between the left and right hemispheres of the brain. They believe that something has gone very wrong with the "wiring" between these two units. Researchers who see the origins as psychological look to the person's early relationships with the primary caregiver.

Neuropsychologists—those who look to hemispheric specialization as the cause of alexithymia—have discovered that the two cerebral hemispheres process the information of mental life differently. The left hemisphere is more verbal, more analytical, more attuned to detail and fact. The right hemisphere, in contrast, is more intuitive and inferential and seems to play a special role in the experience and expression of emotion. This difference in information processing is highlighted among people who have undergone cerebral commissurotomy (the so-called split-brain operation)—a procedure that severs the connections between the right and left hemispheres and is done, for example, to control intractable seizures or to help a person who seems to be unable to execute a pattern of movements. Such people may report being emotionally excited by certain arousing sexually explicit or aggressive imagery but cannot describe why. Without the connection between the verbal–analytical side and the emotional–imagery side of the brain, the source and meaning of emotional reactions remains beyond rational awareness.

Neurophysiologists have pointed out that there are similarities between alexithymics and split-brain patients. Alexithymics behave as if the right and left hemispheres were disconnected from each other; they exhibit a lack of interhemispheric communication. The right hemisphere's passions are inaccessible to the left hemisphere's verbal, conscious integration. Somehow a dampening of signals, or perhaps simply a lack of amplification of signals, occurs between the two hemispheres. Consequently, the person's emotional life remains out of conscious awareness. Because one of the right hemisphere's specializations is processing body image and somatic awareness, what should have been expressed as emotional reactions is channeled into bodily symptoms.

Some psychiatrists and psychoanalysts trace the roots of alexithymic behavior to a lack of transitional space in childhood. They attribute alexithymia to disturbances in the mother–child relationship, suggesting that some overprotective mothers frustrate their child's individuality and attempts at play, not allowing the infant to feel for him- or herself. The infant becomes trapped in an aborted symbiotic relationship whereby extreme dependence is artificially prolonged. Such mothers treat their children as extensions of themselves and keep them under their constant surveillance. They treat the child's body as if it were their property, monitoring closely all bodily signals and disorders. At the same time, the child's natural emotions are stifled, thwarting development of an autonomous feeling of identity, of appropriate affect, of the ability to differentiate and verbalize emotions, and of the capacity to form symbols. As a result, alexithymics ignore the distress signals given by their mind; they are out of touch with their inner psychological world. If that inner world communicates with them at all it is indirectly, through physical distress; they then pass those somatic complaints off as interpersonal communication. Likewise, concrete external details become the substitute for internal fantasy.

The Alexithymic Continuum

Alexithymia is not an all-or-nothing phenomenon. Rather, it exists along a continuum of affective experience and expression. A distinction is sometimes made between primary and secondary alexithymia. The former implies a deficit in experiential thinking and is a lifelong dispositional factor, which can lead to somatic illness. Of the two subtypes, it is the more difficult to change, being a relatively permanent condition. Secondary alexithymia, generally the result of certain developmental restrictions, manifests as alexithymic*like* behavior. In this subtype, alexithymic reactions are a consequence of one's way of processing stimuli under specific conditions. Put another way, stress causes the person characterized by secondary alexithymia to block his or her expressive potential. Rather than a permanent personality characteristic, secondary alexithymia covers a set of coping behaviors that occur in certain stressful situations only. It therefore tends to be of a more temporary and intermittent nature. Because it is more circumstance-specific than primary alexithymia, it is also more prevalent—indeed, all of us might react in an alexithymiclike fashion in certain situations—and is more responsive to efforts to change.

Alexithymia in the Workplace

Circumstances that encourage alexithymia are found with appalling frequency in the workplace. To illustrate how alexithymiclike behavior can be caused by the work environment, I offer the following revealing excerpt from an interview with a CEO:

I sometimes think back to the time when I was a child. I have the image of a person full of life. I remember the tantrums I used to have as a kid. I would scream and yell at my mother if things weren't going my way. Not exactly pretty behavior, but at least I showed that I was alive, that I cared. At university I remember the pleasure I experienced when our team won a soccer game. There was this enormous feeling of exhilaration. Even when I started working, I remember temporary highs—for example, when I was asked to set up a sales office in Indonesia. Now, at the age of 47, all these feelings seem somewhat strange to me. It's as if they're from another planet.

Whatever passions I had, my company has taken care of them. I learned very early on that "Don't show any excitement" is the rule around here. And I've been very good at following that rule. I know that behind my back people call me a cold fish. I've overheard them say that I must have ice water in my veins. They may have a point. I keep myself well under control, and it's not even a challenge anymore.

At this point in my life *everything* seems rather flat. At home my way of interacting isn't much different from at work. Now, with the children gone, when I'm alone with my wife there seems to be very little to say. We go through the motions. We're like two ships passing in the night.

We all know people like this; they populate a good share of the offices and cubicles of the world. That is because alexithymiclike behavior fits in so well with so many organizations. After all, what organization wants to have a reputation for encouraging emotional expressiveness?

Many companies seem to enforce a division of emotional labor. Blue-collar workers are permitted to express emotions while white-collar employees are required to be paragons of emotional control. Thus we often see quasi-alexithymic behavior at the senior executive level. Think about all the corporate types scuttling around the workplace—the men in their gray flannel suits, the women in their severely tailored outfits—who make all the right noises, who behave appropriately, but in whom nothing distinctively human is revealed. They follow the rules, never rocking the boat, but they do not know how to dream or play. The words *vision* and *inspiration* are foreign to them. They cannot create "stretch" in the organization, because they engender no enthusiasm and inspire no peak experiences.

"If it ain't broke, don't fix it" is the slogan of these executives. Dealing with discontinuities in the environment is not their strength. And *encouraging* such discontinuities? Don't even think it! Welcoming change is not their forte. *Incrementalism* is written on their banner.

Interaction with people like this is draining; there is so little emotional resonance that we may wonder whether anybody is home. After a short while, being with them gets to be boring. One feels like kicking them just to get a reaction, *any* reaction. Simply conversing with these people can be exhausting because of their lifelessness. And they do not wear well: it takes a lot of energy to keep emotions under lock and key for long periods of time.

Though few organizations would set out to find a CEO or other senior executive who fits the above description, many nonetheless encourage alexithymiclike behavior. And the years take their toll. Whatever life these people once possessed is driven out of them. Such individuals may not be truly alexithymic, but because alexithymiclike behavior is encouraged in the workplace, behaving in an emotionless way has become second nature. They conform to what their organization expects of them, and this lack of emotionality eventually begins to stick. It turns into the real thing. Whatever playfulness the person once felt has been replaced by ritualism and apathy. The result? A life without pleasure.

Methods of Intervention

How do we deal with alexithymia? Is it treatable? So far the answer is ambiguous. If we are dealing with primary alexithymia, where the etiology seems to be associated with genetic neurophysiological or anatomical deficits (as opposed to secondary alexithymia, where developmental, sociocultural, or psychodynamic factors play a role), psychodynamic forms of therapy—those that are more self-reflective and insight-oriented—are contraindicated. Given the personality makeup of primary alexithymics, such techniques of intervention may actually result in a worsening of the condition, because of the anxiety evoked by psychotherapeutic interventions. But whatever intervention techniques are used with alexithymics, treatment is not an easy ride.

In the case of secondary alexithymia, or alexithymiclike behavior, a variety of interventions can be beneficial. For secondary alexithymics, psychodynamic psychotherapy (with some modifications) can offer some help. But both therapist and client need to be patient; the process of helping alexithymics identify and verbalize their emotions can be long and tedious. It takes considerable time for alexithymics to learn to recognize, tolerate, and verbalize different feelings. They have to practice their capacity for reflective self-observation. On their part, therapists have to come to grips with the boredom such people may engender in them—a very human response to a state of nonrelatedness.

In general, however, from a time-effectiveness perspective, *supportive* psychotherapy seems to have more promise than *psychodynamic* therapy. Group and family therapy can also be helpful, with group members and spouses lending assistance as educators of emotions. Interventions that are anxiety-suppressive, include active reassurance, and demand minimal intrapsychic work tend to be more effective with these people.

Behavioral techniques such as biofeedback, relaxation training, autogenic training, guided imagery, and hypnosis may be of some help with both forms of alexithymia. These techniques give people a sense of control over stressful responses and increase their awareness of the relationship between bodily sensations and environmental events. In certain instances, biological interventions in the form of various forms of medication may be of some help to facilitate communication between the hemispheres. Often the best strategy, however, is a combination of approaches.

In the case of secondary alexithymia, if the organization was part of the problem, it can be part of the cure. If key executives believe that a repressive company culture has had dire effects on personnel, they can improve the situation by changing their tone rather drastically. If they are convincing—if employees believe that emotional expressiveness has become an accepted part of work behavior and will no longer have negative consequences—they will inspire other executives and workers to rise to the occasion. As you will recall, it is secondary alexithymics who have the greatest potential to unlearn dead-fish behavior. Although change may take considerable effort, these patterns, though not integral to the personality, may be deeply rooted, it can be achieved.

Companies in which emotionless interaction is an intrinsic part of the organizational culture face an uphill battle. Unlearning this kind of behavior in such companies may require a specific, major impetus toward change—the sort of corporate "revolution" that is usually triggered from the outside. The catalysts can be many. Perhaps the most typical catalyst is the arrival of senior executives from outside the organization who relate to each other very differently from the way their predecessors did. Given the elevated rank of these new executives, their behavior will be widely noted and gradually imitated. Because the presence of a new cadre of executives is usually the result of a much-needed turnaround, a merger, or an acquisition, it is even more likely that the key players will try to introduce a cultural revolution, making a great effort to change the way people relate to each other. During the process of change and transformation, secondary alexithymics may discover the emotional potential that has been hidden deep within them. Like the Tin Man once he discovered that he had a heart, they may no longer be afraid to express themselves. Such a change in relating will go a long way toward raising morale, making the organization a better place to work.

Managing Personalities at Both Ends of the Spectrum

This review of hypomania and alexithymia, and of the behaviors they result in, was intended to foster a better understanding of troubled employees at both ends of the emotional spectrum. As we have observed, hypomanics, if handled well, can be a great source of strength to any organization. The passion of these people, their enthusiasm, their inspiration, and their vision, goes a long way toward creating a great organization. In contrast, unchecked hypomanic behavior can contribute significantly to the downfall of an organization. Executives under the thrall of alexithymia likewise have the power to bring down the organization. Because they do not emanate the dynamism, inspiration, and vision that a high-performing organization needs, they cannot motivate others to make exceptional efforts or stimulate in them a passion for learning and further development. Because they do not handle discontinuous change well, they impede organizational progress. Their emotional absence has an infectious demotivating effect, putting its stamp on corporate culture, discouraging creativity and strategic innovation, and even contributing to a decrease in organizational performance.

This look at executives who occupy extreme positions on the emotional spectrum—hypomania and alexithymia—highlights the importance of effective emotional management. It is clear that emotions are the lifeblood of organizations. They determine the nature and intensity of interpersonal and group dynamics. They are, however, commodities that have to be handled with care. People at the helm of high-performance organizations exercise that care; they address the emotional factor. They recognize their need to know how to deal with emotional issues, and they appreciate the diversity of emotions among their associates.

This ability to manage emotions is grounded in emotional intelligence, which is the product of an inner journey of self-discovery. Only when we understand our own emotions can we appreciate how emotions affect others. Knowing how to be empathic also plays an important role in emotional management. Yet empathy too comes only through a solid understanding of our own emotions. Only with that understanding of self and others can we try to use the emotional levers that will make employees more effective.

Above the entrance of the temple of Apollo at Delphi was written "Know thyself." That statement is as relevant today as it was when it was first penned. Carl Jung shared basically the same advice: "The man who has not gone through the hell of his passions has never overcome them either." People who know themselves, who have a genuine interest in others, and who are in touch with their feelings are the ones most successful at handling others, whatever the emotional makeup of those others may be, including the extremes on the emotional spectrum: the hypomanics and alexithymics. If executives who possess such knowledge are willing to share their emotional intelligence with others and are prepared to "contain" the emotions of others in stressful situations, they can help their colleagues grow, develop, learn, and be creative. In our knowledge-based society, this kind of learning brings competitive advantage. People with this emotional awareness exemplify the sometimes overused phrase "People are our greatest asset."

References

American Psychiatric Association. (1994). *Diagnostic and statistical manual of mental disorders* (4th ed.). Washington, DC: Author.

Blanchard, E. B., Arena, J. G., & Pallmeyer, T. P. (1981). Psychosomatic properties of a scale to measure alexithymia. *Psychotherapy and Psychosomatics, 35,* 64–71.

D'Este, C. (1995). *Patton: A genius for war.* New York: HarperCollins.

Goodwin, F. K., & Jamison, K. R. (1990). *Manic–depressive illness.* New York: Oxford University Press.

Krystal, H. (1988). *Integration and self-healing: Affect, trauma, alexithymia.* Hillsdale, NJ: Analytic Press.

McDougall, J. (1985). *Theaters of the mind.* New York: Basic Books.

McDougall, J. (1989). *Theaters of the body.* New York: Basic Books.

Sifneos, P. E. (1973). The prevalence of alexithymic characteristics in psychosomatic patients. *Psychotherapy and Psychosomatics, 22,* 255–262.

Taylor, G. J. (1994). The alexithymia construct: Conceptualization, validation, and relationship with basic dimensions of personality. *New Trends in Experimental Clinical Psychiatry, 10,* 61–74.

Weismann, M. M., Leaf, P. J., & Tischer, G. L. (1988). Affective disorders in five United States communities. *Psychological Medicine, 18,* 141–153.

3

Organizational Sleepwalkers: Emotional Distress at Midlife

By passions I mean appetite, anger, fear, confidence, envy, joy, friendly feelings, hatred, longing, emulation, pity, and in general the feelings that are accompanied by pleasure or pain. (Aristotle)

To those who are awake, there is one ordered universe, whereas in sleep each man turns away from this world to one of his own. (Heraclitus)

Man is only great when he acts from the passions. (Benjamin Disraeli)

Do you think my mind is maturing late, or simply rotted early? (Ogden Nash)

This chapter further develops the concept of emotional numbness—the second dysfunctional emotional behavior pattern introduced in the previous chapter—looking in particular at how this phenomenon develops in some individuals as a response to middle age. Although emotional numbness touches all parts of life, this discussion focuses on the organizational context. For some executives, the stresses and strains of midlife (including stresses involving career issues) serve as the catalyst for this dysfunctional emotional behavior. Their reactions are of a quasi-alexithymic and anhedonic nature. Some of the characteristics of this dysfunctional emotional pattern are delineated in the

95

pages that follow, as is the related experience of depersonalization. This chapter then identifies some of the factors that contribute to these phenomena and offers recommendations for dealing
with them.

Introduction

At midlife, a stage typically given to reassessment, many executives are at the height of their powers, exerting significant influence on their organization and supporting a heavy and varied
weight of responsibility. For some individuals this critical midlife period is a time of major revitalization, the prime of life.
Others, however, have great difficulty in passing smoothly
through this life stage; for them, midlife represents a disturbing
period of invalidating reappraisal and self-doubt.

Whether it is experienced positively or negatively, the self-
questioning that characterizes this time is a logical development
in the life of an individual. As Carl Jung once said, ''Aging
people should know that their lives are not mounting and unfolding, but that an inexorable inner process forces the contrac-
tion of life. For a younger person it is almost a sin—and certainly
a danger—to be too much occupied with himself; but for the
aging person it is a duty and a necessity to give serious attention
to himself. After having lavished its light upon the world, the
sun withdraws its rays in order to illumine itself'' (Jung, 1933,
p. 125).

Midlife is a time of greater reflection, of questioning and
seeking, of increased interiority. Personal relationships and work
activities, the two anchors of emotional stability, generally begin
to be regarded in a different light at this stage. The ways in
which people respond to these reflective impulses vary greatly,
however.

There is no escape from the conflicts of middle age. Consciously or unconsciously we protest that there are limits to our
omnipotence, that there are limits to what life has left to offer

us. Many people cope with this well, adapting to aging more or less gracefully. They see midlife as an important transition point from which to review and assess the past and make plans for the future. But not everybody responds constructively to the transition of middle age. For some, the passage through middle age turns into a full-blown crisis. Consider Dante's words in *The Divine Comedy* (1304/1954):

Midway in our life's journey, I went astray
from the straight road and woke to find myself
alone in a dark wood. How shall I say

what wood that was? I never saw so drear,
so rank, so arduous a wilderness!
Its very memory gives a shape to fear. (p. 28)

It was in recognition of these conflicts that scholars introduced the notion of the midlife crisis. According to psychoanalyst and sociologist Eliott Jaques, such a crisis is precipitated by the growing, inescapable awareness of the inevitability of one's own death, which awakens fantasies of annihilation and abandonment. Jaques noted that the resultant serious psychological disturbance could lead to manic behavior, depression, and breakdown (1965). Developmental psychologist Erik Erikson viewed the middle years as a time when the individual has to deal with the opposing forces of generativity and stagnation (1963). In other words, a person has to either adjust to feeling alive through contact with others (particularly the oncoming generation) or risk entering a cocoon of self-concern, isolation, and psychic deadness.

For many people this crisis point stimulates the sense that they need to act before it is too late, that they should disrupt the comfortable routines of life, make dramatic changes. They recognize that if they fail to act, the alternative will likely be stagnation. These confrontations with the self can be accompanied by great stress. For people who find this dilemma—generativity versus stagnation—anxiety-provoking, getting older is accompanied by considerable psychological pain.

The stress of this experience can be expressed in many ways. Some people give in to dysfunctional, impulsive behavior, often fortified by drugs or alcohol. Other people become prematurely old and excessively routine-bound, wary of trying anything new. Still others begin to lose interest, energy, and concentration. Another group experiences depressive reactions. Unfortunately, none of these symptoms, these states of negativity, augurs well for a person's longevity.

For many people a major source of stress is found in midlife changes in the home environment—children moving out on their own, for example. Relationships at work, however, can also be major stressors. At midlife many executives ask themselves whether they should be content with what they have achieved in the workplace or strive for something more. They evaluate whether their original career goals match what they have achieved to date. What sets this evaluative process in motion is the fact that the discrepancy between aspirations and current achievements becomes more noticeable at midlife. For some executives this process of internal questioning is quite alarming. They may feel dead-ended at work and become painfully aware that time is running out. They may have difficulty dealing with the changes in life's circumstances. Some become frantic; others acquire a zombielike quality. Although people in this latter group are *present* at work, they appear to sleepwalk. For these people the comment of one wit—''The brain is a wonderful organ; it starts working the moment you get up in the morning and does not stop until you get to the office''—seems appropriate.

These people, instead of adding value in the workplace, seem to be only going through the motions. Merely spending time at work—looking at the clock and shuffling papers—replaces being truly engaged in creative work. These workers lack passion for what they are doing; they have little sense of joy, affection, love, pride, or self-respect. Strong emotions of any sort, negative as well as positive, seem to be absent. Even outside the workplace, there is little if any pleasure.

The Challenges of Midlife

Physiological Changes

Many things, experiential, behavioral, cognitive, and physiological, happen simultaneously at midlife (Diamond, 1997; Greer, 1991). Let us start at the end of that list. A major catalyst for the transition and reappraisal process of middle age appears to be physical wear and tear. Painful and pleasurable physical experiences having colored the early developmental processes, the primacy of bodily experiences continues throughout adulthood. To paraphrase Freud's comment that "anatomy is destiny," physiology is destiny. As we know all too well from having been sick, the ego is foremost a *bodily* ego. Bodily sensations determine our way of relating to the external world. When there is something wrong with the body, all other problems tend to take second place.

One subtle way of experiencing the reality of bodily change is by simply looking at ourselves. For some people, the daily process of staring in the mirror once the bloom of youth has faded is like looking at death on the installment plan. The mirror is where, incrementally, the decline of the body can be observed. And when the integrity of the body image begins to disintegrate, that process is echoed by a string of associated mental processes.

At midlife these concerns with altered body image come to a head. The changes are no longer dismissible. The physiological implications of aging are there for all to see—baldness, gray hair, wrinkles, sagging breasts, a belly, glasses, hearing loss, a decrease in cardiovascular efficiency, and a slower response time. These transformations, making the maintenance of a youthful image of the self more difficult, force people to reflect on their lost youth.

Sexuality is also an important factor at midlife. Men, although generally referring to this issue rather indirectly, may have concerns about a decrease in or loss of sexual potency. From midlife onward there is a gradual diminution in sexual interest, arousal, and activity. To people for whom sexuality has been an essential part of identity, concerns about failing sexual performance can be devastating. To have this part of the self malfunction can cause considerable agony. Unfortunately, difficulties in sexual intercourse are often translated into a self-fulfilling prophecy. When a person doubts his ability to perform, the risk of failure becomes greater. Thus a considerable number of cases of impotence are caused by psychological rather than physiological factors. Furthermore, two of the major contributors to impotence are excessive alcohol consumption and excessive use of drugs such as tranquilizers and antidepressants—the side effects of stress—rather than aging (Nemroff & Colarusso, 1990; Oldham & Liebert, 1989; Pollock & Greenspan, 1980/1993).

For women the onset of menopause can be stressful. Particularly to those who delayed having children in order to pursue a career, menopause is a forceful and unwelcome reminder of the implications of the biological clock. For some women this change in life is marked by depression, weight gain, tiredness, headaches, palpitations, insomnia, and digestive problems (Sheehy, 1995).

Furthermore, given the premium that society puts on looks, and given that self-esteem and sexual body image are very closely linked, many women become preoccupied with losing their femininity and sexual attractiveness. Having the sense that their youthful good looks are fading and that the time for having a child is running out, some experience serious coping difficulties. Although women are more susceptible than men to self-esteem problems rooted in appearance, many men suffer from such problems as well. Both men and women may resort to cosmetic surgery in order to preserve their youthful appearance.

Changes in Social Relations

For some individuals the stability of the marriage becomes a major concern at midlife. If increased routine has led to a sense of ennui and tediousness, couples may begin to wonder whether they should be content with a boring but untroubled marriage or should look for a new partner as a way of revitalizing their emotional life. What often brings matters to a head is the sense that time is running out, that some kind of action needs to be taken. People troubled by marital ennui feel that if no immediate (and dramatic) action is taken to get them out of the rut, change will *never* happen.

What often sparks these kinds of preoccupations is the empty-nest syndrome, the depression that some parents feel when their children leave home. This depression is not inevitable, however. For many people the empty nest comes as a relief. Those individuals who do become depressed with the departure of the youngest child may have invested so much in childrearing (having found no compensating activities) that they experience a great sense of loss when their offspring cease to be dependent on them. It is difficult for these people to deal with being a twosome once more. In marriages that have been maintained largely through and for the children, there may be very little left to hold the couple together once the children have gone. In some instances this may be a stimulus for divorce. Yet even if such a rupture occurs late in marriage, it has its roots in a much earlier period of the couple's life together.

Changes in male and female roles may also contribute to disequilibrium at this life stage. Men and women often start to take on somewhat different roles as they enter middle age. The traditional stereotypes of men being more active, independent, and assertive and women being more passive, dependent, emotional, and nurturing may no longer be appropriate (if they were ever appropriate at all). A gradual reversal—a redefinition of roles, if you will—sometimes takes place as people enter middle age: at midlife men may shift toward a more nurturing role, while women may become more assertive (Chiriboga, 1981; Jung, 1933; Neugarten, 1970). If partners are unable to adjust to these different ways of interacting, such changes may destabilize a marriage. Furthermore, what may have been good at 20 may not work well at 45. People tend to age at different speeds: chronological, physiological, emotional, and mental ages are not necessarily synchronized, whether between people or within individuals.

In general, at midlife people experience a growing awareness of aging, illness, and the resulting dependence on others. The serious illness or death of a friend, relative, or acquaintance—an event that becomes less of an anomaly with each passing year—is for many an ominous sign of things to come. Some people, wondering when *their* time will be up, struggle mightily with the idea that it is their turn to grow old and die. Especially devastating—because it shatters the unconscious conviction of one's own immortality—is the decline and death of one's parents, an occurrence that can cause a great sense of disorientation.

With the physical decline of one's parents comes a role reversal of another sort. As they grow older, parents begin to abdicate their role as caregivers and need increasing care themselves. This reversal, difficult, certainly, for those who are aging, can be a major source of stress for the younger generation as well. Changes in one's perception of aging parents, along with one's own role-change from "player" to "coach," have a disruptive effect on a person's mental map. It is hard to relinquish the inner perception of the omnipotent parent of childhood, the person who was always able to make things right. When the situation is reversed—the one who could always be depended on now depending on the "child"—many midlifers respond to the stress with depressive reactions, regressive episodes, or hypochondriacal concerns. The care of a demented relative can be particularly stressful, often contributing to emotional disturbance on the part of the caregiver.

Apart from the time and energy needed to take care of aging parents, there is also the psychological drain of seeing what is happening to them. Not all people age gracefully. If aging is a problematic process for our parents, we wonder whether we ourselves will age in a similar manner. Will we follow a parallel pattern into decline, or can we be different? Frequently, in our parents we see caricatures of ourselves.

The problem of care-needing parents is exacerbated if the midlifers are sandwiched between their aging parents and their children. Being in that position often implies a considerable financial burden, especially if the children are in college. For people so situated, midlife is a period characterized by overwhelming pressures and obligations. Various stress reactions are often the consequence.

Above all, the realization of the gradual disintegration of the body, reflected in what is happening to one's parents, evokes very primitive forms of anxiety. Death, which used to be an abstraction, becomes a more personal issue, a tragic reality pertaining to the self. As a result, fear of death becomes stronger. Time, which used to be calculated as time-since-birth, now becomes time-until-death. This can stimulate an overwhelming need to come to terms with unresolved problems before it is too late.

An acceptance of the inevitability of our own death is one of the challenges of midlife. Denial of this prospect cannot be squared with a realistic appraisal of life. This period also initiates a mourning process for our lost childhood and youth, along with a reexamination of our life goals—that greater sense of interiority described by Jung.

Changing Perceptions of Work

Given all these transitions on various fronts, midlife is likely to be a time when ambitions become less abstract. In the workplace,

executives are increasingly influenced by the constraints and opportunities of reality; the grandiose illusions of adolescence and
young adulthood, healthy prerogatives of the younger generation,
are of necessity relinquished. Forced to come to terms with their
limitations, executives give up fantasies of omnipotence and invulnerability and root their activities in the here-and-now. The
instrumental approach to a career, doing things now to benefit
one later, is abandoned, since the postponement of gratification
is no longer attractive or stimulating. It is important for executives at this stage to be able to mourn unattained goals and to
accept what has been achieved. Confronting this necessity can
be very hard, as it involves abandoning old dreams and redefin-
ing the nature of the challenges to be faced.

One of the most difficult of these challenges to accept is the
possibility of loss of effectiveness in the workplace. With the
plateauing of an executive's career, a real possibility at this stage
in life, routine sets in. For some, new learning slows down or
becomes nonexistent. The excitement of exploring new things
disappears and life at work becomes repetitive, leading in some
to depression and a loss of self-confidence.

For some people these transformations in the "inner theater" lead to what the Germans call *Torschlusspanik* (literally,
panic because the gate is closing), the feeling that very little time
is left to pursue old dreams. Such individuals may try to ward
off these feelings via the manic defense; in other words, they
may engage in a frenzy of activities. Sensing that interiority
might set off thoughts of depression and death anxiety, they use
the manic defense as a form of denial, a way of dealing with the
sense that time is running out, a weapon against the encroaching
sense of deadness. These defensive activities often take place at
work, with desperate efforts made to achieve one's original career goals. Frenetic efforts may also be non-work-directed, however. Midlifers may try to appear more youthful through their
social and recreational activities, resorting to age-inappropriate
(and sometimes even promiscuous) behavior as a way to prove

their youth and potency. After all, emotions tend to be more intense in new relationships.

This expansive mode, however, this preoccupation with doing, not being, this illusion that there are no limit to one's abilities, comes at the cost of one's awareness of inner reality. Moreover, given the emotional drain of this kind of behavior, its uplifting effect cannot last. Eventually, the other side of the coin will show, making for feelings of depression and a sense of futility.

Narcissistic individuals, in particular, begin to deteriorate at midlife. As their charm and their good looks begin to wear out, other people within their sphere become less receptive, less willing to provide them with narcissistic "supplies." In addition, the awareness of the limitations of their achievements may lead to feelings of envy, rage, and defensive devaluation of those who are perceived as being more successful (see chapter 5 for a further elaboration of this theme). Envious of youth (even their own progeny) and engaged in self-deception, they lose whatever external and internal sources of support might have still been available. Some narcissists may become more introverted in a world seen as devoid of meaning and perceived as hostile. Relational failures, fatalism, isolation, and rigidity are common patterns.

Given the importance of narcissism in leadership development, many executives are especially affected by this category of midlife problems. Some executives, however, may also have serious difficulties in dealing with the developmental tasks of midlife. Indications of such problems are the inability to enjoy sexuality, the incapacity to relate in depth to others, emotional detachment, and a lack of satisfaction at work.

All these midlife problems seem to have a common denominator: a lack of passion. Feelings of zest and enthusiasm are mere memories; emotions are flattened; pleasure has breathed its last. People in whom the challenges of the middle years trigger a midlife crisis live in a world permeated by deadness.

Alexithymia and Anhedonia

As we saw in the previous chapter, the label *alexithymic* is used for people characterized by emotional numbness, for whom feeling, understanding, and communicating emotions and moods is foreign territory. Alexithymics radiate a mechanical quality that leaves them unperturbed even by what other people would find emotionally devastating. They respond to every eventuality with a bland inexpressiveness (see chapter 2).

A close cousin to alexithymia in the mood disorder family is *anhedonia* (Chapman, Chapman, & Raulin, 1976; Laos & Boyer, 1993; Snaith, 1993). While hedonism reveres pleasure, its obverse, anhedonia, negates it. Anhedonia is characterized by a sense of apathy and a loss of interest in and withdrawal from pleasurable activity. Anhedonics, with their lowered ability to experience pleasure, are unwilling to seek out new sensations. Lacking a zest for life, their attentional function is diminished. For anhedonics, activities that used to provide pleasure and satisfaction, that provide pleasure to "normal" people under "normal" circumstances, do not do so any longer.

Pleasure, in the context of anhedonia, can be grouped into three categories. The first is physical gratification; the pleasures of eating, touching, feeling, sex, temperature, movement, smell, and sound. The second category is interpersonal social pleasures; being with people, talking, doing things with others, interacting in many different ways. The third category is intellectual pleasures and the pleasures of achievement. In the case of true anhedonia, all of these pleasures are either absent or seriously diminished.

Full-blown anhedonia is a worrisome phenomenon. As revealed in interviews, anhedonics have a disturbing paucity of inner life. The prolonged, marked flattening of affect that characterizes anhedonia has been associated with various forms of mental illness, such as schizophrenia and schizoaffective and bipolar disorders. The nature of the connection between anhedonia and serious mental illness is unclear. However, neurobiological disturbances akin to those associated with some mental illnesses have also been implicated in anhedonia.

People in a depressed state have many symptoms similar to those of anhedonia. A lack of energy, a decrease in activity level, reduced concentration, loss of appetite, weight loss, lack of sexual activity, slowness of thought, inability to respond to the mood of the occasion, insomnia, suicidal thoughts, and feelings of fatigue—all depressive symptoms—resemble some of the indicators of true anhedonia. However, depression, with its quasi-anhedonic behavior, can be transient and does not imply the life-long characterological defect in the ability to experience pleasure that is found with real anhedonia.

Apart from depression, there are other mental states that result in quasi-anhedonic behavior, mental states whereby an individual no longer enjoys a previously pleasurable activity or pastime. My observations, which reveal that quasi-anhedonic behavior often comes to the fore at midlife, support the conjecture that the way people cope with the process of aging is a contributing factor. As with true anhedonics, people adopting such behavior at midlife are characterized primarily by a loss in the joy of living, a defect in the experience of pleasure. In its milder forms, this anhedoniclike reaction is expressed as a difficulty in maintaining concentration and interest in normal activities. It may also be symptomized as a steadily increasing reluctance to take part in normal activities.

People struggling with midlife quasi-anhedonia keep to a minimum the effort they expend. As their energy level fades, things that used to be of interest to them lose consequence. These individuals, now bored as often as not, let their participation in activities drop off; those undertakings that they continue are conducted in a desultory fashion. Negativity prevails, though emotional expressiveness is weakened. Decisions are put off; indecisiveness becomes increasingly troublesome. Sexual intercourse, if it takes place at all, gives little or no pleasure. To a large extent these midlife quasi-anhedonics withdraw from "worldly activities"; they become unnaturally introverted, cut off from life, no longer interested in other people.

One senior executive I interviewed described his experience as follows:

> I realize now that the only time I've been creative, if that's the right word to use, is when I've been passionate about things. But that seems ages ago now. I can't remember when I last felt passion, when I really felt alive. I don't know what's happening to me. I've lost interest in most things. Very little gets me excited these days. I feel very distant from people. Oh, I put up a nice front, but that's all it is. I go through the motions.
>
> The same thing is happening at home. My relationship with my wife and family has become ritualistic. My sex life is nonexistent. I assume that what keeps my wife and me together is sheer inertia.
>
> This lack of interest also applies to other aspects of my life. For example, I used to be quite passionate about food. Not any more: I don't much care what I eat these days. The same thing with reading. It used to be one of my favorite pastimes. Now my concentration isn't what it used to be. I start reading a book every now and then, but I lose interest quickly and put it down. I spend quite a bit of time watching television. Maybe *watching* isn't the right word. I play with the remote control. One program seems like any other. As a matter of fact, I forget immediately what I've seen. I know things can't go on like this. There's no pleasure in what I'm doing. I can't keep up this facade much longer. Something has to happen.

It is not always obvious that these changes in behavior and attitudes, these shifts from passion and fervor to anomie, are taking place. The process can be very subtle. Often people who have lost their spark may not even be consciously aware of it, although subliminally they may realize that there is something wrong. In fact, many executives whose behavior could be termed quasi-alexithymic or quasi-anhedonic comment on their sense of detachment, their capacity to be observers of their own actions.

A Sense of Unreality

In psychiatry the term *dissociative disorders* refers to disruptions of the usually integrated functions of consciousness, memory, identity, and perception of the environment (Fewtrell, 1986; Jacobson, 1959; Lynn & Rhue, 1994; Steinberg, 1993). Within this group of disorders we find *depersonalization disorder,* which is characterized by a persistent or recurring feeling of being detached from one's own mental processes or body (although reality testing seems to remain intact). This disorder might be described as a feeling of unreality or strangeness regarding the self, a feeling of numbness or death, a feeling that parts of the body are disconnected. People suffering from depersonalization complain about a discontinuity in physical reality, in one form or another. A central part of the experience is their disconnection or disengagement from the self and/or the physical surroundings. Depersonalized individuals feel themselves to be detached from their own ongoing perceptions, actions, emotions, and thoughts. What should be familiar is perceived as strange and unreal.

This psychological detachment from the physical environment makes for a reduction in the intensity and vividness of experiences. Diminished capacity to experience emotions is an especially worrisome part of this phenomenon. People troubled by depersonalization experience a sensation of being an outside observer of their own mental processes. It is as if these people were watching a dream or a movie about themselves. No matter what they are thinking or doing, their participation does not seem real; it no longer has a personal relation or meaning. These feelings of depersonalization are more common than one might think. Most people, however, will not admit to them without prompting. A Swedish CEO touches upon depersonalization in these comments:

> When I was chief executive of *Dagens Nyheter* [a major Swedish daily newspaper], my collaborators started to complain about me. . . . To my horror, I noticed my tendency to emotionally disappear in the middle of a presentation. Suddenly I would be gone, closed, no longer part of the surroundings. People would notice; they would become edgy, as evidenced by the way they would cross their arms and legs; their attention span would wander off. . . . To this strange state of mind was also added my incapacity to listen and function in company. (Douglas, 1993, p. 71)

Another senior executive made the following comments to me:

> Here I am sitting in my office. People come and go, but there's nobody
> home. I hope you realize that I'm talking about myself. Oh, they don't
> really seem to notice. I ask the right questions; I take notes; I make an
> effort to laugh with whomever is there. They assume I'm with them,
> but I'm not. I'm looking at myself doing all those things and feeling
> strange. It's like I'm on automatic pilot. Whatever happens, it doesn't
> seem to touch me. Things seem to take place outside me; I feel quite
> removed from the experience. Sometimes I look at my reflection in the
> window to see if it's really me, if I'm still there. I seem to oscillate
> between being part of what's going on and feeling like a spectator. If
> I'm in the latter state, it's like I'm in a movie or a dream from which
> I can wake up at any moment. It reminds me of the story of the sage
> who once dreamed about a butterfly. Afterward, being awake, he would
> wonder if he was a sage who had dreamed about a butterfly or a butterfly
> dreaming about a sage.

As these quotes show, depersonalized individuals experience a
split between the observing and the participating self. Because
bodily actions seem to happen on their own, there is a height-
ening of the function of self-observation. The self can merely
observe; it cannot experience emotions or thoughts. Although
reality testing remains intact during depersonalization, all experiences have an "as if" quality to them: the person feels like
an automaton, physically numb, as if bodily sensations were
happening at a distance. There is also, however, somewhere, the
awareness that what is happening is only a feeling, that one is
not really an automaton.

Because of the quality of unreality and estrangement
attached to personal experiences, the depersonalized individual
has the dual perception that everything is the same as it has
always been but is at the same time different, since it lacks
personal involvement. *Derealization* may also be present: in
other words, perceived objects in the external world may have
the same quality of estrangement and unreality.

Depersonalization is viewed as a mechanism to mask anxiety, one that results in a loss of affect. As such, it can be seen
as a primitive defense allied to denial, an emergency measure

used when the more usual defenses (such as repression) fail. We can also view it, however, as an adaptive mechanism, a response to danger that makes for a heightened alertness on one hand but a dampening of potentially disturbing emotions on the other. One potential precipitating factor for this strange state of mind is the stress of the middle years, when work-related factors may play an important role.

Passion and Work

An exploration of alexithymia, anhedonia, and depersonalization provides us with a certain amount of insight into the emotional malaise some people are troubled by. We have seen how these processes can be viewed both as defensive reactions and as adaptive mechanisms to assist in dealing with stressful situations that may include the vicissitudes of midlife.

As a caveat, it should be noted that it is executives at midlife, at the peak of their careers, who are most often responsible for critical decisions in organizations. Some of these decisions, such as downsizing, with its negative effects on other people's lives, may take their toll in the form of stress reactions. For some people, the combination of the stress associated with such difficult organizational decisions and the stress of the challenging midlife transition can be devastating.

Defensive Reactions

Some individuals at midlife resort to psychological *withdrawal* as a way of removing themselves from active participation in interpersonal problem solving. For them, the outer world feels full of threats against their security and identity. They become emotionally numb as a means of defense.

Others, despite appearances, are not truly emotionally numb. They give the impression of numbness because they have withdrawn from the outside world to hide in their own private space. While they may appear dull and boring, the inner world of their imagination may be quite exciting. But in creating a split between the self and the outside world, they experience a sense of estrangement.

As we have seen, there are also individuals who resort to *isolation* as a way of dealing with painful states of mind—the isolation of feeling from knowing. These individuals may recognize conscious experiences, somebody died or someone is very ill, for example, but the emotional meaning behind those experiences is absent. This way of coping with painful reality makes for emotional numbness.

I have also mentioned that some people, as a strategy for dealing with the unpleasant sensations associated with midlife, engage in *vigorous activity* to induce sensations of an intensity that can breach the wall of numbness. However, this manic way of dealing with the stresses and strains of midlife (although much more attractive than withdrawal or isolation) also has its problems. Manic behavior does not make for a stable state; it is only a temporary solution. It is a kind of "flight" behavior, a way of escaping from painful emotions. The manic's many grandiose schemes, racing thoughts, and apparent freedom from normal physical requirements (such as food and sleep) eventually lead to a serious state of emotional and physical exhaustion. In the long run, manic behavior does not make for enjoyment; on the contrary, it leads to mental impoverishment. It is a very ineffective way of dealing with the challenges of middle age, serving only as a postponement of the dreaded depression.

Dysfunctional Leadership Behavior

As is to be expected, reactions such as social withdrawal, loss of a sense of purpose, and depression not only cause serious problems at home but have a considerable impact in the workplace. Studies of leadership have shown that emotional presence, the energizing role of leadership, is a key ingredient in successful company performance. A leader's passion can make others feel alive, involved, and motivated. Without passion, there is no inspiration; and inspiration is essential if others are to share and enact a leader's vision and create a high-performance organization.

Another important component of leadership is the ability to create an atmosphere that allows employees to enjoy their work. Many of the most effective CEOs have discovered that people work harder when they have fun. A sense of pleasure at work makes for greater productivity and encourages playfulness and creativity. It connects with one of the major motivational need systems of humankind (as described in the Introduction): the need for exploration (Lichtenberg, 1989). Thus the ability to instill pleasure in the workplace is an important contributing variable to effective leadership.

Leaders, at whatever level they may be in the organization, can be compared to psychiatric social workers: they are "containers" of the emotions of their subordinates. One of their tasks is to provide a sense of security, trust, and confidence. Truly effective leaders possess a kind of "teddy bear" quality. Their presence is reassuring. They know how to create a safe and comfortable holding environment for their employees. Their emotional presence and "aliveness" puts people at ease (Lichtenberg, 1989). They are extremely good at picking up elusive signals in conversation. And because of that teddy bear quality, their employees are willing to do more and better work than they would otherwise do. Empathic leaders also have a strong sense of generativity. They take pleasure from helping the next generation as mentor and coach. They do not suffer from the envy that characterizes some people who experience difficulties at midlife. This sense of generativity is critical for organizational learning. Without it, organizational learning is stifled and the future of the organization is endangered.

Obviously, leaders in the pangs of quasi-anhedonic and quasi-alexithymic behavior, and those prone to depersonalization, are not organizational teddy bears, neither do they demonstrate a passion for learning and further development. Their emotional absence is noted by those they work with. And given the power that senior executives wield in their organizations, their negative mood states and their emotional absence, if prolonged, can be quite infectious, coloring corporate culture, strategy, and structure and eventually contributing to a decrease in organizational performance.

Love of Life

The key question in all of this is how the stresses of midlife can be transformed into a progressive process. How can midlifers retain an energizing role and recapture lost passion? What can they do to maintain a sense of vitality? Regaining a love of life takes a lot of work, but midlifers have to make it happen if they are unwilling to stagnate (or worse).

We should keep in mind that as adults our life situation is quite different from what it was in the days of childhood. When we were very young, everything was new; everything was worth giving attention to; it was a world full of new experiences. But retaining that sense of freshness into adulthood is not easy. We have to search out ways to stimulate our exploratory disposition. A continuous effort has to be made to renew ourselves (without resorting to manic defensive solutions).

Various steps, in both private life and the workplace, can be taken to maintain or regain this sense of aliveness. We may not always be able to take these steps alone, however. We may need professional help to get the process underway. Understanding what is happening to us if we falter at midlife—that our emotions are flattening, for example, or that we are losing our zest for life—is not easy, given the blind spots we all have about our own character. Others may help us acquire the courage to address the issues we are struggling with. Psychoanalysis, dynamic psychotherapy, personal coaching, and/or participation in group dynamics seminars where feedback about personal style is part of the process may provide us with insights into our own behavior.

Self-knowledge is the first step in the process of disentanglement from an unhealthy situation. Thus it is imperative that anyone attempting to address midlife concerns acquire a certain amount of emotional intelligence. Awareness makes for insight about one's own motivation; and from insight, strategies can be developed to deal with the problematic situations represented at midlife.

In private life, marriage can be revitalized when children leave home. Breaking established routines and doing things as a couple can be a means of avoiding mourning the empty nest. In fact, once the children are out of the house, there may be many new opportunities for renewal within the marriage relationship.

New relationships can be built with children who have left home as well. Parents and children relating to each other on an adult basis can discover different interaction patterns. Stepping out of the parent–child role enables parents to see their children from another perspective. The possible new role of grandparenthood may be of help in creating these new relationships and may come with its own satisfactions.

Making new and different friends can be a very effective therapeutic exercise. Most people have a tendency to associate with people in the same socioeconomic bracket, in similar occupations. Mixing with people from different backgrounds can be a learning process for both parties. Joining different organizations is another way to meet new people.

Some people may take a very different route. They may find excitement in starting an affair or divorcing a spouse and finding a "trophy wife." For many, sexuality becomes the major avenue toward a renewed sense of aliveness. Not surprisingly, there is a peak in the divorce rate at midlife. When a marriage has become completely stale and both parties are merely going through the motions, when the partners truly have very little in common anymore, a divorce and a new relationship may be a good way to engage in a new beginning.

Some people may see middle age as a good time to pursue completely different interests or go back to interests abandoned earlier in life. This may mean doing something for humanitarian, political, or social organizations, becoming involved in a social cause, or pursuing altruistic concerns. Time can be made now to take up different, less strenuous sporting activities or to rediscover old interests in aesthetic and recreational activities.

In the work setting, midlifers can set stretch goals as one means of maintaining passion. Tackling new, challenging tasks makes for a sense of exhilaration about the workplace. Learning new things is the best way of making the most of humankind's pursuit of exploratory needs. Recognizing that fact, organizations that put an emphasis on learning create opportunities for creativity and innovation; they make self-improvement a cultural imperative. Learning from experience and adapting successfully to changes in the business environment keep workers alive.

Some people "do a Gauguin," an expression coined from the name of the artist who gave up his job as a successful stockbroker to paint full time and later went to a Polynesian island to paint. "Doing a Gauguin" means starting something completely new, making a dramatic change in one's career. The catalyst for such a move is the feeling that unusual action is needed to get out of a rut. At midlife it dawns on some people that they have chosen their career for the wrong reasons—for example, to please a parent. They may now, with their new sense of the imminence of death, be ready to make the jump and do what makes them feel most alive. To experience a sense of renewal, to feel passion once more, they make a complete break from their previous career and take on new challenges.

Others revitalize themselves through mentoring. Getting involved in the development of young people, enjoying vicarious gratification by sharing disappointments and victories, can be an exhilarating and enriching experience. It keeps the mentor young, interested, and involved. As mentioned before, taking the generativity route also helps to establish continuity in the organization. It institutionalizes learning, making it an intrinsic part of the corporate culture.

Mentoring is one way in which midlifers can respond to their "generativity script," their plan for how they intend to leave a legacy for the next generation. The generativity script charts the way to attaining a kind of immortality; it lays out something through which the person will be remembered and which will outlive the self. This creation can be tangible or intangible; be it a child, a book, a business, an idea, or a good deed that becomes a statement of the self, it is a self-expression that is shared with others. In generativity the person gives guidance to the next generation through parenting, teaching, leading, and/or doing things for the community. Something of a lasting nature is done, something that will outlive death. Because generativity promotes continuity from one generation to the next, taking that route indicates faith in the value of human life, a sense of hope for the future.

As someone once said, life is not a rehearsal. Therefore, one of our major life tasks is to die young, but as late as possible. We must do all we can to avoid being diminished by circumstances and sleepwalking through life. It can be a daunting task, especially as we face the struggles of midlife, but what is the alternative? Socrates said that "the unexamined life is not worth living." While I do not dispute that, I would equally maintain that the passionless life is not worth living. The passions are the gates of the soul. At midlife, we must be alert to the dangers of inertia, the tendency to detachment and emotional absence, the panicked rush into action—all negative responses to the crises that accompany this stage in the life cycle. Believing with the French writer Diderot that "only the passions, only great passions can elevate the mind to great things," we must recognize and create new sources of energy and excitement.

References

Chapman, L. J., Chapman, J. P., & Raulin, M. L. (1976). Scales for physical and social anhedonia. *Journal of Abnormal Psychology, 85,* 374–382.

Chiriboga, D. A. (1981). The developmental psychology of middle age. In J. Howell (Ed.), *Modern perspectives in the psychiatry of middle age* (pp. 67–98). New York: Brunner/Mazel.

Dante Alighieri (1954). *The divine comedy* (Vol. 1; J. Ciardi, Trans.). New York: New American Library. (Original work published circa 1304)

Diamond, J. (1997). *Male menopause.* Naperville, IL: Sourcebooks.

Douglas, G. (1993). Jag skulle aldrig vaga möta nittiotalet i enbart glada grabbars lag (I would never dare to meet the nineties in the company of only men). In *Arvets utmaning* (The challenge of inheritance). Stockholm: Brombergs Bokforlag.

Erikson, E. (1963). Identity and the Life Cycle. *Psychological Issues,* Monogr. 1. New York: International Universities Press.

Fewtrell, W. (1986). Depersonalization: A description and suggested strategies. *British Journal of Guidance and Counselling, 14,* 253–269.

Greer, G. (1991). *The change: Women, aging and the menopause.* New York: Ballantine.

Jacobson, E. (1959). Depersonalization. *Journal of the American Psychoanalytic Association, 7,* 581–610.

Jaques, E. (1965). Death and the midlife crisis. *International Journal of Psycho-Analysis, 46,* 502–514.

Jung, C. (1933). *Modern man in search of a soul.* New York: Harcourt, Brace.

Laos, G., & Boyer, P. (1993). Relationships between anhedonia and depressive symptoms in major depressive disorder. *European Psychiatry, 8,* 42–51.

Lichtenberg, J. (1989). *Psychoanalysis and motivation.* Hillsdale, NJ: Analytic Press.

Lynn, S. J., & Rhue, J. W. (Eds.). (1994). *Dissociation: Clinical and theoretical perspectives.* New York: Guilford Press.

Nemroff, R. A., & Colarusso, C. A. (1990). *New dimensions in adult development.* New York: Basic Books.

Neugarten, B. L. (1970). Adaptation and the life cycle. *Journal of Geriatric Psychology, 4,* 71–87.

Oldham, J. M., & Liebert, R. S. (Eds.). (1989). *The middle years.* New Haven, CT: Yale University Press.

Pollock, G. H., & Greenspan, S. I. (Eds.). (1993). *The course of life: Vol. 6. Late adulthood.* Madison, CT: International Universities Press. (Original work published 1980)

Sheehy, G. (1995). *New passages.* New York: Ballantine Books.

Snaith, P. (1993). Anhedonia: A neglected symptom of psychopathology. *Psychological Medicine, 223,* 957–966.

Steinberg, M. (1993). *Dissociative disorders: A clinical review.* Lutherville, MD: Sidran Press.

4

What's Playing in the Organizational Theater? Collusive Relationships in Management

What is our life? a play of passion,
Our mirth the music of derision,
Our mothers' wombs the tiring houses be,
When we are dressed for this short comedy . . . .
(Orlando Gibbons, *The First Set of Madrigals and Motets in Five Parts*)

Ah! Vanitas Vanitatum! *Which of us is happy in this world? Which of us has his desire? or, having it, is satisfied?—Come, children, let us shut up the box and the puppets, for our play is played out.* (William Thackeray, *Vanity Fair*)

Plays are like mantras. You just keep repeating them over and over and over and it makes inroads in your personality and sometimes you walk the line between sanity and madness. (Kathy Bates, interview, *International Herald Tribune*, April 18–19, 1998, p. 24)

This chapter takes as its point of departure concepts derived from couple therapy to better understand collusive relationships in organizations. It identifies four main types of collusive superior–subordinate interaction patterns—the narcissistic, the controlling, the paranoid, and the sadomasochistic—and explores the consequences of each such dyad in organizations. It also presents a number of recommendations for recognizing collusive arrangements in the workplace (taking leadership behavior

121

as a point of departure) and suggests preventive steps that can be taken to avoid such arrangements.

Introduction

On August 24, 1994, Jeffrey Katzenberg, head of Walt Disney Studios, resigned. His acrimonious departure came as a shock after his 18-year collaborative relationship with Michael Eisner, the chairman of Disney. Katzenberg's defection sent ripples through the entertainment industry and became front-page news. Most industry analysts saw Katzenberg's exit as a major loss to the company. He was perceived as the architect of a series of highly successful animated films (including the fabulously profitable *Lion King*), which were the primary engine for Disney's growth. Katzenberg's departure endangered what was to have been a smooth succession process following the accidental death of company president Frank Welch (particularly in light of the fact of Eisner's quadruple bypass surgery). In addition, Katzenberg soon became a partner in a new company called DreamWorks SKG, a company that became a serious competitor for Disney (Huy, 1995).

Ten years earlier, after leaving Paramount together, Eisner and Katzenberg had taken over a moribund Disney. At that time, 1984, the company had relatively disappointing revenues of $1.4 billion. By 1993, revenues had reached $8.5 billion. Pretax profits of the film studio (which was Katzenberg's responsibility) had risen from $2 million in 1984 to about $800 million in 1994. No film studio had reported greater profits over the previous decade. Given that financial success, the Eisner–Katzenberg breakup was surely a matter not of business but of human relationship. What went wrong with the chemistry between the two men? What soured their 18-year collaboration? What *really* happened?

The messy, much publicized Eisner–Katzenberg breakup had all the elements of a marriage gone bad. As with so many divorces, in this one it was hard to identify reality. Observers took sides and, depending on their perspective, assigned one man the villain's role and the other the hero's. Each protagonist was accused of being an abrasive megalomaniac by the other's supporters. Some people felt that Katzenberg had claimed undeserved credit for Disney's success, while others faulted Eisner for tolerating yea-sayers and leading the company in a disastrous direction.

While, as in most breakups, there was certainly fault on both sides, there is a bigger issue here that can teach us much about human interactions in the workplace: the manifest and latent demands of the relationship got out of sync. The various reports of the Eisner–Katzenberg divorce that were circulated in the press tell a tale of dependence and counterdependence, of autonomy and control, of narcissism and emotion. From my vantage point, with the benefit of both hindsight and psychoanalytic experience, it looks as if a kind of equilibrium existed between the men as long as both played their "appropriate" roles in the partnership. But when Katzenberg tried to change his role, asserting himself by requesting the number two job in the organization after Frank Welch's death, Eisner's hackles went up.

According to people familiar with the two protagonists, Eisner had always been rather aloof toward his star performer. These observers noted that Eisner was slow to give credit for a job well done and had become tougher and more arrogant over the years. They suggested that he liked keeping Katzenberg in the one-down position, forcing him to search for approval and play the role of supplicant. On the other hand, they commented that Katzenberg was not exactly Mr. Nice Guy himself; he had a reputation for playing hardball, though he was apparently trying to change his image, presenting a more softened, conciliatory side at times (Grover, 1994, p. 46).

From the information given, we can hypothesize that when Katzenberg made it clear to Eisner that he wanted to be a more equal partner, the equilibrium was shaken. Apparently Eisner was not prepared to give in to Katzenberg's demands. A change in their working relationship was evidently unacceptable to Eisner; he appeared unwilling to compromise. He may have felt that Katzenberg had become too pushy. Whatever the ''glue'' had been between the two of them, it seemed no longer to be holding.

Unfortunately, it is likely that neither party ever understood the real nature of this glue. In spite of the many years that they worked together, these colleagues appeared to have very little insight into their interlocking roles or interpersonal chemistry. Thus the ''tragedy'' ran its inevitable course. As Ken Auletta wrote in *the New Yorker,* ''Katzenberg left a job that he loved and Disney lost a talented executive that it didn't want to lose. Primal forces were at work, which could not be controlled by the mind'' (1994, p. 69).

Who was to blame? Who was the major culprit? Could the outcome have been avoided? What can be said about the roles Eisner and Katzenberg played in this drama? What kind of psychodynamic forces were at work? In a fundamental way, we are all actors, all on stage. We love playing theater, and what is more, we like to get others involved in our plays. Wherever we look around us, we can see various cameo performances: comedies, tragedies, romances, you name it. Theater is part and parcel of daily functioning in both private and organizational life.

Within organizations, as in private life, great masterpieces are continually being performed. Organizational leaders, those at Disney being a good example, are in the theater business. Playacting is an important part of their job, a way of influencing their subordinates. Leaders have to inspire their followers, get them to share their vision of where the company should be going, and enlist their help in enacting the leaders' ideas. To accomplish those tasks, leaders find ''impression management'' essential. They need their subordinates to play along, to help them to get things done.

Spontaneous as all these forms of interaction between senior executives and their subordinates (or even colleagues) appear to be, some of the "plays" we witness at the office are carefully (if not consciously) plotted. Perceptive observers detect a certain regularity to some superior–subordinate encounters; they see that the ways in which particular superiors and subordinates deal with each other fall into specific set patterns, ways of interacting that have "hardened" over time and can contribute to various forms of organizational malfunctioning. Not all interpersonal operational modes are destructive, of course. In most office relationships, employee interactions, though occasionally stressful, lead to maturation, creativity, peak experiences, transformation, and change. Many relationships possess the qualities of intimacy and autonomy that set the stage for further personal and professional development. But not all of them do, and it is those that are not constructive that interest us here.

What are some of the collusive interaction patterns that can be found in organizations? How do they begin? What are their salient characteristics? And how do we deal with them?

The Meshing of Fantasies

Collusive arrangements begin with a sort of "courtship" during which the future partners assess each other's suitability for projective processes. In organizational terms this courtship display is acted out during the selection and socialization process of new people into the organization, as well as in training and development programs during which employee behavior is being shaped. A person's initial entry into an organization is an important occasion for assessing the newcomer's preparedness to participate in the particular interaction patterns enacted by the key players in the organization, the actors who set the tone and define the corporate culture.

The Process of Projective Identification

During this time of courtship, both parties, through the process of projective identification, give off signals, conscious or unconscious, that are received by the other party. Each partner may recognize in the other disowned, denied, or projected parts of the self; each searches the other for a willingness to participate in the prevailing "script."

Projective identification, a complex, subtle, almost mysterious process whereby a part of the self is expelled and "deposited" into someone else, is an attempt to apprehend and influence another person's subjective world. An interpersonal process, it is an intrusive, primitive form of communication whereby the initiator gets the receiver to experience a set of feelings similar to his or her own (Ogden, 1982). Through this process of projective identification, both parties, again, whether consciously or unconsciously, are drawn together. The person who does the projecting evokes in the recipient of the projection feelings parallel to the ones projected. In other words, the initiator becomes understood by the recipient, who then experiences similar feelings. The empathy is sometimes so great that the recipient starts to behave in accordance with the projected fantasies (rather than simply understanding them). In some situations the initiator uses the recipient as a kind of garbage disposal, trying to make him or her the recipient of undesired qualities. (We should not, however, interpret the phenomenon of projective identification in a purely negative way, because it forms the basis for empathy, intuition, leaps of nonverbal synchronicity, experiences of mystical union with another person, and the ability to "read" another person's mind.)

Thus in projective identification the projected psychic content is not gone after projection has occurred. This is in contrast to simple projection, where one's own wishes and feelings are attributed to another person because they spark intolerably painful emotions in the self. That content is simultaneously projected and retained; indeed, the process of projective identification allows the projector to maintain some influence over it.

Collusive Relationships in Organizations

During the courtship stage, each player, employer and new employee explores the extent to which the other will be a good "receptacle" for projective identification. The exact content of the script is not openly articulated, however; it is alluded to subtly. But the tentative feelers that go out at this stage often constitute the beginning of a secret alliance or collusion. If the employer–employee fit is uncomfortable, the newcomer will have no choice but to eventually leave the organization.

The word *collusion* is used here to label relationships in which both parties are stuck in mutual projective identification that hampers future growth and development. In this context, *collusion* should be understood as an out-of-awareness, repetitive pattern of interaction between people, instigated and maintained in such a way as to manage and master anxiety about certain past conflictual experiences. The psychiatrist Jürg Willi defines the collusion principle as "the unconscious interplay of two partners who are looking for each other in the hope of coming to terms *together* with those conflicts and frustrations in their lives which they have not yet managed to resolve" (Willi, 1982, preface).

These collusions, which can be seen as a neurotic form of collaboration, often take up an enormous amount of psychic energy. They occur when certain behavior patterns resonate between two people, two actors in the play. Usually, the initiator keeps the partner bound to a set of complementary reactions, striving to get from the partner what is felt to be missing from the self. Thus, through the process of projective identification, the initiator uses the partner as a vehicle for those aspects of his or her own personality that the initiator would like to integrate within him- or herself. And in organizations, given the dynamics of power, employees who are not willing to "play" with the senior executive are not likely to last.

Such unhealthy collusions contrast sharply with more flexible encounters, the norm, that leave both parties a considerable amount of transitional space where new learning can take place and where new solutions to problems can be discovered. In the latter situations, the outcome is not predetermined; the players do not find themselves stuck in frozen positions; new permutations and combinations are possible. The partners are involved in a process of ongoing growth and development.

Usually, the invitation to participate in collusive activities operates at three different levels of awareness. It is the first level that is the most clearly verbalized. In the workplace, this first level occurs at a person's entry into an organization, when much effort is exerted by the employer to make the new employee aware of the unique features of the prevailing corporate culture—its preferred interpersonal style and way of relating to others. More specifically, an attempt is made to articulate the kind of partnership arrangement the person will be subjected to. This verbalization does not always mean that the receiver truly understands the message, of course, because the process of projective identification is prone to distortion. There can be a substantial difference between one's understanding of such a message at a cognitive level and one's understanding at an emotional level. Thus the new person does not always react as expected to the signals given.

While the first level of awareness is quite corporate, saying, in effect, "This is how the *company* expects you to interact," the next level is more personal. At this second level, the initiator is conscious (or at least subliminally so) of the "contract," of what it means to be associated with the other, but has not yet articulated it for fear of a negative reaction. Only gradually is the other party made aware of what "signing up" is all about, as the initiator tentatively tests and then establishes boundaries of each role: who will be in power and control, what will be the degree of closeness versus distance, who will play the more active and who the more passive role, and so on.

The last level of the "contract," more personal still, addresses those aspects that are predominantly outside conscious awareness. Though occasionally the themes that will dominate the relationship in the future are close to the surface, giving the parties in question a fleeting sense of what is to come, generally these themes take some time to unfold. As they do, the many subtleties of the "script" specifying how the parties will relate to each other come to the fore. No longer is it a question of the generalities of the "play"; now an exact description of each person's role during the different acts is outlined. Here repetition plays a major role, as disavowed, denied, or projected parts of the self based on unresolved childhood conflicts come to dominate the relationship.

Given the existence of these three levels of awareness, it will not come as a surprise that the partners who become actors in these dysfunctional "plays" may not initially be completely cognizant of what they are getting into. Yet before long, the participants may find themselves stuck in a vicious circle, caught up in an activity that seems interminable.

A "mental gridlock" often occurs in collusive situations as dysfunctional interaction patterns follow the same themes and are played out according to specific rules. Certain acts tend to be repeated over and over again. The participants seem to be trapped in a kind of "parasitic" bond symptomizing arrested development (McDougall, 1985). A deconstruction of these repetitive theater pieces indicates that the involved parties are trying to get from each other what they lacked at an earlier, critical point in their development.

The cast of characters in these repetitive plays is carefully preselected. There appears to be a kind of "fatal attraction" between certain types of people, given their ability to complement each other in these performances. In such collusive situations, the players seem to be inextricably tied to one another. Although they may superficially act as polar opposites of each other, deep down they share a similar kind of conflict. One person finds an unconscious sounding board in the other. The roles people play in these activities constantly shift (though even the shifts are carefully scripted). For example, if the initially passive party becomes more active, passivity will increase in the partner. It seems that an equilibrium has to be maintained, whatever the costs may be.

Soon the dysfunctional aspects of collusive interchanges become quite obvious. The players may become involved in formalized fighting rituals; for example, rituals that take so much time and energy that there is very little left for constructive, creative work. In such instances there is no free interplay between the partners. They are stuck in plays without end.

The strikingly irrational quality to these interaction patterns is the giveaway that we are dealing with deep-seated, unresolved childhood experiences and conflicts. The players lack the ability to see their relationship objectively. They do not know how to restructure or get out of it. Resolution of these peculiar interpersonal scripts is particularly difficult because of the presence of irrational fears and conflicts that have deep-seated, transferential roots.

Given the fact that much of this sort of behavior is unconscious, we should not be surprised that the actors vehemently deny that games are being played when asked about a relationship. Game-playing is a deeply suppressed part of their personality. But if we make the effort to delve a little bit deeper, we soon find out that there is a specific division of labor in these collusions. Such an exploration also reveals in each party an underlying wish that, with the help of the other, his or her own deep-rooted conflicts might be resolved.

The drama and the strain that these dysfunctional forms of interaction cause can be substantial. Executives working under collusive conditions often end up suffering from various kinds of stress disorders. Worse, other executives may become contaminated by the collusive arrangements, leading to an enormous amount of tension in the organization. When it comes to looking for the culprit among the main parties in the plot, however, it is difficult to talk in terms of victim and victimizer because both "actors" are addressing unconscious needs. Victim-victimizer seems a valid distinction when such a relationship is looked at from the outside, but closer investigation reveals that both parties are attracted to the plot and get some form of enjoyment from it. After all, it takes two to tango.

Methodological Considerations

The kinds of collusive interpersonal relationships I am referring to are most clearly visible within marriages. Many couple therapists, particularly Jürg Willi, quoted above, have written extensively on destructive collusive arrangements. I have discovered in my research on the relationship between personality, leadership style, organizational culture, organizational strategy, and organizational structure that some of their findings are equally applicable to work settings, though perhaps these experiences are not of the same intensity there. Consequently, concepts from couple therapy will be applied in this chapter to the study of superior–subordinate relationships in organizations.

To understand the underlying scripts that determine these collusive arrangements, we have to find out what is happening in the "inner theater" of the executives involved. Because this inner theater organizes the way information is processed and acted upon in interpersonal situations, we have to be organizational "detectives" in our efforts to decipher "deep" structure. In playing this role, we have to be alert to underlying themes, hidden agendas, meanings behind metaphors used, reasons for the selection of certain words, and deeper implications of certain behaviors and activities of the individual in question.

To be able to decipher these deeper motives, to tease out the emotional, cognitive, and experiential components of the inner scripts of executives, requires the capacity to "listen with the third ear.'' This capacity in turn requires a certain level of emotional intelligence. As noted in chapter 2, that encompasses both an awareness and an understanding of our own feelings and an appreciation of emotions in other people (empathy). It also implies the ability to recognize affective contagion (projective identification processes in action) and make sense out of these elusive, transferred, nonverbal signals. Moreover, it requires the capacity to deconstruct and find the deeper meaning in the complex relational processes that take place in any human encounter.

Because the ideas presented in this chapter are exploratory, the presentation of collusive arrangements is not exhaustive; I address only the most frequently encountered patterns. Other permutations and combinations are certainly possible.

I gleaned my information about collusive interaction patterns largely from leadership seminars I led at INSEAD. Most of the executives in the seminars were the ''hub'' of a set of relationships. During the interviews, we keyed in to the most prominent of these relationships. From the interviews, it appeared that the majority of the discussed relationships were collusion-free. In these healthy relationships, each party's individuality seemed to be preserved. A certain number of additional relationships, however, were described by these executives as characterized by various degrees of enmeshment. The enmeshment was then further explored in the interviews. It will not come as a surprise (given the importance of the narcissistic dimension in leadership) that more than half of the collusive arrangements were primarily of a narcissistic nature. Next in frequency were interaction patterns of a controlling type, followed by paranoid and finally sadomasochistic enmeshments. Given the preeminence of narcissistic enmeshments, these controlling, paranoid, and sadomasochistic relationship patterns could, at times, be enveloped in a narcissistic collusion.

For each type of collusive arrangement seen in these executives, and discussed below, I will give an example of a ''script'' and present some of the major themes in the ''play'' that tied both parties together. I will also make some comments about the characterological development of the executives who participated in these enmeshed relationships.

Types of Collusion

The Narcissistic Collusion

> Subordinate: I very much enjoyed your presentation about the new direction our company should be going. You were great!
> Superior: You really liked the way I made my presentation? Was my position made clear?
> Subordinate: Very much so. You really dazzled everyone. As a matter of fact, I think you lost Smith and Bricker; they were obviously lagging far behind you in their thought processes. They may be on the same level on the organization chart, but they're just plain out of it as far knowing where our industry is going. I'd like to ask you if I could help you develop the new strategic marketing plan you mentioned in your presentation. It would be such a great learning experience. I'd very much like to be part of that project. I know I have a lot to learn, and you'd be a great mentor.
> Superior: What makes you say that?
> Subordinate: Everyone knows that you're the best in the business. You're the one who sets the rules for this industry.
> Superior: You really think so?

The most common form of "play" revealed through the interviews (the above script being a good example) was the narcissistic collusion. Although there were many variations on the narcissistic theme, closer analysis revealed that the basic message remained the same. The person in the one-down position in the script would say, in effect, "I can't function without your assistance. I can't do it on my own. You're the world to me. You're the one who knows the way. You're the only one on whom I can rely. I'll do anything for you. I'll follow you anywhere." Individuals with a great need for admiration and applause who found themselves in the more dominant position were only too happy to oblige, acting as a counterpart to this subservient attitude. And their follow-me invitation—"All your worries are over when you stick with me''—was all too eagerly listened to by the subordinates in question.

The intensity, and thus the danger, of narcissistic collusion seems to depend on how well the principal actors, those in the dominant position, are able to manage their strong narcissistic disposition. We all need a solid dose of narcissism for our day-to-day functioning; an excess, however, can become troublesome. Extreme narcissists are bound to create havoc around them. Preoccupied with wanting to be unique and superior, they exaggerate their talents, engage in boastful and pretentious behavior, conduct themselves in a strongly self-centered and self-referential manner, show an overriding need for attention and admiration, are prone to grandiose fantasies, and often possess vindictive characteristics.

Excessive narcissism can be interpreted as a compensatory strategy for early disappointment in relationships. The predominant feeling of extreme narcissists appears to be that a wrong has been done to them and that the world is therefore deeply indebted to them. They seem to possess a great hunger for recognition and experience a chronic need for external affirmation to feel internally secure. A cohesive sense of self appears to be absent, resulting in an imbalance in the psychic structure, incoherent behavior, and serious problems centered around self-esteem regulation. Extreme narcissists are always in search of an admiring audience to support their yearning for a grandiose self-image and to combat their feelings of helplessness and lack of self-worth.

Characteristic of these people is a history of parental overstimulation, understimulation, or nonintegrative, inconsistent intervention during the early period of development (Kets de Vries, 1979; Kohut, 1974; Miller, 1975). Some extreme narcissists may have been (unconsciously) exploited by their caretakers for the maintenance of the caretakers' own self-esteem; they may have been forced to become narcissistic extensions of these caretakers, assisting them in their own search for admiration and greatness.

The strong concentration of such caretakers on appearances and outward signs of achievement, and their disregard for their children's own personal feelings, may leave these people with a lack of an integrated sense of self; they remain confused about the life they are supposed to lead. They may end up not feeling comfortable in their own skin; many never acquire a secure sense of inner value. The result may be an individual engaged in a lifelong compensatory struggle for self-assertion and self-expression.

When this kind of personality makeup predominates, it is not hard to predict the consequences as far as relationships with others are concerned. The likely outcome of this kind of dysfunctional upbringing is that the narcissist fails to see the people around him or her as individuals in their own right, with demands of their own. In fact, it appears that the relationship between the narcissist and his or her admirers is not a relationship at all in the true sense of the word. In the same way he or she was "used" by caretakers in the early years, the narcissistic individual considers other people as possessions. They fall into the same category as a car, a horse, or a house: they may be used to show off; they are "things," taken for granted; their only function is to act as accessories in the narcissist's pursuit of grandiosity.

It goes without saying that such a collusion will work only if the personality makeup of the two players is complementary. A requirement for the excessive narcissist, then, is a self-effacing quality in the other party—a readiness to offer continual, unconditional admiration. All attention has to be directed toward the narcissist. Nobody else is allowed to share the spotlight. Others are around to act as a positive, reflective mirror. They have to provide a lot of action in order to make the narcissistic party feel "filled up" and able to overcome the inner emptiness he or she experiences. Those permitted to join in with the narcissist's play have to be prepared to remain in his or her shadow.

Often the person in the one-down position suffers from a sense of inferiority and feelings of low self-esteem similar to those of the narcissist, but because of his or her past developmental history, the submissive party is used to being deprecated. His or her dependency needs as a child may have been highly frustrated. He or she may have been brought up in a family where there was little love to go around. This background may have set the stage for a lifelong search for idealized figures to compensate for early emotional deprivations. Such individuals, those with a predisposition toward self-subjugation, sacrifice, and self-compromise, are often actively looking for others they can idealize as a way of boosting their own deflated sense of self-esteem. These people seem to make desperate efforts to counteract their internal anxieties and to feel more "safe" by attaching themselves to someone who is perceived as omnipotent and omniscient. Behind these primitive idealizations may be the fantasy of having all one's needs met unconditionally. In an indirect way, these "ideal-hungry" personalities are trying to obtain narcissistic supplies by searching for others onto whom they can project their fantasies. Through idealization and identification, they obtain such supplies by proxy. Willi calls these people "complementary narcissists." They seem to be trying to appropriate an idealized self from the partner.

Apart from complementary narcissists, people who act as a mirror image for active narcissists, there exists another group of people likely to join into a collusive, narcissistic arrangement: individuals with a personality makeup that can best be described as *dependent* (Storr, 1979). Due to excessive parental protection as developing children, these individuals may have been prevented from properly going through the process of separation-individuation. Thus they may never have been allowed to become completely differentiated beings, to satisfy their own wishes, and to learn to fend for themselves. Frequently, contributing factors to such an outcome are revealed to have been overanxiousness in the mother, a tendency toward sickness in the child, and/or being an only child (with the parents' concomitant excessive fear of losing him or her).

Other permutations are possible, but the end result in the case of both mirror-hungry and dependent individuals is a personality structure characterized by excessive neediness and submissiveness. These individuals seem to lack self-confidence. It is as if they possessed a negative cognitive scheme: they never feel good enough, and they belittle their own achievements. They seem to be unable to function without the help of others. Because doing things independently is a struggle, they allow others to take responsibility for their lives. Consequently, these people may quickly attach themselves to others who can give them direction. Their dependency needs may even take them so far as to agree to things that they know are wrong. Their uncritical acceptance of the behavior and actions of the other party, unrealistic though these may be, seems to be a price they are willing to pay for closeness. Evidently, more frightening than the prospect of doing something wrong is the thought of losing the support of, and being abandoned by, those people on whom they desperately rely for direction. Thus they willingly submit themselves to others at almost any price, often making extraordinary self-sacrifices in the process.

In their intrapsychic world, it appears that the followers see their own happiness as completely dependent on the person they admire. Their boss seems to be always the center of their attention and conversation. This intensive relationship may even turn into an addictive one. There appears to be an unspoken wish to merge, to become one with the other person. The underlying fantasy seems to be one of total symbiosis, a longing for an earlier, happier time when there was a real or imagined perfect relationship with the primary caretaker.

This sort of possessiveness on the part of admirers, however, does not always go down well with the narcissistic target. It may be experienced by him or her as anxiety-provoking. Being idealized and idolized can be a very stifling experience. The admirers' wish to protect their boss from what they see as inappropriate influences, their self-cast role as guardian of the person admired, can be experienced as a straitjacket by the latter. Attempts to shape their idol according to what they consider to be appropriate and inappropriate behavior may (rightfully) be seen as an intrusion. Furthermore, being put on a pedestal is often the precursor to being knocked off it. Living up to exaggerated expectations is highly unrealistic for anyone. When the inevitable disappointment ensues, the idealized person generally becomes at least subliminally aware of the aggression that has been aroused in the admirer when the "idol" who promised so much failed to deliver.

Many leaders fail to realize the extent to which they are caught up in collusive relationships. They do not comprehend the dangers of narcissistic patterns of interaction. Consequently, they are swept away by the seductive forces of narcissism. As the late U.S. politician Adlai Stevenson is alleged to have said, "Flattery is all right as long as you don't inhale." Unfortunately, all too many people inhale far too much, contributing to a lack of critical thinking in the organization, a lack that can have serious dysfunctional consequences.

Yet some leaders on the receiving end of idealization are not flattered; feeling like prisoners of their admirers' glorified portrait, they may become angry and act aggressively. Such reactions, unfortunately, are often to no avail. Whatever unpleasantness these leaders engage in seems to make little difference. The "victims" are quick to find excuses for their idol's unacceptable, abrasive behavior. In many instances, the person being abused by the frustrated leader seems willing to take anything, and what's more, even enjoys the state of martyrdom.

An interesting phenomenon in this process is what Anna Freud described as identification with the aggressor (1936/1965). This is a special form of identification, one that does not necessarily take place at a conscious level, whereby the individual, through impersonation of the "aggressor," assumes the latter's attributes and thus transforms him- or herself from threatened to threatening, pretending that he or she is not the helpless victim but the powerful actor in this drama. It is a defensive maneuver, a way of controlling the severe anxiety caused by the aggressor. The person in the one-down position hopes to acquire some of the power that the aggressor possesses. This wish, to obtain some of the dominant person's power, can explain why people remain in such destructive relationships in spite of the abrasive behavior of the aggressor.

This process of identification with the aggressor, the inducement to participate in a form of group-think, can have terrifying results. In extreme cases, it can lead to the complete destruction of an organization, as demonstrated by the behavior of such executives as Robert Maxwell and John DeLorean.

The Controlling Collusion

Superior: Remind me of when you plan to visit the country managers in Asia.
Subordinate: I'd like to go at the beginning of February.
Superior: I don't think that's such a good idea. More than two months from now—that's too far off. Given our planning cycle, I want to have greater clarity about the figures for the budget proposals sooner. I'd like you to go next week.
Subordinate: I'll do what I can. I'll try to make the arrangements. You do know that it's their peak season now. It may not be the best time to come and hang over them, to pester them with questions. They may need more notice.
Superior: I don't think so. They'd better cooperate. I need these figures. And the only way to get realistic ones is to visit them personally. Remember, you need to assert your authority; otherwise they'll try to pull the wool over your eyes. I want these figures by the end of the month. Things have been slipping too much in the Far East.
Subordinate: I very much agree. I've been thinking along similar lines.
Superior: And one more thing. It's come to my attention that some people in the company are flying business class, using various pretexts that they *need* to do so. One lame argument is that they need to be fit on arrival—as if business class were the answer. I always flew coach when I was an area manager, and I was fit enough. Our expenses for travel are far too high. You know that it's company policy to fly coach.
Subordinate: You have a point there. I'll go and make the travel arrangements. I'll warn the country managers that I'm coming.

From the interviews, the next most common type of collusion identified was one that can best be described as controlling. Here a common script adopted by the executive in the one-down position is as follows: "I'll remain passive. I want you to take the active role. I want you to be in control and take a leadership position." Given the dominant partner's need for power and control, he or she is generally ready to oblige.

The origins of the development of a controlling personality, like those of the other personality types we have seen, can usually be found in a person's early childhood. Starting with exact feeding times, unduly rigid toilet training, and very specific sleeping hours, continuing with narrowly prescribed schedules for all aspects of functioning, the families of compulsive people are often dominated by the theme of control. The parents of these people may be unreasonably exacting, prematurely demanding, and/or condemnatory. Any spontaneous activity may be strongly discouraged for fear that it may bring chaos and disorder. With this sort of background baggage, the control-driven individual derives self-esteem from meeting the harsh demands of the eventually internalized parents.

The predominant feature of the inner world of these compulsively inclined people is their extreme reluctance to find themselves at the mercy of events; they want to master and control everything and everyone around them. The people who flourish in controlling collusions tend to have a personality pattern characterized by rigidity, perfectionism, punctuality, orderliness, meticulousness, and frugality. An inclination to hair-splitting discussions, an exaggerated sense of duty, and meticulous attention to detail are other prevalent traits. Often such individuals can be stubborn, obstinate, inhibited, and unbelievably tense; they lack adaptability, are overly conscientious, and love order and discipline. As members of an organization, they may become preoccupied with factors such as hierarchy, conformity, status, and adherence to formal codes, elaborate information systems, and tightly prescribed procedures and rules.

We can distinguish several varieties of the controlling collusion. In one of them, both parties have a similar mind-set: both are obsessed by the themes of dominance and submission. In this type of controlling collusion, one partner takes the dominant role while the other adopts a submissive position. The person in the one-up position expects total obedience. Any initiative or autonomy on the part of the other is unwelcome. This is a world of master and servant, of superiority and inferiority, of suppression and subordination. The need for order is paramount, founded on both partners' underlying anxiety that chaos will follow otherwise, that things will fall apart without strict authority and control. This type of controlling collusion is also animated by each partner's continuous fear that the other partner may try to reverse the situation. In fact, the partner in the assumed one-up position frequently possesses only the *illusion* of control. In reality, he or she is manipulated by the one-down partner, who is downplaying his or her own desire for control.

In the second type of controlling collusion, the one-down partner may possess a more *passive–aggressive* character structure. The behavior of such an individual is characterized by both passivity and aggressiveness. Passive–aggressive people seem to be ambivalent about everything and cannot make up their mind whether to be dependent or independent, active or passive. They may give vent to their underlying aggression through indecisiveness, contradictory behavior, and conflicting attitudes. Apparently afraid of showing disagreement openly, they express indirect resistance to control through such means as procrastination, dawdling, stubbornness, intentional inefficiency, and forgetfulness. An aura of compliance and cordiality may mask negative resistance. In passive–aggressive individuals, this kind of behavior may be the common pattern for dealing with people in the position of control.

Passive–aggressive behavior patterns often originate in the fact that these people, as children, were unable to assess clearly what was expected of them. Dominated by their parents' frequently erratic and conflicting demands, they led a life characterized by a lack of consistency and clear indicators for appropriate conduct. As a result, they may have failed to learn what kind of behavior pays off. Another possible contributing factor may be a perceived lack of control over decisions when growing up. Because of the domineering style of one or both parents, the option to say no may have been absent in childhood. The wishes of the children may simply not have been taken into consideration. Over time, saying yes but then not doing what they had been asked to do became their solution to this particular conundrum.

In the third type of controlling collusion, the dominant actor may be partnered by someone with a dependent personality structure, someone who gladly submits to the controlling figure. This match is generally the most complementary one, causing the least amount of friction between the partners, since both play out a role that naturally suits their respective personality structures. This combination starkly contrasts with cases where the one-down partner is of a more compulsive type or possesses a passive–aggressive personality makeup. In collusions made up of these latter two combinations, the central action consists of a power struggle fought by both partners in order to decide which one is to take on the leadership position and which one the submissive role. The drama focuses on which of the two is going to take charge. Endless power plays may be the result.

Many organizations offer great opportunities for people to act out the controlling collusion. These kinds of organizations tend to be exceedingly rigid, centralized, and administrative. Formalized controls are used as a way to check the potential abuse of power. Plans are often so explicit as to admit no flexibility; strategy is narrowly focused and unadaptive. The consequences of an emphasis on bureaucracy tend to be predictably dysfunctional. Such rigidity in outlook is bound to have serious consequences in a world characterized by rapid change. A lack of speedy adaptability and an obsession with details can easily become the downfall for organizations run by people engaged in the theater of controlling collusions.

The Paranoid Collusion

> Superior: I'm very unhappy with company sales, given the number of salespeople we have. I wonder how the sales reps spend their time. Do they give their full attention to the company, or are some of them spending their time doing other things? I'd really like to know. Wouldn't it be nice to have a way of monitoring the time they spend on different tasks through our computer system? It would help me catch some of the abusers. Ethics be damned, we have a business to run. Why don't you look into that possibility.
> Subordinate: I'll contact the consulting firm we've been using for systems development immediately. I think they're the right people to answer such a question.
> Superior: One more thing. What's your opinion of Mary? Do you think the head office really sent her here to help us with the feasibility study for a new plant, or is that just a pretext? Could it be that the real reason she's here is to study our operations and recommend where we'll fit in the global company restructuring plan?
> Subordinate: You may have a point there. Many of the questions she's been asking have been way beyond the scope of the plant study. I'll try to keep an eye on her and, if needed, do some damage control—feed her the kind of information that will reassure the people at the head office, make sure they have no reason to single us out and make us a target in their downsizing efforts.

The script for both parties involved in a paranoid collusion reads, ''There's danger lurking out there. We can't really trust anybody. We have to be on our guard. Some menacing force is out to get us. We'd better stick together.''

The interpersonal theater of executives with paranoid tendencies seems to be dominated by the thought that the world is a very dangerous place. There appears to be very little room for trust. People affected by such perceptions feel that they have to be continually prepared for imminent danger. They live in chronic fear of bad surprises, and they take unnecessary precautions. Hypervigilant, they constantly scan the environment for confirmation of their suspicions. They are overly concerned about others' hidden motives and intentions, which may lead to distorted perceptions, thoughts, and memories. They see plots to harass and humiliate them everywhere. They take everything very personally, are easily slighted, and can be extremely litigious.

This paranoid way of thinking and behaving may create a sense of isolation, but it also compels those afflicted by it to seek the validation of their perception by others. There exists an extraordinary wish to pull others into their camp. Unfortunately, such tendencies are easily supported by reality: after all, if one really looks for it, one can always find some confirmation of this kind of distorted view. People do unpleasant things to other people all the time. That this is the state of things only reinforces an already dysfunctional situation.

A major contributing factor in the etiology of paranoid thinking is the presence of a suspicious attitude among a person's principal caretakers. They may have instilled into the belief system of the developing child the tenet that the outside world is very dangerous, that only family members can be trusted. They may have continually come up with "evidence," much of it contrived, to support this distorted point of view. As could be expected, such parenting practices do not enable a child to develop a basic sense of trust.

In other instances, people who show paranoid traits may come from homes where criticism and ridicule ruled, creating an atmosphere of persecution that made it necessary for the developing child to be always on his or her guard. Individuals with this particular background have a tendency to lash out in order to divert the harm they think is approaching them, rather than wait passively for real or imagined dangers.

An essential element in the functioning of the paranoid personality is the attribution of one's perceived negative personality characteristics to others. This projective defense mechanism becomes a powerful tool in the repertoire of paranoid executives. As a matter of fact, these executives may feel persecuted even by the despised image of themselves! In addition, these "delusions of persecution," which serve to combat their sense of inner vulnerability, may be accompanied by "illusions of grandeur."

The combination of such dysfunctional behavior patterns can make these people very hard to live with.

In the context of paranoid collusions, folie à deux (shared madness), should be mentioned (Kets de Vries, 1979). Basically, that concept implies the sharing of a delusional system by two (or more) individuals. People who are prone to folie à deux lack an integrated self-concept and thus have strong dependency needs. They seem to be in desperate need of having others provide them with a structure for their lives. Colluding with an executive with paranoid features thus suits their own personality structure. They generally prefer colluding with someone perceived as powerful (who provides them with the direction) even when it leads to clearly dysfunctional organizational activities. They will go to great lengths, even so far as to sacrifice reality, to please the person to whom they feel attached. They tend to uncritically accept the behavior of the dominant person, and adopt it themselves, in spite of its delusional content. They are willing to hang in persistently; it takes a lot before they are ready to quit.

Naturally, it is highly unrealistic to run an organization in such a way. When a leader of an organization is preoccupied with suspicion and distrust, when attitudes of folie à deux reign, his or her way of thinking and behaving may reverberate throughout the organization, with devastating effects. If power is highly concentrated at the top, such behavior will color the whole organizational culture. If subordinates are going to survive in an organization run by a paranoid executive, they may have no choice but to share their boss's distorted way of looking at the world; otherwise, they will soon be rejected by him or her.

Some of the subordinates joining in this collusive drama may themselves have a paranoid outlook on life and thus adapt easily to a leader with paranoid tendencies. Others who are willing to play along with this game may have frustrated dependency needs and be willing to suspend reality as long as the position of closeness to their leader is maintained. Such distorted perceptions, however, tend to have a very negative effect on sound decision making, eventually affecting the company's bottom line in a negative way.

Characteristic of the kind of organization created by people with a paranoid outlook are elaborate information systems and an extreme emphasis on the power of information. Strategy making is usually reactive, conservative, overly analytical, and secretive. There is great uniformity in values and beliefs; a very narrow point of view reigns. Trust is not one of the qualities that characterize this type of organization. On the contrary, conflict and distrust prevent effective communication and collaboration. Suspicion causes power to be centralized at the top, resulting in too little grassroots adaptation.

The Sadomasochistic Collusion

> Superior: Where's that report on the plant extension that I asked you about yesterday?
> Subordinate: Didn't you find it on your desk? I left it there this morning.
> Superior: Oh, you mean *that* piece of garbage. I had a quick look at it. I thought it was just preliminary notes. What about the projections I asked you about? They haven't been worked out. It certainly isn't what I had in mind when I was talking to you. I'm beginning to wonder if you're in the wrong job, if not the wrong company. Do you plan to produce something better?
> Subordinate: I'm sorry; I guess I misunderstood. My mind must not have been completely there when you gave me the assignment. I'll rework the report right away. I'll stay as long as it takes to come up with the figures.
> Superior: You'd better. Otherwise this may be your last project, at least in *this* company.

The sadomasochistic collusion is acted out in the theater of the abuser and the abused. Deconstruction of our interviews with executives showed the following basic script of the more masochistically inclined party in such a collusion: "I'm worthless. I'm bad. I submit to you. I deserve to be punished for the error of my ways. My suffering is justified."

To sadistically inclined executives, the world is a jungle. Given that worldview, they have to behave aggressively and frighten others into submission; to survive they have to be on the attack. Retaining the upper hand, striking out when danger threatens, remaining in power and control, these goals take precedence over everything else. Fortunately for them, abrasive executives can usually find masochistically inclined people who are willing to put up with such an outlook. The roles of sadist and masochist are not necessarily definitive, however. Often we find a strong sadistic component behind a masochist's facade of self-sacrifice. Some workplace masochists, for example, get a lot of pleasure out of defaming their tormentors by telling others what awful things those tormentors have done to them.

Studying the early personal history of individuals with a sadistic disposition, we often find a chaotic background with weak, depressed, masochistically inclined mothers and explosive, inconsistent, or even sadistic fathers. Substance abuse is quite common in these families. Violence is a regular pattern. Frequent moves, various types of losses, and family breakups are not unusual. A true holding environment is generally missing. Under these circumstances, it is to be expected that normal development will not take place. Hostility breeds more hostility, becoming the model for similar behavior later in life.

The lack of containment during childhood creates a sense of helplessness in these people; because as children they had to deal with what seemed to be uncontrollable forces, they carry into adulthood the sense of being at the world's mercy. To compensate for feelings of inferiority, they often develop a compelling desire for dominance and power. To show signs of weakness or vulnerability is unacceptable to them. Authority figures are not looked upon as positive and benevolent but as tough, dangerous, and abusive. Paradoxically, while these people often reject authority figures when in a dependency position (fearful as they are of being maltreated), when in a position of authority they themselves tend to abuse their power.

Another possible background scenario resulting in sadistic behavior involves parents who signal to their children that they are special and therefore exempt from the normal rules of conduct that conventional society imposes on people and entitled to do whatever pleases them. Anyone trying to set boundaries on their behavior (such as teachers or counselors) invites the wrath of the parents. The children may take notice of that and, with permission granted at least implicitly, do whatever takes their fancy. Such childrearing practices set the stage for antisocial, impulsive, and sadistic behavior. Obviously, sadistically inclined people cannot act out their fantasies in a vacuum; they need others to participate. And, as life in organizations all too often shows, they have an uncanny ability to attract people who are willing to be victimized.

The origin of a *masochistic* disposition seems to be based on the child's attachment needs. Whatever the circumstances of growing up may be; there is always an intense wish on the part of the child to arrive at some form of interaction with the parents. Unfortunately, some parents are able to offer only painful, unfulfilling contacts. If painful contact becomes the established pattern between parent and child, the developing child associates love and caring with the reception of pain. Nevertheless, he or she generally concludes that any attention, even if accompanied by pain, is better than neglect. Eventually, attachment through suffering becomes the chosen interpersonal style of these people, and they seek out situations that recreate early experiences of receiving love through pain. Because they perceive the gratification that come from being abused as outweighing the pain that accompanies it, their emotional comfort comes from being in the role of the victim. Martyrdom becomes the price of relating to others.

Critical, guilt-inducing caretakers can contribute to the development of a masochistic style of relating to others. Role reversals whereby the child (age-inappropriately) is made to feel responsible for the parents, as well as instances of abuse, are also conducive to masochism's etiology. Deep, unconscious guilt feelings can be at the root of this form of relating. Unresolved dependency issues and fears of being left alone also appear to be major driving forces in the development of this interaction pattern. Children brought up under circumstances of guilt and the fear of abandonment may internalize the reproaching quality of their parents toward them. The perception of being bad seems to be a major theme in their internal theater; eventually, they take over the role of the parents and become their own worst critic. The guilt of not living up to the parents' expectations may follow them like an inseparable shadow. Throughout their lives they may feel unworthy, guilty, rejectable, deserving of punishment. As a result, a masochistic style may become their way of relating to others. As a result, identification with the aggressor, mentioned earlier in the context of the narcissistic collusion, comes easily to them.

Masochistic behavior, however self-defeating it may seem, can provide an enormous dose of "secondary gain" in the form of arousing the concern and interest of others. People who see themselves as the victims of unfair suffering often get great satisfaction out of the sympathy and pity others express to them for the way they have been (or are being) abused. Suffering may also give them a sense of moral superiority. In addition, by behaving masochistically and enduring pain and suffering, these individuals may hope (consciously or unconsciously) that some good will come out of it. In other words, they may see tolerating abuse as accomplishing some goal that justifies suffering or averts an even more painful eventuality. These are people who aspire to sainthood. With all the drama they create, however, they can be quite a burden to those around them.

Sadistically and masochistically inclined executives often seem to be a perfect match for each other. In the interplay in this kind of collusion, self-esteem for each seems to be maintained by proving the other party wrong. The interactions between such people can become extremely intense, with a compulsive quality. The nature of the interactions cannot be changed: quarreling becomes a way of life, an extremely distorted way of expressing affection. In the context of couples, a good example of such a situation of abuse can be found in Edward Albee's play *Who's*

Afraid of Virginia Woolf? (1982). As we follow the heated interchanges of that play, it seems that winning boosts self-esteem,
while losing is a major disaster.

At times in organizations we encounter similar dramatic
scenes. When sadomasochistic relationships become an overriding pattern in the organization, it is not trust but fear that rules,
affecting morale, stifling creativity, and hampering learning. In
the fear-ridden organization, the quality of decision making goes
down and the most capable executives leave. Eventually, the
very future of the company is endangered.

Breaking the Vicious Circle

In the above discussion we have seen that a certain kind of group
process allows the behavior of one of the players to determine
the role that the other(s) will assume. If the role assigned to an
individual is not compatible with his or her character, that individual generally quits, moving on to a partner or an organizational setting more suited to his or her personality.

But not every person who quits a job does so because of
collusion, and not every enduring workplace relationship is collusive. On the contrary, as psychoanalyst Wilfred Bion observed,
most work relationships are task-oriented and based on the rational approach of goal orientation and work sharing (1959). The
"basic assumptions" of collusion, the underlying forces that
make people behave in specific ways, are not generally predominant; hidden agendas do not routinely set the tone. In most interpersonal situations, the draining, stressful, adversarial processes
that characterize collusive relationships and make them so exas-
perating are conspicuous by their absence. Our interpretation of
the material gleaned from our interviews supports Bion's view:
most of the interaction patterns studied were not of a neurotic
nature. In many of the relationships there appeared a considerable amount of transitional space; there was the kind of playful

give-and-take that gives people ample space to grow and develop.

Nevertheless, the interviews revealed a fair number of collusive relationships, in differing degrees of intensity. The existence of such relationships is a cause for concern, given the dysfunctional effects of collusive processes on other people in the organization. The destructive potential of corporate collusions makes it important to know how to recognize such processes, or better yet, to prevent them.

A Spanish proverb asserts that fish start to stink at the head. Given the power that leaders wield, and the fact that it is usually they who enlist others in their dysfunctional theater of the absurd, they are largely responsible for initiating these collusive activities. Thus, if we wish to make an attempt at prevention, diagnosis, or treatment, a good place to start is by assessing the quality of leadership in the organization. Recognizing dysfunctional behavior patterns in an organization's leadership is an essential aspect of the diagnostic and preventive process.

The first question we should ask ourselves is whether the people at the top have the kind of personality makeup that renders them susceptible to collusive practices. If the individuals running the organization react in strange, irrational ways that suggest specific personality disturbances, we should become alert to the danger that their conduct might pose for the organization. Symptomatic of potential trouble are such behavior patterns as abrasiveness, selfishness, overambitiousness, arrogance, excessive detachment, overemotionality, vindictiveness, suspiciousness, overcontrol, insensitivity, untrustworthiness, decision paralysis, and excessive detail orientation.

In addition to these troublesome behavior patterns, narcissism is disturbingly insidious. Earlier in this chapter, I described some of the salient elements of narcissistic behavior. Other indicators of excessive narcissism worth mentioning are an executive's preoccupation with being at the center of things, the need to take all the credit or be in the limelight, and an obsession with getting his or her name in the press. With this kind of narcissistic behavior comes a tendency toward one-upmanship over one's peers. Subordinates who are prepared to buy into this game confirm and encourage such behavior.

Another cause for concern is inappropriate reactions on the part of top executives to mistakes. How do these individuals attribute blame? Are they likely to seek out scapegoats? Do they see conspiracies everywhere? If leaders have created the kind of corporate climate where others are always at fault, where they themselves never take the blame for mistakes, the organizational environment is far from healthy. Because such leaders sometimes react violently to realities that inconvenience them—realities such as the hard truth from colleagues—partners can always be found to participate in their collusive behavior, but the effects of collusion on future organizational functioning are dire.

Predictably, executives who behave in such ways create organizations where only yea-sayers survive. Contrarian thinking is not permitted; disagreement with the leader's point of view is not condoned. People are not allowed to question anything. Those who are prepared to participate in collusive behavior are given only a submissive role. A corporate culture evolves in which communication is restricted; a lack of openness prevails. Soon distrust and fear develop and predictably, when fear rules in an organization, the processes of organizational adaptation and learning stop.

A further cause for worry is the presence of a top executive who insists on making all the decisions and allows nobody to think for him- or herself. Overcontrolling everything that affects the organization becomes such a person's major preoccupation. In this kind of organizational culture, empowerment is a dirty word (and delegation is therefore unheard of). A top executive's refusal to plan for succession is a related indication of trouble. The addiction to power and the need to hang onto control make it very hard for some executives to let go (or even begin to think about handing over the reins). Not surprisingly, in an organization dominated by such executives only collusive relationships are possible. And unfortunately, when that is the case, the best people start to leave. In addition to that present crisis, the absence of succession planning leads to predictable crises in the future.

Unpredictability is another warning sign. When a leader becomes unpredictable, his or her behavior is bound to contribute to a climate of distrust and uncertainty in the organization. People who work for such a leader no longer know how they are supposed to act. Furthermore, because of the leader's behavior, the company may adopt a short-term, fire-fighting mentality. In such instances, priorities are unclearly set and tend to vacillate.

An additional question that should be raised in testing an organization's relationships for collusion relates to how realistic the senior executive's outlook is on the business. If his or her strategic initiatives bear little relation to the realities of the company's situation, alarm bells should start ringing loudly.

A decrease in morale is another warning sign of collusive interaction. Companies troubled in the ways described here often become increasingly politicized. Infighting and gamesmanship replace teamwork. Good corporate citizenship behavior is absent, because an increasing number of executives have become turf defenders. Having adopted a parochial outlook, they no longer care about things that are good for the company. A siege mentality prevails.

The list goes on and on. These are only some of the more obvious danger signs that can derive from collusive entanglements. From my observations, I have concluded that the possibility for collusive entanglements is not an abstraction; it is an organizational reality. After all, we all have, at one level or another, some unfinished business originating from our history. We all find ourselves stuck occasionally in a vicious circle, the victims of typecasting. The ultimate challenge, however, is to not let this happen, to avoid the kinds of damaging relationships that result in organizational pathology. It is salutary to remember that such relationships eventually destroy any organization. An important question then becomes, What can be done to prevent (or nip in the bud) such dysfunctional relationship patterns? How can the vicious circle be broken before it threatens the workplace?

Help can be offered in various ways. The presence of countervailing powers in the form of external directors, institutional shareholders, or other powerful stakeholders in the company can do much to reverse collusion. These individuals can emphasize reality testing in relationships and pinpoint dysfunctional interaction patterns. Other senior executives and internal and external consultants may also be in a position to offer a reality check. The most appropriate starting point for the unraveling process, however, is to help executives who are stuck in collusive relationships gain a better understanding of the kind of script that they are acting out in the organization as a whole.

How do we do this? Understanding others requires a solid dose of self-awareness, a recognition of the role of emotional processes in motivation, an attribute that has been described in chapter 3 as the "teddy bear" quality. The development of emotional intelligence through self-knowledge is the first step in the process of disentanglement from an unhealthy situation. The ability to monitor one's own reactions makes it easier to understand how others may become enrolled in a collusive effort (and the effect this kind of relationship can have on the organization). Thus executives would do well to take regular stock of their relationships to others, asking themselves whether these are continually evolving and growing or have become stuck in a repetitive interplay. If executives suspect that someone is trying to draw them into a neurotic play they should have the presence of mind to decide whether they wish to participate or not, and realize the implications of participation.

Understanding one's own role in the interactive process is not generally easy, given the blind spots we all have about our character. It can be hard work to move from a fusional state, where one does not perceive oneself as a person in one's own right but attached to another, to one of true separateness. Superior and subordinate need to be able to sort out their own subjective experiences without the kind of confusion that characterizes collusive interaction patterns. But recognizing these patterns in oneself and others, and gathering the motivation and courage to address these failings, may require outside help. Psychoanalysis, psychotherapy, coaching, or participation in a group-dynamics seminar in which feedback about personal style is part of the process may help an individual disentangle his or her role in the process.

All too many people forget that if we do not like a play in a theater, we can leave, and that is true of organizational dramas as well. We do not have to participate; we always have the option to quit. In organizational life, it is important to retain our sense of individuality and not be swept away by forces that stifle our ability to play and to be creative. In the final analysis, mental health means having a choice!

References

Albee, E. (1982). *Who's afraid of Virginia Woolf?* New York: New American Library.

Auletta, K. (1994, September). The human factor. *The New Yorker,* 70 (issue 926), pp. 54–61.

Bion, W. R. (1959). *Experiences in groups.* London: Tavistock.

Freud, A. (1965). *The ego and the mechanisms of defense.* New York: International Universities Press. (Original work published 1936)

Grover, R. (1994 January 31). Jeffrey Katzenberg: No more Mr. Tough Guy? *Business Week,* 46.

Huy, J. (1995, April 17). Eisner explains everything. *Fortune,* 33–48.

Kets de Vries, M. F. R. (1979, July/August). Managers can drive their subordinates mad. *Harvard Business Review,* 125–134.

Kohut, H. (1974). *The analysis of the self.* New York: International Universities Press.

McDougall, J. (1985). *Theaters of the mind.* New York: Basic Books.

Miller, A. (1975). *Prisoners of childhood: The drama of the gifted child and the search for the true self.* New York: Basic Books.

Ogden, T. H. (1982). *Projective identification and psychotherapeutic technique.* New York: Jason Aronson.

Storr, A. (1979). *The art of psychotherapy.* New York: Methuen.

Willi, J. (1982). Preface. In *Couples in collusion: The unconscious dimension in partnerships.* Claremont, CA: Hunter House.

5

Envy and Its Vicissitudes

The infernal Serpent; hee it was, whose guile,
Stirrd up with Envy and Revenge, deceiv'd
The Mother of Mankinde.
(John Milton, *Paradise Lost*)

Never having been able to succeed in the world, he took his revenge
by speaking ill of it. (Voltaire)

Passionate hatred can give meaning and purpose to an empty life.
(Eric Hoffer)

Whenever a friend succeeds, a little something in me dies. (Gore
Vidal)

Don't get mad, get even. (Joseph Kennedy)

In reviewing management textbooks, I have noticed that the
construct of envy is almost nonexistent. It is, however, a major
preoccupation and motivator in human functioning. The consequences of envy can be observed all around us. To address that
gap, this chapter explores the meaning and origin of envy and
looks at its function in society. After weighing envy against
related topics such as jealousy, greed, revenge, and vindictiveness, this chapter looks at various ways of dealing with envy.
Special emphasis is given to coping mechanisms regarding envy
in the context of organizational life: strategies of an envy-avoidance and envy-inducing nature. Among the alternative strategies

157

discussed are idealization, denial, reaction formation, rationalization, withdrawal, devaluation, the drive to excel, and reparation. I believe that a better understanding of the envy construct
will bring greater realism to the study of behavior in organizations.

Introduction

On August 17, 1661, Nicholas Fouquet, the French finance min-
ister in the early years of the reign of Louis XIV, a man who
loved beauty and pleasure in every form, gave an incomparable
party in honor of his king to show off his original vision of
architecture, decoration, and garden design at his estate Vaux-
le-Vicomte. In France's most beautiful chateau, the guests were
extravagantly entertained with fireworks, theater, and sumptuous
meals. The luxury of his lifestyle, however, raised the envy of
Louis XIV and others and contributed to Fouquet's downfall.

That party led from suspicions about how Fouquet had enriched himself to an investigation into financial irregularities. As
a result of that investigation, he was arrested on the orders of
Louis XIV and sentenced to life imprisonment. The remaining
19 years of his life were spent in Pignerol, a small fortress in
the Savoy Alps. As an epitaph, we can say that envy of Fouquet's
gaiety and magnificence was the motivating factor that led to
his downfall.

As the example of Fouquet illustrates, although envy is an
often unrecognized and repressed factor, it is one that nonetheless greatly affects human motivation, behavior, and action. It
plays a major role as a motivator in society but is a relatively
taboo topic in management circles. In spite of the ubiquity of
the experience—after all, competition, aspiration, and comparison are part of human life—references to this very important
issue in organizations are scarce.

The Ubiquity of Envy

St. Thomas Aquinas listed envy as one of the seven deadly sins. And no wonder, since already in the Ten Commandments there were warnings about the destructive effects of envy: "You shall not covet your neighbor's wife, you shall not set your heart on his house, his field, his servant—man or woman—his ox, his donkey or anything that is his" (*Jerusalem Bible,* 1966, p. 94). The Bible also contains well-known illustrations of the consequences of envy in the stories of Cain and Abel and Joseph and his brothers.

The experience of envy is not restricted to the Judeo-Christian tradition, however. In certain cultures, the idea of the "evil eye" exists as a representation of envy. The universal nature of envy is also attested to in proverbs concerning envy that are prevalent in many different societies. For example, in Bulgaria, "Other people's eggs have two yolks"; in Denmark, "If envy were a fever, all the world would be ill"; in Sweden, the expression "royal Swedish envy," has a strong message not to provoke envy by being conspicuous. Literature is also full of examples of envy, probably the best known being Milton's portrait of Satan in *Paradise Lost,* a being who, seething with envy and wanting revenge, fabricates man's fall from Paradise. Many instances of the effects of envy are also found in the tales of Chaucer and Shakespeare. In addition, philosophers such as Bacon and Kant, fascinated by the phenomenon of envy, have emphasized the critical role of that emotion in explaining human action. Immanuel Kant saw envy as an intrinsic part of human nature:

> The impulse for envy is thus inherent in the nature of man, and only its manifestation makes of it an abominable vice, a passion not only distressing and tormenting to the subject, but intent on the destruction of the happiness of others, and one that is opposed to man's duty toward himself as toward other people. (1785/1922, p. 316)

Sociologist Helmut Schoeck (1969) talked about the universality of an "envy motive," arguing that "envy is a drive which lies at the core of man's life as a social being, and which occurs as soon as two individuals become capable of mutual comparison" (p. 1). For Schoeck, the essence of envy is the rejection of diversity. People have a great need to equalize, he said, noting that even a policy such as progressive taxation is based on envy. In other words, envy creates the social controls on which society depends. In that respect, Schoeck's point of view is very close to that of the advocates of one of the few theories of motivation found in management theory that, albeit not directly, acknowledges the role of envy: namely, equity theory, which essentially argues that managers tend to compare their efforts and rewards with those of others in a similar work situation. Equity exists when employees perceive the ratios of their inputs (efforts) to the outcome (rewards) as equivalent to those of other employees. In the absence of perceived equity (i.e., when people believe they are being treated unfairly) the impact on motivation can be dramatic. Schoeck acknowledged this darker side, mentioning that the envy motive can have both constructive and destructive consequences. Anthropologist George Foster (1972) supported him in this stand, calling envy "a particularly dangerous and destructive emotion, since it implies hostility, which leads to aggression and violence capable of destroying societies" (p. 165).

The Meaning of Envy

What is envy? Is it a conscious or unconscious state of feeling, a defensive reaction, a motive, a cognitive orientation, or all of these? The psychoanalyst Wilfred Bion (1977) said that "envy is typical of other elements of the personality in that everyone would be prepared to admit its existence. Yet it does not smell; it is invisible, inaudible, intangible. It has no shape" (p. 54). Bion may have been too optimistic about the willingness of people to admit to being motivated by envy. Envy is seen as so shameful a passion that we rarely dare to acknowledge it. Certainly we are embarrassed to own up to it. Acknowledging envy does not enhance our self-image; indeed, it feels tantamount to admitting a sense of inferiority.

Whatever envy is, it is treated with a great deal of ambivalence. For the purpose of simplification, envy as an emotion can be looked at as an organizer and coordinator of the physiological and psychological processes that make up behavior. We need to remember though that emotional processes are at the borderline not only of the ideational and physiological but of the voluntary and involuntary (Goleman, 1995; Knapp, 1963, 1976). A complex relationship exists between states of feeling and thinking; that is, emotional reactions and evaluations are tied in to cognitive and perceptual encoding processes, behavior, and actions.

Deconstructing Envy

When we look at the etymological source of the word *envy,* we discover that it is derived from the Latin noun *invidia* and the verb *invidere,* meaning, according to the *Oxford English Dictionary,* "to look maliciously upon." The examples in that dictionary indicate that envy has to do with malignant or hostile feelings, a wish to cause harm or mischief, a feeling of mortification and ill will occasioned by the contemplation of superior advantages possessed by another, and the desire to emulate and equal the other in the achievement of excellence. *Webster* speaks of the painful or resentful awareness of an advantage enjoyed by another, accompanied by a desire to have the same advantage. From these definitions, it appears that at the heart of envy there is an unpleasant feeling caused by the desire to possess what someone else has, such as wealth, power, status, love, or beauty. Such a reaction may give rise to feelings of frustration, anger, self-pity, greed, and vindictiveness.

The clinician sees envy as a more complex reaction than many other emotions because it deals with a *mixture* of feelings. As an example, Karl Abraham noted that "the envious person shows not only desire for the possessions of others, but connects with that desire spiteful impulses against the privileged proprietor'' (1968, p. 382). Envy is a strange term in that it both characterizes a type of activity and makes a prediction about the actor. Moreover, envy is Janus-faced: it generates not only fear of the consequences of one's own envy but fear of the envy of others.

In disassembling the components making up the envy construct, we can differentiate four affect states (Spielman, 1971, p. 77). First, there is a desire for emulation based on a perception of excellence, which leads to a wish to equal, imitate, or surpass the envied individual. Second, there is a narcissistic wound, or the sense of lacking something, connected with feelings of inferiority, inadequacy, and injured self-esteem. In other words, the person devalues him- or herself in comparison with someone else or some specific ideal. Third, there is a longing for the desired possession. Finally, there is a feeling of anger at the possessor, which may be expressed mildly (as chagrin or discontent), moderately (as resentment or ill will), or severely (as an impulse to spoil or destroy the envied object or to engage in malicious, spiteful action).

A certain amount of confusion exists between the terms *envy* and *jealousy*. Although these labels for human passion are often used interchangeably, there is a fundamental difference, depending on the interpersonal context in which each occurs. That difference, on which most psychologists agree, is that envy applies to two-person relationships whereas jealousy applies to three. Rivalry with a third party is the critical variable that distinguishes jealousy. Basically, the jealous person fears that a third person will intrude upon a two-person relationship and take possession. In other words, jealousy is not a wanting-to-have but a wanting-to-hold-on, a protest against loss.

In differentiating envy from jealousy, Harry Stack Sullivan, one of the original researchers of the concept, defined the former as:

[An] activity in which one contemplates the unfortunate results of someone else's having something that one does not have.... [E]nvy may be an active realization that one is not good enough, compared with someone else. Although it involves primarily a two-group situation, one of the two may be a more-or-less mythological person.

Jealousy, on the other hand, never concerns a two-group situation. It is invariably a very complex, painful process involving a group of three or more persons, one or more of whom may be absolutely fantasized. Jealousy ... involves a great complex field of interpersonal relations. (1953, p. 348)

Melanie Klein, another major contributor to the concept of envy, made a similar distinction between envy and jealousy:

Envy is the angry feeling that another person possesses and enjoys something desirable—the envious impulse being to take it away or to spoil it. Moreover, envy implies the subject's relation to one person and goes back to the earliest exclusive relationship with the mother. Jealousy is based on envy, but involves a relation to at least two people; it is mainly concerned with love that the subject feels it is due and has been taken away, or is in danger of being taken away from him by his rival. (1975, p. 181)

While it is embarrassing to admit to envy, jealousy is much more acceptable and thus less masked. Newspapers, songs, and literature, mute on the subject of envy, are full of examples of jealousy. Despite the basic difference between envy and jealousy developed earlier, and this additional difference in the social acceptability of the two constructs, the behavior, cognitions, and emotions associated with envy and jealousy are not that different. As an example, both envy and jealousy result in anger. Given this bridge of commonality, while from a conceptual point of view it may be interesting to differentiate the two, from a pragmatic point of view the distinction is less meaningful. Because jealousy is based on envy, as Klein noted above, and because society favors the term *jealousy* even when *envy* is more appropriate, we may have to accept that in everyday conversation the terms are used synonymously.

The Origins of Envy

What are the origins of emotions in general? Where does envy fit into that overall picture; how do we explain its development? Henry Krystal, an astute observer of the general development of emotions, remarked that:

> [T]he affective responses of the infant represent two basic patterns: a state of contentment and tranquility and a state of distress. These two states represent affect precursors out of which evolve pleasurable and painful affects respectively. In the normal course of maturation the mixed affect precursor pattern separates out into specific entities. The several emotions of anger, shame, guilt, envy, jealousy, anxiety, depression, and so on identifiably evolve out of the general distress response. The process continues into the progressive refinement of emotional experiences, so that in the adult these major groupings differentiate into finer nuances of meaning. (1982, p. 365)

Most researchers do not object to this point of view, although there is disagreement about the point in human development at which feelings of envy first arise, and how it evolves. For example, Sigmund Freud traced the origins of envy to that stage of life when the child becomes aware of the anatomical differences between the sexes (1905/1953, 1925/1961). This led him to postulate the controversial concept of penis envy, the female's conscious or unconscious envy of the penis and the feeling that she is handicapped or ill treated because of the lack of it. Freud argued that such recognition of difference may give rise to injured self-esteem and may contribute to the character trait of jealousy, envy being only a precursor. In response to this supposition, others have postulated man's envy of the woman's procreative abilities, which can lead to similar feelings. In contemporary psychoanalytic theory, however, the notion of penis envy (if the term is still used at all) is looked at more as a metaphor for certain milestones in human development having to do with mental imagery about unification with and separation from the primary caretaker(s), the awakening of sexual aware-ness, and societal attributions of power and helplessness.

Although Freud recognized the preoedipal antecedents of envy, he saw envy as basically a universal phenomenon of child-hood related to the Oedipus complex. Subsequent child studies have shown, however, that one must go to the preoedipal period to solve the riddle of envy; considering only the mother–fa-ther–child triad is not sufficient. Melanie Klein, for example, considered envy an oral–sadistic and anal–sadistic expression of destructive impulses operative from the beginning of life. Al-though that passage suggests that envy is an innate characteristic, Klein emphasized the developmental point of view, arguing that envy is one of the most primitive and fundamental of emo-tions—one that comes to the fore as soon as the infant becomes aware that the mother's breast is the source of all gratification and good experiences. Along with the wish to preserve and pro-tect these good feelings come the first stirrings of an envious desire to be the source of such perfection oneself. Thus envy is bound up with both the experience of gratification and the experience of a lack. Envious feelings start when children be-come aware that they do not have the power to give the pleasures they themselves enjoy.

In older children, the arrival of a new baby in the family stirs up these envious feelings. The original envious feelings are intensified and transformed into jealousy when the child watches the mother suckle or take care of a sibling. Such actions are an additional source of rivalrous feelings and lead to comparison of one's own qualities with those of the other. A sense of compet-itiveness is born, as alluded to in a passage from St. Augustine's *Confessions* (398/1961):

> He was not old enough to talk, but whenever he saw his foster-brother at the breast, he would grow pale with envy. This much is common knowledge. Mothers and nurses say they can work such things out of the system by one means or another, but surely it cannot be called

innocence, when the milk flows in such abundance from its source, to object to a rival desperately in need and depending for his life on this form of nourishment? (p. 280)

Envy becomes further crystallized as the child continues to develop. Originally linked to orality, being preoedipal, envy seems to be the matrix that determines many of the child's later relationships. The intensity of envy as determined by the holding environment provided by the parents strongly affects relationships to siblings and, later in life, other persons.

Jealousy (triadic envy) comes into its own at the oedipal stage, the time in life when the child is around 4 or 5 years of age. Interestingly enough, this transformation of envy into jealousy can make emerging envious feelings less guilt-inducing and more acceptable to the person involved. Indeed, jealousy can be seen as a *defense* against envy, because in multiperson relationships, hostile feelings can be "split off" and displaced onto others. Through jealousy, then, the sense of guilt over envying a loved person can be avoided.

Because envy is viewed as a shameful reaction, and as such is a motivator that individuals usually do not dare to acknowledge, myriad forms of self-deception are used to conceal its appearance. And the competitive world of organizations, with its many different cultures and reward structures, provides numerous opportunities for envy to flourish, albeit in disguise.

In the following pages I will explore some of the more prominent ways in which people deal with envy. These different expressions are not mutually exclusive, however, nor are they necessarily stable. One way of dealing with envy frequently evolves into another, depending on the intensity of intrapsychic conflict. The strategies employed combine, in an intricate way, envy-avoidance and envy-inducing components; that is, they are often a mixture of those reactions that are a form of self-protection against the envy of others and those used to negate one's own envious desires.

Destructive Ways of Dealing with Envy

Idealization

One common way of managing envy is through idealization. By idealizing individuals, groups, organizations, or other objects, one puts them out of reach. Exaggeration, which places the envied object beyond the range of common mortals, can be seen as an attempt to diminish envy. With idealization comes the rationalization that it is one's fate not to belong to this privileged group; others have just been "luckier." This strategy tends, however, to be a precarious answer to the problem. Whether the idealized subject be person, group, or organization, the idealizer will soon find reasons to diminish or devalue it. No person or institution can live up to excessive expectations for too long.

Idealization is essentially a way of managing aggressive impulses. It is an effort to prevent a "good" image from being contaminated by a "bad" one, an attempt to retain satisfying experiences as a source of inner strength. Idealization indicates that the individual tends to resort to "splitting" as a defense. What this means, as we saw in chapter 1, is that the person's sense of self is too weak to tolerate the feeling of ambivalence, with its implication that the same "object" (meaning the other) can have both good and bad qualities. Instead, good and bad experiences, perceptions, and feelings are polarized, kept apart to prevent the world from being polluted by spoiled objects and the corollary bad feelings.

A good example of idealization as a defensive strategy against envy can be seen in the way many executives act toward their leaders. To illustrate, consider the following comments made by a director of a telecommunications company:

> I really like to work in this organization. The main reason I'm still here is Richard. Compared to other executives I've worked for, he's the best. Without doubt, he's one of the most creative CEOs in this industry. I view him as a true visionary. When he was appointed I felt a little bit like a wounded prince. I had hoped I would get the job. But

> I no longer feel that way. I really admire him. I hope to learn from him, although I don't think I'll ever have the kind of insights he has about new market developments. It's unfortunate that our board of directors doesn't realize the gem they have in Richard. All too often they block some of his more innovative proposals. Many times I've told him to go ahead anyway and do what he wanted to do. If he does a little repackaging, the board members won't know that he's moving ahead without their okay. Whatever action he takes, I'll always stand behind him.

People who choose the idealization strategy as a way of dealing with envy often keep their envious impulses under control by exaggerating the leader's qualities and directing negative (destructive) feelings onto scapegoats. Thus excessive praise and admiration of superiors can be a (relatively transparent) way of concealing envy. Individuals who choose this defense feel the need to create superpersons. But as astute observers of organizational life know so well, being on the receiving end of idealized admiration is a very delicate proposition. The "hero" inevitably, and soon, turns out to have clay feet. Very little is needed for the pendulum to swing in the other direction, pushing the leader off the pedestal.

Withdrawal

Complete withdrawal from competition is an extreme envy-avoidance strategy. While people who choose this strategy often seem to be driven by the desire to be inconspicuous, the real reason for the choice may be their inability to tolerate feelings of envy and destructive fantasies concerning others. What the outsider notices, however, is simply a person who does not try to compete but instead devalues him- or herself. Yet withdrawal is a countermeasure with extreme consequences. Because it leads to feelings of helplessness and reactions of dependency, in an organizational setting it transforms good workers into unpromotable problem employees. Consider this example:

Two friends from the same engineering school were taken on by a consulting company. For some years, both had almost identical career paths, following the normal route from assistant to full-fledged consultant. Then one of the two was made a partner and director. Soon after that promotion, a change was noticeable in her colleague. She began to come in late, stopped participating in meetings, and gave poorly prepared client presentations. Most seriously, her colleagues noticed that she was neglecting her contacts with her clients. After an increasing number of people in the company had become concerned, the human resource department suggested that she see a therapist who had previously been employed by the firm. In discussions with the therapist, it became clear that envy was a key theme in this woman's life.

She came from a family of three girls, of whom she was the second. Her younger sister had been her mother's favorite, and her older sister had grown up in her father's footsteps. The sisters had always been fiercely competitive, and she had never felt that she had a chance. She had always been third best. After years of frustration, she had basically withdrawn from the competition.

The fact that she had been able to excel in engineering school and then become successful was due in large part to the attention given to her by one of her high school teachers, a man who had encouraged her to develop her engineering talents. All had gone well for this person professionally until the promotion of her friend and colleague brought things to a head. Life at the consulting firm then seemed very much a rerun of the past, although this was not a conscious realization at the time. When her friend was favored over her, she fell back into her old way of behaving: withdrawal.

The fear-of-success syndrome is closely related to simple withdrawal. Those with this syndrome become depressed when successful in their work, afraid, though not necessarily consciously, that success will arouse the envy (and potential retaliatory action) of others. Herodotus's story of Polycrates, tyrant of Sumos, offers a good illustration of this fear. Terrified by his exceeding good fortune and wishing to forestall the envy of the gods, Polycrates threw a priceless ring into the sea. But the ring returned in the belly of a fish served to him. Polycrates then knew that Nemesis, the goddess of divine retribution, had refused his sacrifice and that misfortune would inevitably come his way. Self-defeating behavior, snatching defeat from the jaws of victory, as it were, is all part and parcel of this pattern. In the organization, we see the fear-of-success syndrome embodied in organizational "hobos," individuals who continually get themselves into the same kind of trouble, be it fights with superiors, procrastination on the job, shoddy work, or unethical practices, and have to move on to the next organization.

Devaluation

Devaluation is probably not only the most destructive but also the most complex way of dealing with feelings of envy. It is also the most common, since both idealization and withdrawal, along with denial, reaction formation, and rationalization, generally end up in devaluation's abyss. The logic behind this strategy is that a spoiled object will not arouse envy.

People who choose this strategy are usually guided by vengefulness and bitterness, but they may disguise their base motives and justify their actions with a veneer of moral righteousness and indignation. Driven by a need for revenge, they attempt to prove that they are as good as or better than the envied object. Backbiting, destructive criticism, and humiliation are common ways through which envious feelings are expressed. Another insidious way of dealing with these feelings is by stirring up envy in others. Take this case in point:

One of the VPs of a biotechnology company was known for his negative attitude. For him, the glass was never half full; it was always half empty. Nobody was spared from his criticism. At one time or another, most people in the company had been exposed to one of his sarcastic comments. A company-wide 360-degree feedback session brought things to a head, however. Although this VP had rated himself very high on the various dimensions of this instrument, he received extremely low ratings from nearly all his colleagues and subordinates and from his boss. It was hard for him to ignore this kind of feedback; this time it was difficult to rationalize the results. Because his style of relating to others was now recognized as a serious problem, he was asked by his CEO to do something about it. And because the ratings were a serious blow to his self-esteem, he was motivated to look for help. With the assistance of an organizational coach, he began to understand that envy of others, originating from a problematic relationship with his sister earlier in life, was at the heart of the problem. Because he had successfully used devaluation as a survival strategy to protect a fragile sense of self-esteem at that time, he had continued to do so later in life. It had become his way to create a perception of control over his environment, to turn passive exposure into active mastery.

Ritualistic behavior (symptomized by excessive documentation of activities, turning a company into a paper factory) and scapegoating practices in organizations, both of which can have serious dysfunctional consequences in diverting energy from formal organizational responsibilities, are often perceived as ways of defending against anxiety about losing control. If we go one step further in examining these behaviors and their origins, however, we can often find envious feelings at the core.

Envy and Vindictiveness

In many of these situations, because of the narcissistic injury (the deflation of one's self-image that accompanies envy), the wish to return injury for injury stands central. This urge for revenge or sense of vindictiveness was dissected by Karen Horney, who distinguished three forms. First, she postulated, there is openly aggressive vindictiveness that is uninhibited in action. Second, there is self-effacing vindictiveness whereby subversive and indirect means are used. In this case, the one who is envious takes on the role of the victim; the presentation of suffering is an unconscious act to make the other feel guilty. Finally, there is detached vindictiveness. In this case, the envied person is simply frustrated by such things as not being listened to, the discarding of his or her needs, the withholding of praise from him or her, or treatment as an unwelcome intruder. In all instances, that is, in all three categories of vindictiveness, what people seem to be after is a "vindictive triumph," the satisfaction that comes with restoring injured pride. To use Horney's words, "This seems to be the flame sustaining their lives" (1948, p. 12).

People who make vindictive triumph the governing script of their lives suffer from what has been called the "Monte Cristo complex.'' This peculiar behavior pattern is named after the protagonist in Alexandre Dumas's romantic story of suffering and vindication. Edmond Dantes, the self-named Count of Monte Cristo, was the victim of an injustice that led to the loss of everything dear to him and a prolonged incarceration in the Chateau d'If. This wrongdoing made him bitter and eager for revenge. During his imprisonment, he became close to a fellow inmate, the Abbé Fario, who resided in an adjacent cell. The latter gave him the secret of Monte Cristo, a buried treasure. Dantes found the cache and, helped by his new fortune, singlemindedly tracked down his enemies and took his revenge. Similar behavior patterns can be observed in organizational life, particularly in those instances when a number of subordinates are jockeying for the attention of a superior. Collusion and power games in organizations often have their origin in envy.

Generational Envy

Envy of the next generation can be most clearly observed in the relationship between parents and children, specifically, when parents take on an attitude of moral righteousness as a way of rationalizing actions rooted in envy. Some parents deprive their children of certain privileges and pleasures out of envy at not having had those privileges themselves, disguising their envy in rational-sounding justifications. A parallel pattern can be found in organizational settings, where senior managers sometimes, by various subtle means, act vindictively toward younger managers. The bitterness they feel at not having succeeded where newcomers might do so induces them to set up traps or impediments. Under the guise of giving new executives ample opportunity and wide discretion, they give them more than enough rope to hang themselves.

A good example of this particular way of acting is exemplified in the behavior of the vice president of a global bank who became known as being a ''people consumer'':

Rare was the young executive who managed to survive in the department run by the vice president of sales. Some quickly recognized that working under Ted was bad news and managed to be transferred. Others, more naïve, didn't see through the emptiness of his statements about creating a learning organization and developing high potentials. Usually, the honeymoon between Ted and the new recruits didn't last very long. The common scenario was one whereby new recruits found themselves being fired after having been accused of gross incompetence. Closer examination of these terminations showed that Ted had the habit of setting his subordinates up, sending them on "missions impossible," assignments that were bound to fail. When behind his back people had begun to give Ted the nickname "Bluebeard," senior management felt that the situation could no longer be ignored. Ted's inability to develop people eventually caught up with him given top management's desire to further leadership throughout the organization and he suffered the same fate as his victims.

The drama that often accompanies management succession is another clear example of the workings of these processes, particularly in those instances where potential "crown princes" come to a bad end, having aroused the envy of their bosses. The succession dramas around former business tycoons such as Harald Geneen of ITT, Armand Hammer of Occidental Petroleum, Peter Grace of W. C. Grace, William Paley of CBS, and Robert Allen of ATT may contain elements of generational envy. Even though the "rules of the game" necessitate planning for management succession, the shift of power that comes with the appointment of a crown prince is not taken lightly by those not selected. Vindictive action may follow. In many organizations the credo seems to be that the prime task of a CEO is to find his or her likely successor and "kill the bastard."

Denial and Reaction Formation

Other common envy-avoiding strategies include denial and reaction formation. As was noted earlier, having envious feelings at the conscious level is too destructive to the self-image for some people. To avoid such feelings, they may try to reassure themselves that there is nothing to be envied. In concert with that denial, they may use excessive compliments and flattery to cover up envious feelings, a strategy known as reaction formation.

People for whom envy is an unacceptable emotion may use similar tactics in order to prevent the arousal of envious feelings in others. They trivialize their own personal accomplishments, denying reasons to be envied. As an example of such behavior, consider the president of a very successful company who always responded to the question, "How is business?" with "Terrible!" (even when his business was doing better than ever). It was his way of not raising the envy of others. Undue modesty—not flaunting his success—was seen as the "safer" response. In addition, he used various forms of rationalization to make it seem that what appeared to be envied was not all that important.

But, as in the case of the defensive strategy of idealization, these forms of self-deception rarely make for a stable solution. Envious thoughts and feelings can be disavowed for only so long. Because powerful feelings make their way to the surface eventually, no matter how strong our defenses, envy inevitably makes itself known through backbiting, rumor-mongering, character defamation, malicious gossip, the cold shoulder, or other means.

Constructive Ways of Dealing with Envy

The Drive to Excel

The Spanish philosopher Gracian once said that nothing arouses ambition so much as "the trumpet blare of another's fame." That response can be seen as a form of identification with the accomplishments of others. Compared to the other strategies for dealing with envy, trying to excel over others is a constructive response. The rationale behind it is that if we are successful in our own pursuits, there is no reason to be envious. (The downside of this strategy is that it may induce envy in others by increasing competitive feelings.)

While the drive to excel is often constructive in its consequences, it is sometimes nothing more than disguised vengefulness. As Horney (1948) stated, "The wish to vindicate oneself in the spirit of defiant triumph can be the determining force in any drive for success, prestige, or sexual conquest" (p. 9). In many organizations, this way of dealing with envy is manifested both overtly and covertly. The "search for excellence" involves competition with other organizations, departments, and colleagues. As a defense against unacceptable feelings of envy, the drive to excel is a great motivator and can lead to performance beyond expectations. As long as companies and individuals recognize the darker side of competitiveness and take care that it does not get out of hand, the drive to excel can lead to very positive results.

Reparation

Finally, the most constructive way of dealing with envy is to engage in a reparative effort. Insight into one's own motivations and into envy's destructive potential can help to break the vicious circle of vindictiveness. In an interview with *Fortune* magazine, Lee Iacocca showed that he had gone beyond the state of vindictive triumph over Henry Ford II that colored his early years at Chrysler. (The full story of Iacocca's feud with Henry Ford II, which has passed into popular legend, can be found in Iacocca's autobiography.) Later, Iacocca engaged in what appeared to be a more reparative effort, trying to view his relationship in a more balanced way and recovering the good memories that he had about it:

> My difficulty with Henry Ford was over long before he died . . . . Most people were remembering the last years of his life, when Henry was sick with a bad heart, realizing that he was mortal and worrying about his health day and night. I tried to remember the years beginning in 1960, when we were buddies. We hunted together, we went to parties together, we caroused in Europe together. So I try to remember the 16

good years, and not the two bad ones in 1977 and 1978. (Taylor, 1988, p. 25)

Unlike vengefulness, reparation tries to *help* the envied party. With reparation, we make a positive effort to undo and overcome destructive fantasies; we try to change the nature of the fantasies about the envied object in order to develop a more constructive attitude. Doing so means giving up wishing for what we cannot have, realizing that certain realities in life cannot be changed but have to be accepted, and that expedient defenses such as idealization, denial, and reaction formation are not appropriate.

Reparation necessitates an elaborate working-through process to deal with a sense of loss, with having to let go of long-held, emotionally charged wishes. But that difficult course of action leads to a greater sense of satisfaction. As Melanie Klein observed, "Envy spoils the capacity for enjoyment . . . . For it is enjoyment and gratitude to which it gives rise that mitigate destructive impulses, envy and greed" (1975, pp. 186–187). A sense of responsibility and mutuality and the willingness to engage in vicarious gratification—those are the real solutions for discontinuing envy's destructive impact.

Concluding Comments

"Envy never takes a holiday" as Francis Bacon once said. Envy is part and parcel of the human experience, influencing all of our behavior and actions. It is an intricate part of organizational life and must be taken into consideration when making predictions about human behavior in organizations. Including envy in the equation will make for a more realistic approach to organizational analysis. We may not like being possessed by envy, but we cannot avoid having to live with it. And it is not all bad: having a certain amount of envy directed toward us may be viewed as a sign that we have achieved something of value. As

Schoeck said, "Every man must be prone to a small degree of envy; without it the interplay of social forces within society is unthinkable. Only pathological envy in the individual, which tinges every other emotion, and the society entirely designed to appease imagined multitudes of enviers, are socially inoperative" (1969, p. 10).

Envy can appear in many guises, some constructive, some destructive. It is the insidious excesses of both envy-avoiding and envy-stimulating behavior for which we must be ever alert. The critical challenge for each individual is keeping his or her own level of envy within acceptable boundaries. That is no easy task, because, human nature being what it is, envy is quickly aroused and easily gets out of hand.

From an organizational perspective, certain preventive measures can be taken: reducing hierarchical arrangements, engaging in power equalization or participative management, eliminating highly visible executive perks, introducing profit-sharing plans and stock options on a large scale, and doing away with extreme differences in salary scales. The avoidance of envy-inducing behavior springing from various forms of conspicuous consumption can also have a tension-reducing effect:

On the individual level, individuals can work to direct envy into more constructive channels, thus fostering creativity and adaptability, by choosing the route of reparation and the constructive pursuit of excellence. Those strategies are much more positive than the other strategies that have been discussed. People can choose not to be prisoners of a self-created illusory balance, not to live in a world of self-deception where they are consumed by anxiety and tension. But to make that choice they need emotional maturity characterized by the capacity for honest self-evaluation, compassion, gratitude, responsibility, commitment, and a sense of generativity (taking pleasure in developing the next generation). The ability to face reality and the capacity for empathy—both of which take us beyond purely selfish concerns—are, in the final analysis, the best antidote to the destructive effects of envy. Only the person freed from envy is able to see things as they really are.

References

Abraham, K. (1968). *Selected papers on psychoanalysis.* New York: Basic Books.

Augustine of Hippo. (1961). *Confessions* (R. S. Pine-Coffin, Trans.). Harmondsworth, U.K.: Penguin. (Original work published A.D. 398)

Bion, W. R. (1977). Attention and interpretation. In *Seven servants: Four works by Wilfred R. Bion.* New York: Jason Aronson.

Foster, G. M. (1972). The anatomy of envy: A study in symbolic behavior. *Current Anthropology, 13,* 165–202.

Freud, S. (1953). Three essays on the theory of sexuality. In J. Strachey (Ed. & Trans.), *The complete psychological works of Sigmund Freud* (Vol. 7, pp. 123–243). London: Hogarth Press. (Original work published 1905)

Freud, S. (1961). Some psychical consequences of the anatomical distinction between the sexes. In J. Strachey (Ed. & Trans.), *The complete psychological works of Sigmund Freud* (Vol. 19, pp. 241–258). London: Hogarth Press. (Original work published 1925)

Goleman, D. (1995). *Emotional intelligence.* London: Bloomsbury.

Jerusalem Bible. (1966, p. 94)

Horney, K. (1948). The value of vindictiveness. *American Journal of Psychoanalysis, 8,* 3–12.

Kant, I. (1922), Grundlegung zur Metaphysik der Sitten (Foundations of the metaphysics of morals). *Samtliche Werke* (Vol. 3, 4th ed.). Leipzig: Vorlander. (Original work published 1785)

Klein, M. (1975). *Envy and gratitude and other works, 1946–1963.* New York: Delta.

Knapp, P. H. (Ed.). (1963). *Expressions of emotions in man.* New York: International Universities Press.

Knapp, P. H. (1976). The mysterious split: An inquiry into the mind–body relationship. In G. Globus, G. Marwell, & J. Savodnik (Eds.), *Consciousness and the brain.* New York: Plenum Press.

Krystal, H. (1982). Alexithymia and the effectiveness of psychoanalytic treatment. *International Journal of Psychoanalytic Psychotherapy, 9,* 353–378.

Schoeck, H. (1969). *Envy: A theory of social behavior.* New York: Harcourt, Brace, & World.

Spielman, P. M. (1971). Envy and jealousy: An attempt at clarification. *Psychoanalytic Quarterly, 40,* 59–82.

Sullivan, H. S. (1953). *The interpersonal theory of psychiatry.* New York: W. W. Norton.

Taylor, A. (1988). Iacocca. *Fortune Magazine, 118,* 25–31.

6

High-Performance Teams: Lessons from the Pygmies

What is not good for the beehive cannot be good for the bees.
(Marcus Aurelius, *Meditations*)

Tell me the company you keep, and I'll tell you who you are.
(Miguel de Cervantes, *Don Quixote*)

You don't lead people by hitting them over the head; that's assault, that's not leadership. (Dwight Eisenhower)

What is a committee? A group of the unwilling, picked from the unfit, to do the unnecessary. (Richard Harkness)

The purpose of this chapter is to describe best practices for effective work teams. Taking the behavior of the pygmies of the African rain forest as a primary model of human behavior, the chapter offers a number of suggestions for creating successful teams. It also examines some of the factors that can destroy teamwork and explores themes relevant to high-performance organizations.

Introduction

Most readers are probably familiar with the label *pygmy,* an anthropological term referring to various populations of a Negroid type inhabiting central Africa, whose adult males average

181

less than 1.5 meters in height. The word *pygme,* in Greek, represents the length between a person's elbow and knuckles, a mea-
surement applied descriptively to this group of unusually small
people. The pygmies are thought to be among the earliest inhabit-
ants on the African continent and are probably the oldest human
dwellers of the rain forest. The pygmy culture has existed since
prehistoric times, and there is a great deal we can learn from it.
It is a window on our past, a primary model of human behavior,
giving us a glimpse of the way people behaved before the rise of
agriculture some 10,000 years ago. Already in ancient Egyptian
history, some 2300 years before Christ, the existence of the pygmies was noted in the record of an expedition looking for the
source of the Nile. A message sent to Pharaoh Phiops II of the
6th Dynasty by Prince Herkhuf of Elephantine, the commander
of this expedition, described the discovery of "dancing dwarfs
from the land of the spirits" (Siy, 1993, p. 16). Reference to the
existence of the pygmies can also be found in Homer's description of a battle between Greek and Trojan forces in the *Iliad.*
According to a description in his *Historia Animalium,* Aristotle
was also aware of the existence of pygmies living in the land
from whence flows the Nile.

Unfortunately, humankind's knowledge of the pygmies ad-
vanced slowly from these early reports. Over the centuries, the
pygmies were turned into a mythical tribe through increasingly
fictitious depictions. Early Arab traders, for example, told stories
about dwarfs who jumped at them from underground, killing the
unfortunate with poisoned arrows. Tall tales about this group of
people continued well into the 19th century. Most of these stories, however, recent as well as ancient, were clearly figments
of the imagination, fanciful, extravagant descriptions far removed from reality. (Consider, for example, stories in which
pygmies were depicted as subhuman monsters who, like mon-
keys, flew about in treetops using their tails.) In short, the pygmies remained a people of mystery.

Starting with the explorers of the Congo at the beginning
of the 20th century, a more realistic picture of the pygmies

emerged. In 1870 the German explorer George Schweinfurth rediscovered the pygmies about 4000 years after Prince Herkhuf's first encounter. Shortly afterward, the British journalist Henry Morton Stanley, reporting for the *New York Herald* about his adventures in Central Africa, mentioned the existence of the forest pygmies. Gradually, through the writings of various explorers, more was learned about the pygmies' seminomadic hunter–gatherer existence. Those who observed the pygmies reported accurately about their ability to survive in a harsh forest environment by hunting game and gathering honey, fruits, nuts, roots, plants, and certain insects, and trading with nearby villagers for vegetables, tobacco, metal, tools, and cloth (Bahuchet, 1991; Bailey, 1989; Hallet, 1973).

Pygmies are now defined as a number of tribes scattered among the rain forests of central Africa in small, temporary settlements. Although the basic unit is the nuclear family (that is, mother, father, and their children), several extended families generally make up a camp numbering from 10 to 35 people. Each nuclear family builds its own dome-shaped hut; these are then placed in a circle around a common area (Bahuchet, 1991; Duffy, 1984).

Life in a pygmy camp is lived mostly outside. There is very little privacy in the camp; pygmies are rarely alone. Eating, drinking, bathing, and even sexual intercourse take place in close proximity, necessitating considerable sharing and tolerance. Empathy and cooperation are therefore important qualities of pygmy society.

Pygmies have no written language. Their history and knowledge are preserved in an oral tradition. Their detailed knowledge of the rain forest ecosystem is kept alive in the minds of the people and passed on verbally from generation to generation. Pygmies also possess a rather enlightened moral code, one that was in place long before missionaries tried to impose their worldview on them. Included in that code are injunctions against killing, adultery, lying, theft, blasphemy, devil worship and sorcery, lack of love for children, disrespect for elders, and other forms of misbehavior. It is not surprising, then, that the pygmies, in contrast to many other tribes in their region, have never indulged in cannibalism, human sacrifice, mutilation, sorcery, ritual murder, intertribal war, debilitating initiation ordeals, and other cruel customs (Hallet, 1973).

The 20th century has not been good to the pygmies. Encroaching civilization has taken its toll as other population groups have pushed them out of an ever-shrinking habitat. A low birth rate, high infant mortality rate, and extensive intermarriage with invading nonpygmy tribes have added to their decline. Furthermore, missionaries and government officials have been settling the pygmies in permanent villages, forcing them to abandon the life that their people have lived for thousands of years. Because the pygmies' entire upbringing and culture are geared toward a nomadic forest existence, becoming sedentary has often led to moral and physical disintegration. There are very few pygmies left who still live in their original state; and at the pace things are going, their world will soon be gone forever.

I spent some time among the pygmies in the rain forest of Cameroon. As my guides in the jungle, they taught me some of the basics of jungle lore. It was with considerable awe that I observed their knowledge of the forest, their ability to read the signs made by different animals, and their expertise with respect to edible mushrooms, fruits, tobacco, and vegetables. What to the untrained eye would have no significance was full of meaning for the pygmies.

From the first day of my visit, it was clear that to the pygmies the forest is the main source of well-being; it is the center of their existence. For an outsider, however, the forest can be frightening, particularly when thunder and lightning conspire with rain to turn small streams into raging torrents and topple heavy branches or even whole trees. Drama of that sort makes a person feel small and insignificant; it is a very intimidating experience. But for the pygmies, the forest remains a source of beauty and goodness despite its potential for harm; the forest is the great provider.

I was intrigued by the relationships I observed among the pygmies in a variety of contexts. I saw them operating as a hunting team; I watched their dances; I listened to their songs. I was struck, in all their interactions, by the degree of mutual respect and trust they showed toward each other. I also noted that they seemed to be a generally happy group of people. Their outlook toward the world appeared to be of a very positive nature, perhaps because trust is a core characteristic.

The Importance of Basic Trust

As we attempt to understand this positive outlook toward the world, we need to remember that the anchor point for basic trust is the primal relationship with one's initial caregivers (Erikson, 1963). Because of the influence child development has on later behavior, adult attitudes are a giveaway of the kind of early relationships people experienced. As child development studies have shown, primary interaction patterns color all later experiences; one's original ways of dealing with caregivers remain the model for all future relationships. Thus the earliest social experimentation of children toward the people close to them leads to a lasting ratio of trust versus mistrust and creates a sense of mutuality (a reciprocity that, as they depend on each other in the development of their respective strengths, determines their later *Weltanschauung*). In consequence, if a child is brought up in a caring environment, it is to be expected that the adult he or she becomes will feel safe and secure.

Trustworthy parental figures who respond to the needs of children with warm and calming envelopment make for a positive world image. Pygmy society seems to be full of this kind of adult. As an example of their caring environment, everyone in the same age group as one's parents is called "mother" or "father," while the older ones are called "grandparents." As far as pygmy children are concerned, then, all adults are their parents and grandparents. Given the nature of pygmy society, there is always someone around to take care of children's needs; kids are rarely without physical contact. Fathers are actively involved in the direct care of their infants. In fact, they engage in more infant caregiving than fathers in any other known society. They spend almost 50% of their day holding or within arm's reach of their infants (Hewlett, 1991). Child neglect and abuse are almost unknown in pygmy society; cruelty to children is the most serious violation covered by pygmy laws and commandments. No wonder pygmies have such a positive, trusting way of relating to each other. We can also hypothesize that the pygmies' deeply anchored sense of independence and autonomy are a consequence of their early exposure to their parents' egalitarian role in the family model.

This positive attitude toward the world, these feelings of independence, and this sense of basic trust are reflected in the attitude toward the forest mentioned earlier. The pygmies' strong faith in the goodness of the forest is probably best expressed through their great *molimo* songs. When pygmies celebrate or are upset about something, they sing. They simply cannot do without dancing, singing, and making music. They believe that such expressions awaken the forest, and that in time this makes everything right again.

Molimo is the name given by the pygmies to a ritual embodied primarily in songs sung nightly by the men. In the *molimo,* often referred to as "the animal of the forest," participants make believe that the sounds they produce are made by an animal dancing around the camp. The same name, *molimo*, is given to the long, trumpetlike instrument that plays an important part in this ritual. The *molimo* is called out whenever things seem to be going wrong, especially in times of crisis: the hunting is bad, somebody is ill, or someone has died. By calling out the *molimo,* the pygmies initiate the process of making things good again.

Pygmy Society as a Metaphor for Effective Teamwork

Although the pygmies are not necessarily better than more "civilized" folks, there is something about the relationships among these relatively simple people, and the relationship they enjoy with the forest, that is fascinating. The intensity with which they live and the joy they feel despite their hardships, problems, and tragedies are worth studying in greater depth. Could it be that their simple wisdom and the good-nature reflected in their human relationships hold a lesson for humankind in our postindustrial society? When I first read of the pygmy way of life, I became curious to learn more about their ancient, primordial culture, their ways of doing things. I also wondered whether their effectiveness in operating as a team—an effectiveness that I later experienced in my personal dealings with them—could teach us something about operating in small groups in the workplace.

This issue is very topical, since most of the work in organizations is done in small groups or teams. The capability for effective teamwork is essential to success in the "global village," with its rapid changes in product and market conditions; to success in the postindustrial organization, with its networking focus and its need for a cross-functional process orientation. Organizations that know how to use teams effectively can get extraordinary performance out of their people, while companies that lack that knowledge encourage mediocrity. Thus it will not come as a surprise that effective teamwork has been identified by researchers as one of the core values in high-performance organizations. Companies that continue to perform successfully have cultures where teamwork occupies a central position.

Labels such as *teamwork, quality, respect for the individual,* and *customer orientation* can be overheard in most organizations, but they quickly turn into clichés. Returning to the slogan *teamwork,* what does it mean? Expressing the wish to be a team-oriented company is both easy and popular; actually *implementing* that wish, however, is difficult in the extreme. Many of the companies I have studied have a long way to go to reach a genuine team orientation. The pygmies, however, as described in the seminal work of Colin Turnbull and other anthropologists (and as observed by me), seem to make teamwork happen (1961, 1965). Their approach to teamwork makes them less susceptible than most corporate teams to the processes that corrode group efforts. Many of their practices are models for effective human behavior.

What Destroys Teamwork?

Many factors can hamper successful teamwork. If we identify those factors, perhaps we can find ways to counter them in the workplace. In the "cry for help" that follows, a senior executive of a new biotechnology company talks about the situation in his organization. In his description, we can identify many of the factors that hamper successful teamwork—factors that in his case have led to a climate of mistrust and a dangerous decline in innovation and production.

In this company we lack an overarching, solid framework. The signals given from the top executive team are very confusing. There just isn't enough clear direction coming from these people. Looking at it from my perspective, it seems as if our top team doesn't share any common values or goals. This has a terrible effect on the rest of the organization.

Because we get no clear signals from the top group, we end up with distracting political battles. Turf fights are the norm. Since there's no clear mandate from the top, a few people want to control everything. This obviously discourages frank, open communication and sharing of information. I don't think people trust or respect each other. Everybody seems to be looking out for themselves, making sure they look good at their colleagues' expense. It makes you feel quite alone. That's been my experience anyway. I know I can't expect much support from others. I have to make things happen on my own.

The "rot" in the top team has trickled down; there are many other work teams that are going nowhere. It makes life in this place very chaotic. Look at the lack of discipline: there's no accountability, so people do what they want. And the results are very disturbing. We're hemorrhaging money. We miss deadline after deadline. In the meantime, our competitors aren't sitting on their hands waiting for us to solve our problems. We're in an industry where innovation is essential. If we don't keep ahead of the competition, we could very quickly lose our market share. Our competitors are probably delighted with our situation. I don't know how long we can go on like this.

In my opinion, it all has to do with leadership. Our new CEO means well, but in his desire to create a participatory ambiance, he abdicates responsibility. He seems unable to set clear boundaries and to communicate about priorities. Decisions that need to be made *aren't* made. And even when decisions are made, they aren't adhered to. As I said, there's a lack of accountability. I know what I'm talking about. I've been present at some of the meetings of the top team. And I can tell you, being there takes a lot of energy. As these meetings drag on, some of these people can't do anything but argue. Their personal agendas often overshadow very exciting business ideas. In the end, it takes too much effort to contradict them; a lot of us end up just going along with what they say. We want the meeting to end; we want to have it over with. I'm sure some of our institutional investors will start screaming for changes before long.

This senior executive raises issues that occur frequently in organizations that have trouble developing effective work teams: conflict, powerhoarding, status differences, self-censorship, and groupthink.

Conflict

One of the most obvious team destroyers is conflict, whether covert or unresolved and overt. Although occasional tension is inevitable in teams (by virtue of their nature as collective phenomena), conflict has to be brought out and addressed. When conflict is left unresolved, hidden agendas take over, detracting from the real work at hand. Even a discussion that seems to be centered on substantial issues may, at a deeper level, concern issues of power, prestige, and other personal needs. The fact that lack of trust between team members is often the catalyst for conflict-concealing dysfunctional behavior makes the problem especially insidious, because the cure is all but out of reach: in the absence of at least a minimal level of trust, constructive conflict resolution is a daunting task. In the meantime, crucial decisions are tabled and deadlines are missed; meetings flounder, sometimes degenerating into rituals whereby everyone assumes a fixed position and plays a stereotyped role. When team members are merely going through the motions, constructive and creative ideas are stifled.

Power Hoarding

Another common weakness of teams is their susceptibility to control at the hands of specific individuals or small coalitions. Power hoarding has two primary negative consequences: to those in power, winning may become more important than constructive problem solving; while to those lacking power, participation may seem futile. Those in the latter category, who are generally the majority, take on the role of silent bystanders, keeping their real opinions to themselves and limiting their involvement. Convinced that they are not being heard, they stop putting their opinions forward and simply give up. As a consequence of this dysfunctional behavior, agreements may be realized prematurely, mediocre compromises may be reached, and courses of action contrary to what each team member envisioned may be chosen. Any team members who do not feel committed to the resulting action plan may resort to tacit subversion, insubordination, and even outright sabotage. This is a group that probably includes all members who did not contribute or whose contributions were ignored.

Status Differences

This kind of self-limiting behavior may be exacerbated if one or more team members are perceived as having special expertise, as being especially qualified to take decisions about the issues to the table. In addition to this respect-conferred status, status differences due to position may confound teamwork: lower-status members may doubt their ability to contribute. Hidden agendas may also play a role. As an example, lower-status team members may be more concerned with making a favorable impression on senior team members than with solving the problems.

Self-Censorship

Members of the team who believe that they are the odd person out may opt to keep their opinions to themselves. They may keep quiet in group deliberations and avoid issues that are likely to upset the group, a lack of action they may come to regret later on. Because people assume that those who are silent are in agreement, self-censorship often leads to an illusion of unanimity among the members of the group—a sort of pseudo-consensus. Sometimes self-censorship also turns into censorship of others: those who feel the need to protect the team leader and/or other key members of the team from information that might shake the complacency of the group put "mind guards" in place.

Groupthink

In this context, the phenomenon of "groupthink," the pressure to conform without taking seriously the consequences of one's actions, should be mentioned (Janis, 1972). Team members suffering from groupthink may intimidate members who express opinions contrary to the consensus, creating enormous pressure to conform, to submit to the "party line" and avoid rocking the boat. People who verbalize their disagreement may be labeled *obstructionists*. If team members succumb to that overwhelming drive for consensus and compromise, dysfunctional group dynamics sway the decision-making process and inhibit the potential for healthy dissension and criticism. This is dangerous not only because of the bad decisions that may result. Groupthink also leads to an absence of individual responsibility: those who wanted to dissent but felt pressured to keep quiet feel no responsibility for team decisions and consequently behave less carefully than they would have done otherwise.

In situations of groupthink, team members may also develop the illusion of invulnerability, the perception that there is safety in numbers. The consequence may be excessive risk taking, as manifested in a failure to regard the obvious dangers of any chosen course of action. Team members may collectively construct rationalizations that discount warnings or other sources of information that run contrary to their thinking; they may discount sources of negative information in their group deliberations. Stereotyped perceptions of other people or groups may come to the fore, clouding the group's judgment and blocking possible relationships with the colleagues in question.

All these factors can and do stifle the efficacy of successful teamwork; they turn teamwork into a waste of time and energy, and they dissipate synergy. Whatever the objectives of a team ruled by these factors, the outcome will be disappointing.

Into the Heart of Africa: Effective Teamwork

In light of all the things that can go wrong in teamwork, we must ask ourselves, How can we avoid the pitfalls? What are some of the qualities of successful teams? What makes for effective teamwork? More specifically, in this case, we ask, What do the pygmies do to make teamwork happen? Are there lessons to be learned from pygmy society that are relevant for organizations in our postindustrial age?

Lesson 1: Members Respect and Trust Each Other

Among the pygmies, given the potential hardships of the forest, there is a great dependence on one another. Staying alive can be an arduous challenge; simple things that we take for granted can be major burdens. Food is not always plentiful, for example, and hunting can be dangerous. After all, the forest is inhabited by vicious red buffaloes, short-tempered forest elephants, swift-footed leopards, deadly snakes, and frightening army ants. These dangers have to be dealt with, not once but almost daily. To overcome such threats, trust and mutual dependency play an important role. Because without trust the hazard of these existing dangers would be magnified, trust is an essential factor for survival in the pygmy community. Each person needs to be able to count on every other team member. This mutuality and trust anchor the pygmies' hunter–gatherer society and allow it to function. When there is trust, whatever the forum, rain forest or Western workplace, many other things fall into place. Trust simplifies life in whatever organization a person is part of. It is an antidote to a proliferation of rules and regulations.

Pygmy society is a good example of what trust can do to simplify and expedite decision-making processes. Although to outsiders life in a pygmy community may be striking in its simplicity and apparent lack of organization, it is undergirded by a complex, though informal, system based on trust; the informal rules that make up this system help the community function effectively. While an *excess* of rules and regulations (and massive paperwork) is a good indicator of a trust disorder and paranoid thinking, a high degree of trust allows the informal organization to dominate the formal one. In other words, implicit rules become more important than explicit rules.

Trust also implies respect for the other members of the group. In a trust-based community, differences are appreciated. And as students of high-performance teams understand, diversity can be a competitive advantage. Pygmies know how to harness the energy from the different parts of the small group into a well-functioning whole. They also exhibit great fluency in relationships and roles; rigidity in behavior is absent.

The mutual respect so essential to good teamwork also characterizes male–female relationships among the pygmies. Unlike in other populations of Africa, the woman is not discriminated against in pygmy society. As mentioned before, male–female relationships are extremely egalitarian. Sex-role flexibility is the norm. A good indication of that is the fact that pygmy language is genderless. Husbands and wives cooperate in a wide range of activities, at the same time respecting each other's feelings and peculiarities. They never force the other to do something against his or her will.

Apart from spear and bow-and-arrow hunting, there is very little specialization according to gender. Women are essential partners of the work team. They contribute substantially to the diet and are actively involved in the distribution and exchange of food. Both men and women net-hunt, usually together. A man collects mushrooms and nuts when he comes across them, gathers firewood, fetches water, cooks, washes up, and cleans a baby when needed. A woman participates in the discussions of the men and does heavy work when required.

The moral in all of this is that if we want teams to work, we need to build trust and mutual respect among team members. If such feelings are not present, other factors conducive to effective team behavior become irrelevant. When there is no sense of mutuality among the members of a team, the group soon becomes dysfunctional and suffers from many of the problems listed earlier.

Trust does not occur instantaneously, however. It is like a delicate flower that takes time to blossom. Trust grows best if the basics were met for each team member in childhood—if each person developed a trusting attitude as one of the anchors of his or her personality (as is the case in pygmy society). In such instances, the trust equation falls more easily into place. When there is a solid foundation, however, trust can be learned, just as we can cultivate honesty, integrity, consistency, credibility, fairness, competence, and the ability to listen. Leaders who ''walk the talk'' and do not kill the messenger of bad news exhibit behavior patterns conducive to a culture of trust.

Lesson 2: Members Protect and Support Each Other

One corollary to trust and respect is a system of a mutual support and protection among the members of a team. Members of any work team should share the conviction that they can rely on each other. An important component of that mutual support equation is the maintenance of each person's self-esteem.

Let us again take the behavior in pygmy society as a point of departure. In spite of the mutually supportive nature of male–female relationships, marital conflicts do occur. Physical violence against women is almost nonexistent, however. Quarrels are usually resolved through dialogue, mediation, jokes, physical separation, or the reframing of the conflict. In general, however, women are more outspoken than men in showing their displeasure. One common way in which women show their anger with their husbands is by tearing down the house. (Because women tend to be better house builders, the huts in which the pygmies live are considered to be the woman's property.)

Turnbull gives an example of a domestic quarrel that got out of hand and led to a surprising sequence of events, a sequence that, as I understand from my discussions with the pygmies, is not uncommon. In Turnbull's example, the matrimonial argument had come to an impasse. The wife, to express her displeasure, began to methodically pull all the leaves off the hut. Usually in such a case the woman would be stopped halfway by the husband. In *this* case, however, the husband was a rather stubborn fellow and did not budge. Consequently, his wife saw no alternative but to keep going. Eventually, the hut was stripped of all its leaves. At that point, the husband commented that it was going to be awfully cold during the night. Because the woman felt that her husband still had not reacted in an appropriate way that would settle the dispute she saw no choice but to continue. Hesitantly, she began to pull out the sticks that formed the frame of the hut.

By this time the whole camp, party to the quarrel since the beginning, was upset. Clearly things were going too far; the boundaries of mutual care were being transgressed. The woman was in tears, and the husband was equally miserable, because the last thing he wanted was to lose his wife. (If the hut were completely demolished, the woman would have no choice but to pack her belongings and return to the home of her parents.) The question became how to reverse the situation, how to stop the conflict while preserving each person's self-esteem and allowing each to save face.

In this instance, the husband had a flash of insight into how he might solve his predicament. He "reframed" the whole

conflict. He mentioned to his wife that there was no need to pull
out the sticks, as it was only the leaves that were dirty. Initially
puzzled, she quickly understood what he was trying to do, and
asked him to help her carry the leaves down to the stream. There
they both pretended to make an effort to wash the leaves; then
they brought them back. She cheerfully started putting the leaves
back on the frame, while he went off with his bow and arrows
to see if he could bring back some game for a special dinner.
He had defused the argument by pretending that the leaves were
taken off not because she was angry but because they were dirty.
Everybody knew what had *really* been the matter, but people
were happy that the quarrel was over. As a matter of fact, to
show solidarity and support some of the other women took a
few leaves from their own huts to wash in the stream, as if this
were a common procedure.

This incident illustrates an important factor in effective
work teams. Conflict is inevitable; indeed, it is part of the human
condition. But while that may be the case, when push comes to
shove in an organization, each team member must be willing to
support, protect, and defend the others. In effective teams, members go to great lengths to sort out differences between themselves while maintaining individual self-respect. Whenever
possible, what can be interpreted as *conflictual* is reframed as
collaborative. It is part of the mind-set of team members that
they all have a stake in a constructive outcome. Such an attitude
of mutual support and protectiveness provides the glue that
makes for teamwork and helps a team survive when times are
tough.

Lesson 3: Members Engage in Open Dialogue and Communication

In pygmy society, participation is an essential part of the group
culture. Everyone can expect it; everyone can demand it; everyone is supposed to give it. Obedience to authority figures is

minimal among the pygmies. Nobody has the right to force someone to do something against his or her will. Because there is not much of a power gulf between the various members of the group, nobody is afraid to speak his or her mind. There is interaction by and involvement of all members, with everyone having a say in decisions that affect the group. Disputes are settled in an informal manner. Constructive conflict resolution is the norm. Although each individual has the personal responsibility to *attempt* dispute settlement, he or she also has the right, if this effort fails, to get others involved in the matter until it is resolved.

For example, if a pygmy male has an argument with his wife that disturbs him so that he cannot sleep, he simply has to raise his voice—remember, the huts of a particular community are in close proximity—and ask his friends and relatives to help him. His wife will do the same, getting the whole camp involved until the dispute is settled. Conflicts are not allowed to fester among the pygmies. They are dealt with up front as they occur, to minimize bad feelings; problems are faced, not pushed underground.

Various techniques used to diffuse disputes among the pygmies work well with workplace teams also. Jokes and laughter are common methods of resolving problems between team members. Humor helps people overcome the stresses and strains that are an inevitable part of group togetherness. Diversions are also useful; they help people forget what the conflict was all about.

Emotional management, a concept introduced in chapter 2, also plays an important role in conflict resolution. Pygmies are not at all self-conscious about showing emotions. They love to laugh; they love to sing. Their willingness to express emotions makes conflict resolution much easier. In fact, a *silent* pygmy camp is a camp that has problems. As pygmy interaction patterns illustrate, it is better to err in the direction of "noise." Furthermore, a willingness to show emotions by all members of the team helps reduce defensiveness and leads to more honest communication. The ability to drop one's defenses and bare one's soul is not for everyone, however; it necessitates considerable self-confidence. But one's efforts at self-revelation are generally well rewarded.

When there are pressing issues on the table, it helps to talk about them. Thus open dialogue and communication are important ingredients in making teams work. As can be observed in the pygmy community, effective teams share their ideas freely and enthusiastically; team members feel comfortable expressing opinions both for and against any position. Teams that meet these criteria are the ideal vehicles for creative problem solving.

Frankness and candor are also key to team effectiveness. In well-functioning teams, shared open, honest, and accurate information is the norm. In addition, members are prepared to provide feedback about the quality of each other's work when appropriate. Critical reviews are viewed as opportunities to learn and do not result in defensive reactions. Moreover, team participants learn to defuse narcissistic injuries and to minimize damage to a person's sense of self-esteem by letting critical comments center around ideas, not people. Substantive issues are separated from those based on personality. Furthermore, members of high-performance teams avoid as much as possible disruptive behavior, such as side conversations or inside jokes.

Lesson 4: Members Share a Strong Common Goal

Pygmies have a strong sense of communal responsibility. Indeed, cooperation is the key to their society. Pygmies are "the people of the forest," a forest that provides them with all the necessities of life. To benefit from the bounty the forest can provide, however, they need to share common goals. Certainly one of the overriding goals in pygmy society is survival in an extremely difficult environment.

Hunting for meat is one of the major survival tasks for this population. A pygmy can take his bow and arrows and try to shoot a bird or a monkey by himself, of course, and this is done regularly. The most effective way of obtaining meat, however, is through communal hunting—driving animals into nets. Net hunting *cannot* be done alone; it would be impossible for a single hunter to cover sufficient territory to drive the prey, an antelope, for example, into a net. A necessarily cooperative affair, net hunting therefore implies shared interests and a common purpose among the men, women, and children of participating families. This shared purpose encourages teamwork. At the time of a hunt, the nets owned by each family in the group are joined together in a long semicircle. Usually, the women and children drive the animals into the nets while the men stand behind the nets and kill animals that become entangled. But it does not *have* to be this way. It can be the other way around, the men playing the role of beaters while the women do the killing. Afterward, the meat is shared among the various participants according to a set of very specific rules.

In organizations, as in pygmy society, teamwork is ineffective without mutually agreed upon goals. To give team members a sense of purpose and focus, what needs to be accomplished by the team and the ways to go about that task need to be articulated clearly. If a goal is ambiguous or ill-defined, the group will lack motivation and commitment. Although goals have to lie within realistic boundaries, offering a vivid description of what the organization expects of its members, they should also encourage team members to "stretch." When met, stretch goals give a sense of pride; their execution creates a sense of achievement among the members of the team.

In conjunction with a clear sense of purpose, certain mutually agreed upon qualitative and quantitative targets need to be expressed. Such targets help team members determine the degree of their success in pursuing their given tasks. These targets serve as a roadmap, creating order out of chaos and generating excitement about future direction.

Lesson 5: Members Have Strong Shared Values and Beliefs

Closely related to a sense of purpose is the group's culture—its shared values and beliefs. Because these values and beliefs define the attitudes and norms that guide behavior, they play the role of social control mechanism. They also provide another form of glue binding the members of a work team. Hence the internalization of shared values and beliefs by team members is extremely important in the realization of the organization's goals.

Although to the uninitiated observer forest life among the pygmies may seem to be happy-go-lucky, that appearance deceives. Beneath the apparent disorder of the community lies considerable order. As mentioned earlier, we should not underestimate the importance of informal systems. All pygmies in the camp, from early childhood onward, internalize rules of behavior that are transferred orally from generation to generation. Cultural values and beliefs are at the base of these rules; they make this small society work.

To understand the making of culture we have to start at the beginning. In other words, we have to take a closer look at early socialization patterns. As indicated before, in pygmy society all adults participate in the upbringing of the children, contributing to their training and helping them understand the rules. They also help the children internalize strongly held social expectations about appropriate attitudes and behavior. What pygmy elders attempt to do is to make effective hunter-gatherers of their younger generation, teaching children the art of survival in the rain forest. They train them early to become autonomous and acquire subsistence skills. They provide them with the collective wisdom that has accumulated over thousands of years, instilling in the children the lore of pygmy society.

Pygmy elders want their youngsters to share a common heritage. To reinforce the behaviors deemed appropriate by that heritage, rewards and punishments are handed out when needed. To make sure that the rules are adhered to, pygmy society imposes a number of deterrents. For the most terrible offenses, no action is taken by the other members of the group; indeed, none is needed, because it is expected that some form of supernatural retribution will follow. While in the case of minor infractions the accused is given the opportunity to argue his or her case with the other members of the group, serious incidents become the affair of the *molimo,* which acts on behalf of the community. The *molimo* players may show their public disapproval of a violation of social standards by attacking the hut of the transgressor, for example, or by attacking the transgressor him- or herself during an early-morning rampage. The *molimo* is an important part of pygmy tradition, representing in this kind of situation the collective conscience of the group.

Sharing, cooperation, independence, and autonomy are among the basic values in pygmy society. Another strongly shared value is the maintenance of peace among group members. This desire for peace sometimes transcends even the rights and wrongs of a particular case. Turnbull describes an incident in which one of the younger pygmies had gone on an amorous expedition to the hut of his neighbor, who had an attractive daughter (1961). Shortly after entering the hut, he was thrown out by a furious father, who was screaming and yelling and throwing sticks and stones at the intruder. Because of all the noise, the whole camp woke up. The father yelled that he was upset not because the young man had tried to sleep with his daughter but because he had had the nerve to crawl right over him and wake him in the process. *This* he felt was unacceptable. Any decent person would have made a date with the girl to meet her elsewhere.

In this particular incident, the argument was not quickly resolved; the commotion kept on going, keeping everyone awake. Finally, one of the elders told the father, in a no-nonsense way, that he was making too much noise; the elder was getting a headache, he said, and wanted to sleep. When the father continued shouting, the elder commented that he was ''killing the forest and he was killing the hunt.'' Although the father was right—the behavior of the young man *was* inappropriate—he was causing a greater wrong by disturbing the whole camp, making so much noise that he was frightening the animals away and spoiling the hunt for the next day.

Although this may seem a rather far-fetched example, it does illustrate the application of norms of social behavior. In this instance, we can see how one norm supersedes the other; how everyone buys into what is viewed as suitable behavior. The lesson that can be learned from this relatively primitive society is that any organization or smaller work team needs to articulate its core values and beliefs and define appropriate attitudes and behavior for its members. The do's and don'ts of social behavior need to be first clarified and then reinforced through stories and traditions. The latter in turn reinforce the group's identity. A specialized language may further add to the bonding of the group. To strengthen this bonding process, successful organizations make a great effort to select as employees people who are likely to subscribe to the core values of the organization. Furthermore, these organizations go to great lengths to socialize their new members, helping them internalize the group's core values and beliefs. Finally, these organizations clearly articulate sanctions for transgressions of the shared values and beliefs.

Lesson 6: Members Subordinate Their Own Objectives to Those of the Team

One of the stories I heard while among the pygmies concerned the breaking of a major rule of proper behavior. Apparently, one of the hunters had committed one of the greatest sins possible in the forest. During a hunt, frustrated because of his poor luck—he had not trapped a single animal all day—he had slipped away and placed his own net in front of the others, catching the first of the animals fleeing from the noise of the beaters. Unfortunately, he was not able to retreat in time and was caught committing the serious crime of placing his own needs before those of the community.

In a small hunting band, as I have noted, survival can be achieved only by close collaboration and a system of reciprocal obligations that ensures that everyone gets a share of the daily catch. This particular pygmy had clearly broken this unwritten rule. He had been selfish. Humiliation and ridicule were the punishment meted out by the group for his unacceptable behavior. He was laughed at by the women and children, and nobody would speak to him; he was ostracized. (This may not sound like much in the way of punishment, but what disturbs pygmies most is contempt and ridicule. Ostracism in pygmy society can be compared to solitary confinement in ours.) The ostracism was only temporary, however. Pygmies do not carry hard feelings for a long period of time. In a very small community, hunters cannot afford to ignore a fellow hunter.

What this example from pygmy society illustrates is that good team members operate within the boundaries of team rules. They understand personal and team roles. They do not let their own needs take precedence over those of the team. They control their narcissistic tendencies and subordinate their personal agenda to the agenda of the group.

Teamwork is an interesting balancing act. A form of participation that can flourish only in an atmosphere that encourages individual freedom and creative opportunity under the umbrella of the overall organizational goals, teamwork represents an interdependent balance between the needs of the individual and the needs of the organization. To make such a balance work, however, each member of the team needs to recognize the limitations on his or her freedom; and this requires considerable self-discipline.

Lesson 7: Members Subscribe to "Distributed" Leadership

Pygmies are strong believers in the concept of "distributed" leadership. As mentioned earlier, pygmy society is characterized by a disarming informality. Among the pygmies, it is difficult to talk about a single leader. Unlike other African societies, pygmy groups have no "big men" among them; leadership is not the monopoly of one glorious leader. There is no person who has

ultimate authority. Because there are no real chiefs or formal
councils, pygmy behavior is extremely egalitarian and participatory. The pygmies are probably as egalitarian as human societies
can get. Among the pygmies it is considered bad taste to draw
attention to one's activities. Many subtle means are used to prevent this from happening. Bragging about one's abilities is an
invitation to become the butt of rough jokes, a very effective
leveling device.

Pygmies are not intimidated by rank, seniority, or status.
All members of the group are empowered to make decisions.
Respect may be given to elders, but it is based not on wealth or
status but on knowledge and expertise. Likewise, if certain people are listened to more than others in the making of a decision,
it is because of their special ability or skill, be it bow making,
hunting, or playing an instrument. Although some members'
opinions may be more valued than others—those members having become somewhat more "equal" than their peers—every
member of the pygmy community is prepared to challenge authority whenever he or she believes that the team effort is jeop-
ardized. As a result, each team member is likely to accept
ownership for the team's decisions.

The pygmies seem to have figured out that the best form
of leadership is a configuration whereby leaders are distributed
throughout the community and everyone can be involved in decision making. However, individuals who are accorded exceptional
respect are expected to subscribe to a number of leadership practices that foster effective teamwork. If they fail to, they are
reminded of their obligation by the group.

Look behind the scenes at a high-performance organization,
and you will find a similar attitude toward leadership. Among
the practices that successful team leaders use to encourage full
participation is a willingness to share goals with the other members of the team. Effective team leaders avoid secrecy of any
kind at all costs. They treat members of the team with respect,
listen to feedback and ask questions, address problems, and display tolerance and flexibility. They offer guidance and structure,

facilitating task accomplishment, and they provide a focus for action. They encourage dialogue and interaction among the participants, balancing appropriate levels of participation to ensure that all points of view are explored (and withholding their own point of view initially to prevent the possible swaying of opinion). They capitalize on the differences among group members when those differences can further the common good of the group. They give praise and recognition for individual and group efforts, and they celebrate successes. They accept ownership for the decisions of the team and keep their focus sharp through follow-up. By acting in these ways, they create an atmosphere of growth and learning. In the process, they encourage group members to evaluate their own progress and development.

Authoritative (Not Authoritarian) Leadership

In discussing these lessons from the pygmies, I have emphasized the important role of team leaders in making successful teamwork happen. Team leaders, and their own leaders in the corporate hierarchy, have to set up the matrix within which teamwork can be most effective. They have to create the right ambiance and lead by example. The old paradigm of command, control, and compartmentalize has to be discarded. In fact, rules and regulations should be minimized.

The Need for Transitional Space

In the context of team leadership in the workplace, a few more caveats are needed. First, however participatory one likes to be, there is a need for direction from the top, with clear communication about the organization's priorities. Second, executives and team leaders must create an atmosphere that encourages people's natural exploratory capabilities. People need room to *play*—and they need to see top management's commitment to that endeavor—because with play come creativity and innovation. Without innovation, an organization stagnates and dies. Thus senior executives must not only encourage people to take risks but also accept occasional failure, protecting those who stick their necks out in a good cause.

While strong, committed leadership is necessary to foster innovation, that leadership need not, *should* not, be authoritarian. On the contrary, *authoritative* leadership is a prerequisite of the supportive climate. What organizations need is leaders who are respected because of what they can contribute; who "walk the talk"; who get pleasure out of developing their people; who are willing to play the role of mentor, coach, and cheerleader; who know how to stretch others. Authoritative leaders accept contrarian thinking and encourage people to speak their mind; they want people to have a healthy disrespect for authority. They also know how to celebrate a job well done, how to recognize achievements, and how to put the appropriate reward systems into place to align behavior with desired outcomes.

In our time of transformation and change, conflict in organizations is a fact of life, a given. The ability to solve conflict is therefore an important competency for people in team leadership positions. Those who are effective at leadership in the years to come will be masters of clarity and candor, skills that are important enablers in diffusing conflict. They will communicate what has to be done in clear, unambiguous terms that leave little room for misinterpretation. They will deal with conflict in such a way that it is transformed from an obstacle into an instrument for creative problem solving and increased performance.

Teamwork remains, above all else, a balancing act. On the one hand, every member of the team deserves to have his or her place in the sun, to have his or her achievements recognized. On the other hand, team members need to recognize the value of collaboration, subordinating their own needs to those of the group. Yet collaboration is rarely easy. An atmosphere of constructive give-and-take goes a long way toward making it happen.

A community like the pygmies, operating in a harsh environment like the rain forest, is acutely aware of this need for collaboration. All the problems associated with teams notwithstanding, the pygmies realize that it is harder to operate without teams than with them. Indeed, without teamwork they have little chance of survival, given the challenges of their environment. Members of business organizations would do well to heed these lessons from the pygmies, the product of knowledge accumulated over thousands of years.

Open Versus Closed Systems

Perhaps the most telling lesson of the pygmies is a negative one not yet addressed in these pages. As I mentioned earlier, recent times have not been good to the pygmies. Their way of life is now threatened, because the epicenter toward which their whole being has been directed, the rain forest, is in danger. Their focus on a hunter–gatherer existence has determined their socialization and training practices over the centuries; it created their unique culture and continues to color their outlook on life. As long as there is a rain forest, their world will be aligned; everything will fall into place, and their life will have real meaning. Unfortunately, the building of new roads—allowing large-scale plantation farming to gain a foothold—and the migration of people from other parts of Africa to the rain forest in search of farmland have led to massive deforestation. The world of the pygmies is disappearing at an alarming rate, creating in these wanderers a sense of dislocation. Of those who have been forced to leave the rain forest, many have been unable to find a new focus. In the agricultural and industrial society that surrounds their old world, their particular expertise has become less relevant. Very few pygmies have been able to adjust to the dramatic societal discontinuities that have taken place around them; very few have been able to make the transition into ''our'' world. The consequences for their various communities have been dire.

Thus, as a final lesson from the pygmies, we learn that survival requires not only an inward but also an outward focus; changes in the external environment have to be accounted for. Boundary management is important; building bridges with key outside stakeholders is an essential task. Members of effective teams recognize the need for external relations. In the case of the pygmies, making this external adjustment may simply not be possible. Conforming to the larger society would require a complete reinvention of themselves, a draconian transformation of their culture that would mean the end of the world as they know it.

The world of business organizations is not as closed a system as that of the pygmies, of course, and there are many other differences as well, but still, the parallels are still striking. Like the pygmies, business organizations have no choice but to look beyond their boundaries; they have to look out for emerging discontinuities to ensure at least a chance at survival and success. If they do not look beyond their borders in this fast-moving, competitive, globally interdependent world, they too will face dire consequences: an inexorable winding down of their life cycle, culminating in death.

As described in this chapter, one way of managing for continuity, one way of creating companies that last, is through teamwork. Companies that gain the tools of effective teamwork have a distinct competitive advantage, a leg up toward organizational success. To master those tools takes considerable psychological work, however. The French statesman and novelist François-René Chateaubriand once said, "One does not learn how to die by killing others." The pygmies have taken this statement to heart. They know how to take care of each other. Members of teams in our postindustrial society would do well to gain that same knowledge.

References

Aristotle (1997). *The complete works of Aristotle: The revised Oxford translation, vol. 1,* ed. S. Butler. Princeton: Princeton University Press.

Bahuchet, S. (1991). Les pygmées d'aujourd'hui en Afrique centrale. *Journal des Africanistes, 61,* 5–35.

Bailey, R. C. (1989, November). The Efe: Archers of the African rain forest. *National Geographic,* 664–686.

Duffy, K. (1984). *Children of the forest.* New York: Dodd, Mead.

Erikson, E. (1963). *Childhood and society* (2nd ed.). New York: W. W. Norton.

Hallet, J.-P. (1973). *Pygmy Kitabu.* New York: Random House.

Hewlett, B. S. (1991). *Intimate fathers: The nature and context of Aka pygmy paternal infant care.* Ann Arbor: University of Michigan Press.

Homer (1995). *The Iliad* (Samuel Butler, Trans.). New York: Barnes & Noble.

Janis, I. L. (1972). *Victims of groupthink.* Boston: Houghton Mifflin.

Siy, A. (1993). *The Efe: People of the rain forest.* New York: Dillon Press.

Turnbull, C. M. (1961). *The forest people: A study of the pygmies of the Congo.* New York: Simon & Schuster.

Turnbull, C. M. (1965). *Wayward servants: The two worlds of the African pygmies.* London: Eyre & Spottiswoode.

7

Transforming the Mind-Set of the Organization: An Owner's Manual

Only the supremely wise and the abysmally ignorant do not change. (Confucius)

There is nothing permanent except change. (Heraclitus)

One of the greatest pains to human nature is the pain of a new idea. (Walter Bagehot)

If you want to make enemies, try to change something. (Woodrow Wilson)

No gain without pain. (Jane Fonda)

This chapter explores the processes of individual and organizational change, their characteristics and dynamics, and highlights resemblances between personal and organizational change. The chapter then looks at elements that are central to both individual and organizational change, including a period of distress, a crystallization of discontent, a focal event, and a public declaration of intent. It also outlines the process of working through the loss associated with change, a process that, like the process of mourning, is made up of a number of predictable stages: shock, disbelief, discarding, and realization. It then looks at factors such as social support, locus of control, and hardiness, which facilitate the change process. The chapter concludes with a case study showcasing a company that experienced a dramatic transformation. This case study highlights some of the critical change variables and shows how top management can work toward successful transformation.

Introduction

There is a story of a man who seemed normal in all respects but one: he thought he was dead. Everybody around him tried to persuade him that this was not the case, but to no avail. Finally, so the story goes, he was referred to a doctor. This doctor also tried to convince him that he was not dead. After a long, fruitless conversation, in desperation the doctor asked, "Well, do dead men bleed?" The response of his patient was, "No, they don't." The doctor then took his scalpel and made a little cut in the arm of the patient. "Look at that," the doctor said confidently. But the patient replied, "By golly, dead men *do* bleed!"

As this story indicates, change is not easy. People have a tendency to hold on to dysfunctional patterns, illogical as these may appear to others. They cannot change their perspective on life without expending a great deal of effort. The reasons that people cling so tenaciously to the status quo are not always easy to identify. There are many conscious and unconscious obstacles on the path toward change. To many, the rallying cry seems to be, "Better dead than changed!"

The issue of whether personality can change in any fundamental way has intrigued psychologists for decades. Indeed, the stability or changeability of personality has been a major preoccupation of many students of human behavior: they have tried to determine whether there is a certain malleability to personality, and if so, whether there arrives a time when personality becomes frozen. In other words, is personality change possible; and if so, can that change continue throughout the life cycle?

Both developmental psychologists and psychotherapists have studied these questions from various angles. One school of thought has argued that personality becomes quite stable after a certain point in time. These psychologists subscribe to William James's notion that personality is set by early adulthood. According to them, after the age of 30, and sometimes much earlier, most personality characteristics have become deeply ingrained. Others have taken exception to this point of view, testifying about the great malleability of personality as people move through the life cycle. Still others, recognizing that the dramatic changes of childhood and adolescence are not matched by transformations later in life, have chosen a more intermediate position. They claim that although there is a certain stability in basic personality characteristics, many maturational changes and adaptations take place as people grow older. These moderates have argued that although the more central aspects of a person's personality are less likely to change than the peripheral ones, individuals continue to learn new behavior as they mature. While we may not see in adulthood the kind of dramatic, revolutionary change that people experience in early childhood, some change is possible.

While developmental and dynamic psychologists have cast their net widely, looking at the individual in all his or her diversity, few organizational psychologists have taken a similar approach in studying human behavior. Unfortunately, in spite of the over one million articles on change that have been published, with respect to human behavior many organizational psychologists have taken a fairly narrow behavioral point of view, seeing human beings as simplistic recipients of environmental determinants. In adopting this perspective, however, they deny their research subjects' possession of a rich inner world of wishes, desires, and fantasies. In these models, directly observable behavior becomes the focus of change; very little (if any) attention is given to internal and unconscious processes. As mentioned in the introduction to this book, many of these models assume that people are rational, logical beings and will change their behavior according to the information they receive and according to self-interest. Psychologist Kurt Lewin's famous model depicting the change process as a force field between restraining and driving forces (whereby change depends on the ability to manage an unfreeze–change–refreeze process) is indicative of this rather mechanistic way of looking at the process of change, though with a more social–psychological slant (1951).

Some organizational psychologists, however, have heeded the findings of developmental and dynamic psychologists about the psychodynamics of personality change. Placing the question of organizational change in the context of those research findings, they argue that successful organizational change requires an understanding of individual reactions to the change process. (After all, organizations are collections of people!) In the opinion of these psychologists, a lack of attention to the inner experience of the individual with respect to change condemns organizational change efforts to failure.

Some psychologists and organizational executives take this inner-focused point of view regarding workplace change simply to counteract the unrealistic claims they have heard from change specialists promising overnight transformation through instant ''unfreezing'' and ''refreezing.'' Painful experience has taught them that oversimplistic models of human behavior come with a price. Many recommendations made by change specialists—quick-fix solutions based on oversimplified models of human behavior that disregard deep-seated psychological processes—have no enduring influence. Recommendations that heed the rich underlying dynamics of individual change, on the other hand, can facilitate genuine organizational transformation. That focus on individual change helps change agents appreciate the mind-set of the people in the organization and distinguish between what is feasible and what is no more than a pipe dream.

The objective of this chapter, then, is to explore the dynamics of individual and organizational change processes. I will argue that although things are ever-changing and ever-changeable, and that change is therefore infinitely variable, the underlying principles of the change process are relatively *in*variable. I believe that it is possible, by observing from a clinical perspective the different stages by which individual change takes place, to draw parallels between individual and organizational change processes. Taking this thought one step further, I suggest that by adopting the process of individual change as a conceptual framework, it is possible to induce, facilitate, and speed up lengthy organizational intervention and change processes. This seems especially useful given that such change processes often are set in motion only when the organization's situation is already critical.

The organizational change literature, in spite of its wealth of contributions, is still in its infancy. Given the confusion resulting from myriad conflicting theories of organizational change, a contribution securely anchored in the clinical theory of individual change may shed some light, offering prescriptive value for future change agents.

The Psychic Theater of Change

The comment by one wit that the only person who likes change is a wet baby contains substantial truth. One of the recurring assertions in the vast scope of change literature is that people possess a pronounced inner resistance to change. Social and psychological investments in the status quo make it very difficult to weaken that resistance. Anxiety associated with the uncertainty of engaging in something new or being once again exposed to old dangers and risks, for example, often prompts people to resist change. In an effort to reduce such anxiety, people allow avoidance behaviors, those means by which we keep ourselves out of frightening situations, to become deeply ingrained. Furthermore, repetition compulsion, the inclination to repeat past behavior in spite of the suffering attached to that behavior, is an all too human tendency. In addition, fear of a narcissistic injury, of having to acknowledge that the present state of affairs is not good enough, can contribute to a frozen stance. Ironically, in many instances we seem to prefer the familiar "bad" to the promising unknown.

It is impressive to see the degree to which people make an effort to preserve dysfunctional patterns of operating. They are often willing to put up with extremely unsatisfactory conditions rather than take steps toward the unknown in order to improve their situation. Given the pain that continuing in dysfunctional ways entails, we can surmise that there must be a certain amount of pleasure as well. Indeed, in each individual's adherence to the status quo, there is more than meets the eye; there are unconscious processes that, when understood, explain that person's frozen stance—resistances that have a protective function. In other words, people resist change in part because of the earlier mentioned ''secondary gain''—the psychological benefits (such as sympathy and attention) that accrue to them by manipulating the external environment so as to continue in the same way.

Prerequisites of Personal Change

A number of prerequisites of personal change can be listed: the crystallization of discontent, the focal event, and the public declaration. Each of these plays an important role in facilitating the process of transformation.

The Crystallization of Discontent

If the human tendency is to *resist* change, how does the process of change ever get under way? Why does a person's resistance start to weaken? Given the relative stability of personality, getting the process of change into motion requires a strong inducement in the form of pain or distress. In short, some form of discomfort is usually the catalyst for change.

Studies of personal change support this notion; they indicate that a high level of stress is a major inducement to change. Among the stressors isolated by such studies are family tensions, health problems, negative social sanctions, problematic relationships at work, feelings of isolation leading to a sense of helplessness and insecurity, problem behavior, and even daily hassles and frustrations. In addition, accidents or special incidents of some kind (such as something drastic happening to important others) frequently precede the change process. Among the executives I interviewed and who reported that they had changed, most mentioned the experience of a high level of negative affect in the period just prior to change, generally precipitated by a stressor such as those listed above. This negative affect brought to awareness the serious negative consequences that were to be expected if dysfunctional behavior patterns were continued. Individuals who reported major change said that they found the status quo increasingly difficult to maintain. They found themselves deadlocked in situations that unsettled their psychological well-being. Their negative emotions, and the consequences they anticipated if those emotions continued, led to a weighing of the pros and cons of the problem in an effort to find a solution.

When the study subjects realized that their bad days had turned into a bad year—in other words, that the isolated occurrence of occasional discontent had changed into a steady pattern of unhappiness—they were no longer able to deny that something had to be done about the situation. From this point on, every new disturbance was recognized as part of the general pattern of dissatisfaction. A certain amount of what Roy Baumeister called "crystallization" occurred, turning the complaints into a coherent entity (1994). Gradually, all the undesirable features of life's circumstances compounded to create a clear picture of the situation. Many people reported then having a kind of "aha!" experience, a moment when they were finally able to interpret correctly what was happening to them. They saw clearly that neither the passage of more time nor minor changes in behavior would improve the situation—indeed, that the situation was likely to become even worse. Something drastic had to be done.

While this clarification of the problem, this process of self-assessment, did not automatically compel people to take action, it usually set into motion some kind of mental process whereby they were willing to consider alternatives to the adverse situation. When people finally made the transition from denying to admitting that all was not well, they found themselves at the beginning of a reappraisal process. This was likely to be accompanied by strong feelings of confusion and (at first) even protest. Every alternative to the troubling situation was likely to appear more frightening than the status quo. Gradually, however, a preferable alternative to the stalemate began to crystallize, although the hurdles still seemed insurmountable.

The Focal Event

Among research subjects, accepting the need for change was generally not enough to get them to take an active step toward changing their situation. They needed a push, in the form of what Todd Heatherton and Patricia Nichols described as a "focal event" (1994). While the expression "focal event" signals a significant happening that triggers change, the reality is frequently somewhat different: often the focal event is only retrospectively interpreted as a milestone.

This focal event can be described as the straw that broke the camel's back. That metaphor is very appropriate, because it indicates that the triggering event can be minor, the final additional element (one among many) that puts matters into focus. When latent dissatisfaction has built up to such a degree that a person is prepared, if not actually *ready*, to take decisive action, a minor occurrence may be seen as focal simply because the person is ripe for initiating change. And indeed a minor occurrence *is* focal under such circumstances: it is a facilitating factor that enables the discontented person to take that long-delayed first step. For that reason, it has important symbolic meaning.

Among the interviewees, this focal event was often an incident that happened to someone important to the person in question, that, because it was perceived as a threat, led to a reevaluation of the behavior that caused distress. One woman, for example, remembered as her focal point the sudden death of her boss and mentor; she saw in that death a judgment of her own overdedication to the workplace. The crystallization of her discontent centered around this focal event, which symbolized and called attention to the existing problem and provided the impetus for change.

A person's focal event can also be seen as a kind of "screen memory": while the incident may seem trivial at first glance, it is actually an indicator of a whole range of incidents that are symbolic of the experienced problem. Although it is *objectively perceived* as minor, it is *subjectively experienced* as significant, because it calls attention to a problem that has existed for a long time. It precipitates a moment of insight and leads to a reinterpretation of the person's life history. (Of course, some focal events are objectively as well as subjectively significant, such as the death of a coworker, as in the above example, or one's own illness.)

At this point in the process, with a focal event securely under his or her belt, the person in question is ready to take action. He or she has acquired the inner strength to make a change; the resistances to change have been overcome. New possibilities are seen where before there was only a sense of hopelessness. Emotional energy has been transferred from "objects" of the past (such as dysfunctional behaviors) onto aspects of the present and the future. The person feels as if he or she has received a new lease on life.

The Public Declaration of Intent

Interviews with people who have undergone significant personal change suggest that a good indicator of a high degree of commitment to change is a public declaration of the *intent* to change (Maxwell, 1984; Stall & Biernacki, 1986). Telling others, in a more or less public context, what one plans to do indicates a certain degree of acceptance of the problem. It signifies that the speaker is willing to defend his or her position. It indicates that traditional defense mechanisms (such as denial and projection) have run their course. The person is ready to take new initiatives.

Public commitment works in two ways: by influencing the environment and by influencing the speaker him- or herself. By making other people aware of a desire for change, people initiating change spread awareness that the old conditions are not valid anymore and that they (and others) need to adapt to new ones. At the same time, by pronouncing their wish (and intention) to change, by taking a *public* stance, they give themselves an ultimatum: go through with the change, or lose face. Take smoking as an example. If a man states the wish and intent to give up this addictive habit, acquaintances who see that decision as positive and stand behind it are less likely to offer him a cigarette and will most probably, if they notice that he intends to light up, look at him in a disapproving way. Thus going public with one's intentions is a good way of enhancing one's own determination and enlisting the support of the environment.

Furthermore, a public declaration of intent to change the present situation means a willingness to take a more vulnerable position, a willingness to move the problem from a private to a public stage. The public declaration expresses a wish to establish a ''new identity,'' a different way of behaving. The person wants to distance him- or herself from the former, less desirable self.

The Stages of Change

These prerequisites of successful personal change—a crystallization of discontent, a focal event, and a public declaration of intent—are generally accompanied by emotions that follow a rather predictable sequence. As people progress through this sequence, they show an increasing ability to give up their old identities and roles and to adopt new ones. They begin to reorganize their phenomenal world in a significant way. They reevaluate their life's goals and meanings, letting go of the old and accepting the new.

The fact that what is old and familiar is left behind creates a feeling of privation. Letting go brings to bear memories of separation and loss, themes that touch upon the core of an individual's personality. After all, separation anxiety is a very basic form of anxiety—unconsciously, abandonment is equated with death—that has a unique set of dynamics and follows a specific course. The original model for separation and loss is found in early mother–child interaction patterns. The separation between mother and child becomes the template on which all other experiences of loss are modeled.

From child development studies and related research, we have learned to expect a fairly predictable sequence of emotions in cases of loss. Although the number and nature of the emotions included varies somewhat by researcher, the core sequence remains constant. This process of mourning—the familiar pattern for dealing with stressful experiences, whether the loss is big or small—begins in early childhood and is repeated throughout life. In every experience of loss, variations on this theme can be observed. Recognizing this pattern will help us understand the intrapsychic dynamics of the change process, revealing the logic behind the sequence of crystallization of discontent, focal event, and public declaration of intent. It will also help us in making sense of successful change efforts in organizations. In those firms where change has taken place without major hiccups, we can conjecture that the catalysts of change paid attention to this mourning process.

In his review of the literature on mourning, child psychiatrist John Bowlby was able to discern four general stages that seem quite universal. He noted the following:

> Observations of how individuals respond to the loss of a close relative show that over the course of weeks and months their responses usually move through a succession of phases. Admittedly these phases are not clear cut, and any one individual may oscillate for a time back and forth between any two of them. Yet an overall sequence can be discerned. The four phases are as follows:
>
> 1. Phase of numbing that usually lasts from a few hours to a week and may be interrupted by outbursts of extremely intense distress and/or anger.

2. Phase of yearning and searching for the lost figure lasting for some months and sometimes lasting for years.
3. Phase of disorganization and despair.
4. Phase of greater or less degree of reorganization. (1980, p. 85)

From our investigation of successful change processes, we recognize that this basic emotional sequence of mourning and loss can be applied to the context of personality change as well. In the case of individual change, a conflict takes place between the acquisition of insight into the problem (a necessary precondition for change) and the forces of resistance (in other words, the defenses used by the individual to maintain the status quo). However, in order for a person to change, to move from one state to another, these insights into the dysfunctional situation have to be "metabolized"; resistances have to be dealt with. This brings us to the "working-through process," the various steps the individual has to take to arrive at successful transformation.

Extrapolating the conceptualizations derived from theories on mourning, we can discern four phases in this working-through process: shock, disbelief, discarding, and realization (Kets de Vries & Miller, 1984). We should understand, however, in considering this kind of sequencing, that this succession of stages indicates a *successful* process. When the change process is less than successful, developmental arrest, the inability to proceed from one stage to the next, may be responsible. Such an occurrence can produce dysfunctional and sometimes painful symptomatology.

1. In the first phase, *shock,* the individual is not prepared to consciously acknowledge that something is wrong. Vague feelings of discontent surface, however. These feelings may be ignored or explained away until they grow so strong that this strategy is no longer possible. During this stage, the person may also experience a sense of numbness, sometimes interrupted by feelings of panic and outbursts of anger.

2. Soon the person enters the second phase of the working-through process, which can be described as a phase of *disbelief.* Denial of adverse circumstances is common at this stage. A state

of disarray, confusion, and disorientation prevails, along with a yearning and searching for what has been lost. Irrational anger, sadness, and self-reproach may follow. The person takes a reactive posture; a past orientation is the norm.

3. In the third, *discarding* phase, old patterns of thinking, feeling, and acting are slowly abandoned. Tentative explorations are made toward finding new opportunities and establishing a new equilibrium. The individual in the pangs of change is trying to redefine him- or herself through a process of self-examination. Gradually, that person gains an acceptance of the new situation. He or she experiences a growing sense of hope; new choices seem possible. A more proactive attitude and an orientation toward the future emerge.

4. Discarding prepares the individual for the next stage of the process: the *realization* of a new identity. This fourth stage implies a reshaping of the person's internal representational world, the acceptance of a new reality. A proactive posture is now taken. Past patterns of thinking, feeling, and acting are discarded as the person adopts a more future orientation. This shift in attitude and behavior leads to the redefinition and even reinvention of the self and one's psychic world.

Driving the Wheels of Organizational Change

How can we apply what we know about the dynamics of personal transformation to the organizational setting? How can we proactively drive the process of organizational change? How can we be most effective as change agents? These questions are critical now that change is the rule rather than the exception for those seeking corporate survival and success. The companies that last through the coming decades will be those that can respond effectively to the changing demands of their environment.

As we look at change in a larger context, we can draw a number of parallels from what we have learned about the way individuals change. As with individual transformation, organizational change is a sequential process, and that process requires the impetus of a period of stress. In other words, people in the organization have to become mentally prepared for the fact that change is inevitable.

Stress in the system can be seen as the lever that gets the change process on its way. But pushing that lever is easier said than done, because, as in the case of individual change, there are a lot of resistances to deal with. Organizational participants may not see, at first glance, that the change process is in their self-interest. Even those who are aware that all is not well can find many ways of avoiding the issue of change. The fear that the proclaimed benefits of a particular change will not outweigh the costs involved sets many unconscious defenses in motion. The challenge inherent in this dilemma prompted one observer to comment that creating organizational change evokes the same resistances as moving a graveyard.

Organizational Resistance to Change

For most people in an organization, change brings a fear of the unknown and a reduction in job security. Some people may deal with their anxiety by hanging on to old patterns of behavior. Other people—those who expect that change will require them to learn a new job or work harder—may fear that they lack the skills and stamina needed for change. Still others may be afraid that good working conditions or a sense of freedom will be taken away. Some people may fear that change implies a loss of responsibility and authority, with concomitant status implications. They may dread the perceived loss of status, rights, or privileges that they expect the change to bring. Other people may interpret change as an indictment of previous performance and react defensively. Furthermore, change sometimes endangers existing alliances, threatening separation from important friends, contacts, and familiar surroundings. For those workers who deal with budgets, there is also the question of sunk costs: they may be reluctant to accept a change that entails scrapping certain costly investments. Finally, change may be resisted because of something so pedestrian as a feared decrease in income.

Resistances raised to deal with all these concerns have to be dealt with and overcome in some way. Unless those directing the change effort manage employee resistances, the effort simply cannot be successful. The trick is to make it clear that hanging onto the present state creates more problems than diving into the unknown. People have to realize the implications of not doing anything. They have to be made aware of the personal individual costs of not changing. In other words, they have to be prepared. And, perhaps most important, they have to experience a certain amount of discomfort. As in the case of personal change, pain is an important lever in the process.

Stress in the system, while necessary, is not sufficient, however. (Indeed, *too much* stress leads to feelings of despair and depression, which in turn solidify resistances.) In addition to pain, people also need hope; they need to have something to look forward to. Thus hope becomes the bridge between preparation and transformation.

Fomenting Dissatisfaction

We have all heard the saying, "There's no gain without pain." There is considerable truth to those words in the context of personal change: as we have noted, the willingness to change usually presupposes a high level of stress. Just as discomfort with the status quo is the engine that drives the individual change process, so too does stress drive organizational change. Studying organizations that are prepared to undergo change, we can usually observe a high level of discomfort. There are pressures on the organizational system indicating that some kind of adaptation is needed. In spite of the "pain," however, many necessary organizational change processes get stalled because of defensive routines.

If such routines continue to be manifested throughout the organization in the face of extreme discomfort, we can assume that the resistances of the key powerholders are still intact, that the necessity for change has still not been accepted by organizational leaders. Locked in behavior patterns that have previously proved to be quite effective, these leaders have not yet realized that circumstances have changed, that adaptation is needed, that what once was a recipe for successful performance has become a recipe for disaster, that what once were good practices, a perfect alignment with the economic environment, are no longer viable. As someone once said, "There are two tragedies in life: one is to be unsuccessful; the other is to be successful." But changing the mind-set of key players in the organization is never easy. It generally requires a strong jolt of some kind. Those favoring change must pressure the skeptics into believing that the present state is no longer viable, that the alignment of organization and environment is off.

The best kind of pressure for creating awareness of the need for change is pressure that comes from both inside and outside the organization. Among some of the external factors that can cause discomfort in organizations are threats from competitors, declining profits, decreasing market share, scarcity of resources, deregulation, the impact of technology, and problems with suppliers and consumer groups. Internal pressures can include ineffective leadership, morale problems, high turnover of capable people, absenteeism, labor problems (such as a strike), increased political behavior in the company, and turf fights. All these factors inevitably negatively affect the mind-set of the people in the organization. The resulting malaise affects the corporate culture and has an impact on patterns of decision making. Eventually, as these stressors cause increasing daily frustration, they can no longer be ignored; an overwhelming dissatisfaction with the status quo festers in person after person. Gradually, the majority realize that something needs to be done or the future of the organization will be endangered.

Engendering Hope

To break this vicious circle of organizational despair, hope offered through the role of a change agent is essential. In the best of all worlds, such a person holds a key power position in the organization. Although people at other levels of the organization can (and sometimes must) take the initiative, given the reality of power dynamics it is members of the dominant coalition (particularly the CEO) who are most effective at getting the change process on its way. After all, the ability to effect change depends to a great extent on hierarchical authority, resource control, and dependency relationships within the organization.

It is the role of leaders to identify the challenges the organization is facing. Leaders should point out the source of the distress and clearly present the negative consequences of a failure to act. They should develop and articulate a clear picture of the future under the current direction. By articulating the reality of the situation, they focus the existing state of discomfort. That level of discomfort has to be kept within tolerable margins, however; otherwise, people will tune the problems out. To buffer against excessive stress, leaders must present a viable alternative to the present situation. That change program should be, and must be perceived as, a doable proposition.

In proposing change, leaders need to reframe the cultural guidelines that people in the organization have gotten used to; they should also make an attempt to reframe the positive aspects of the change effort. They need to create pride in the organization's history but also point out how this pride in tradition can anchor the organization to the past. By referring to the organization's greatness but also presenting a new way of doing things, leaders create hope. That dual approach makes for a sense of new beginning.

It is also important that leaders articulate and address people's worries about career advancement. To do so, they must first emphasize the personal implications of continuing as before. Rather than allowing people to follow an ostrich policy, denying reality, leaders must address the likely effects on the careers of people in the organization if nothing is done about the existing threats in the environment. At the same time, they should articulate the opportunities that would be created by doing something about these threats. A new psychological contract, implying mutual obligations and commitments (explicit and implicit) between the employees and the organization, has to be established, clearly setting out the new values required to make the transformation effort a success.

Because cognition without affect cannot bring about change, leaders have to cultivate emotional commitment, thereby creating energy to support the change process. To foster that commitment, leaders should make it clear that they do not see members of the organization as mere pawns in the process; furthermore, they should require everyone in the organization to become involved in the design and implementation of the change effort. Doing so has an emotional impact. Furthermore, involving all employees creates a sense of control over the process, which in turn has a major stress-reducing effect.

In attempting to garner employee commitment for the change process, leaders should use simple language in getting the message across—communications that will resonate within the people who will be affected. Repetition of the message of change is also important, because people need to be reinforced as they deal with the consequences of loss that change implies. Every opportunity should be taken to get this message across verbally and visually, and leaders should also "walk the talk," be role models for the new values that characterize the organization. As leaders provide a focus, articulate the issues in an understandable way, and seek to gain the support of their followers, the role of symbolic action that depicts what the new organization stands for and bridges the old and the new, becomes important (Johnson, 1990).

Getting people on board needs a certain amount of "theater," as a means both to articulate goals in an easily understandable fashion and to draw people into the process. The impact of symbolic action is illustrated in the activities of the new CEO of a consumer products company who began making regular store visits during his travels and talking frequently with potential buyers of the company's products. This interaction was his way of emphasizing that the newly espoused value of customer focus was not just another empty slogan. His obsession with customer satisfaction quickly caught on, reverberating throughout the company. Another CEO who was driving a corporate transformation effort asked all his executives to write a letter of resignation from the "old" company and a letter of application for the "new" one. This activity of rethinking what had been wrong with the company in the past and reflecting on how to make it a high-performance organization had a powerful impact.

In any communication of the change message, leaders must focus on clear, compelling reasons for change, lest employees fear that tradition is being abandoned for naught. To further guard against that fear, leaders should build on aspects of the existing culture that are appropriate for the new organization. Employees must perceive the entire change process as inspired by vision and driven by solid corporate values. They must see that it not only aims at building and maintaining a competitive advantage but also addresses the individual needs of the people who will be affected. Finally, they must know that there are boundaries to the change process, that the proposed change effort has clearly defined parameters.

A dedication to honest, focused, and persuasive communication pays dividends to those spearheading a change effort. Eventually, most people in the organization will have at least a basic awareness that there are problems, and they will be prepared (in spite of lingering resistances) to accept the need for action.

Carrying Out the Transformation

After leaders have convinced their workforce of the need for change, the next step is to get people committed to the new vision, to the new way of doing things. In order to move the change process forward, leaders must align crucial players behind their new view of the future; they must build coalitions with key powerholders in the organization. Those powerholders can then help to spread commitment throughout the organization.

Transferential processes, including both mirroring and idealizing, can play a critical role in this "recruitment." Transferential processes, which result in "false connections" between people, come about because there is no such thing as a completely new relationship; all relationships are based on previous relationships. This means that at an unconscious level, followers generally respond to leaders as though they were significant persons of the past, such as parents or other caretakers. In part because of that false connection, followers tend to identify with their leaders (a transferential process called "idealizing") and project on them their hopes for a new alternative. Through "mirroring," having these projections reflected by the recipient, this process is reinforced. Thus followers often recognize themselves in their leaders. Consequently, they may go out of their way to please them, to make things happen. Leaders, gaining strength from this mutual identification process, reassure their followers, who in turn reassure the leaders (and give them their unqualified support).

Taking advantage of the enhancing force of transferential processes, leaders driving a change effort need to empower their subordinates by sharing information fully, avoiding secrecy, and delegating responsibility. Of these, the first is perhaps the most important: open and honest communication is critical. Leaders should keep surprises to a minimum, clearly delineate expectations, and maintain dialogue that is both ongoing and genuinely (rather than merely superficially) two-way. Furthermore, leaders need to communicate values by setting an example with clarity and consistency. In other words, as we noted earlier, those who drive the process have to "walk the talk."

Employee participation and involvement are the keys to organizational commitment. People at all layers of the organization, not only those at the top, should be involved in the change effort, beginning with a joint diagnosis of the problem. And that participation should be rewarded: leaders can offer incentives, for example, to people who support the change effort, thereby signaling the benefits of change. People who do a good job with change should be rewarded, just as those with other needed skills are. They will then serve as models to others.

Because small wins have a ripple effect, leaders are advised to divide a big change effort into bite-size portions, thereby making the overall task more palatable. Visible improvements (again, small wins) help convince people of the doability of the change effort. Despite striving for small wins, however, leaders should set high performance expectations. By stretching people, by offering them an opportunity to spread their wings, leaders encourage followers to rise to the challenge. Successful stretching benefits both the organization and the individual, since reaching one's stretch goals engenders considerable personal satisfaction.

Staging a Focal Event

If leaders have been employing the techniques discussed above, most people in the organization have probably gone from contemplation of change to action; they are committed to, and working on, overcoming existing problems, changing personal behavior, and making changes in the organization's structure, strategy, and culture. If leaders feel the need to expedite the change process, however, they can try staging a focal event. Again we see a parallel between organizational and individual change processes.

A focal event can be staged in many different ways: it can be an off-site gathering at which members of senior management announce plans for a new organization; it can be a series of workshops, a seminar, or a meeting run by an outside consultant. Whatever the design, such a staged event should allow for, indeed, mandate and focus on, strategic dialogue between top management (particularly the CEO and members of the executive committee) and the subsequent organizational layers.

As a forum for feedback and critique, strategic dialogue offers the opportunity for organizationwide involvement. The resistance that people feel not only to initiating change themselves but to *being* changed is lessened by such involvement, because it gives participants a sense of control over their destiny. Since strategic dialogue is based on a direct feedback loop with senior management, it permits an open and informed discussion of the challenges facing the company. Topics perceived as undiscussable in the day-to-day work context can be put forward and addressed, diminishing the level of employee anxiety (especially among those who have the will to change but are afraid that they lack the necessary skills). Furthermore, strategic dialogue offers an opportunity to mourn the old ways of doing things, to be nostalgic about the past, and to tackle a new beginning.

In the course of the strategic dialogue that takes place at a staged focal event, a number of issues need reiteration. First, even if most people seem to have bought in to the notion that the organization's present state is unsatisfactory, leaders should reemphasize that crucial point. Second, leaders should work to build and reinforce companywide commitment to a redefined corporate vision and mission, to shared goals and expectations. Third, leaders should work with focal-event participants to determine whether the appropriate organizational design, systems, and workforce are in place. Having achieved clarity about vision and mission, they must ask themselves and their followers these questions: Are the existing structure and processes still in alignment with the marketplace? Have the steering mechanisms of the organization become obsolete, outlasting their usefulness? Given the need for change, does the company possess the right mix of competencies? If not, is a training and development program designed to help employees acquire the necessary competencies (and thus reinforcing their belief in their own skills to change) adequate, or do outsiders with specialized expertise need to be brought into the organization? Do performance appraisal and reward systems need to be modified to encourage alignment of behavior with the new circumstances?

Encouraging individuals to make a public declaration of their intent to change during these dialogues can also have a powerful effect. As in the case of personal change efforts, a public declaration strengthens commitment to the organizational change effort; it reinforces the intent to change simply by making it highly visible. A public declaration of intent alone is not good enough, however. It has to be backed up with a way of measuring what has been announced. In other words, a follow-up procedure, perhaps in the form of an individual action plan, has to be tied to each declaration. After all, what is not measured rarely gets done.

It is important during staged focal events to drive the notion deep down in the organization that "the enemy is us," that blaming others for existing difficulties is unproductive. These sessions offer the opportunity to explore the extent to which problems can be traced to practices that were originally good but now are out of alignment. Strategic dialogue should not be overwhelmingly negative, however: focal-event workshops should facilitate a process of self-discovery of *both* the good and the bad, allowing people the opportunity to reflect on what made the organization great, but emphasizing that what was good in the past may no longer be appropriate (given the changing circumstances). Because the opportunity to reminisce, to mourn the past, allows people to build on the old and create the new, strategic dialogue should permit expressions of nostalgia and grief for the past; in doing so, it will encourage expressions of excitement for the future. But this is a slow process: it takes considerable time for a new conception of the organization to be fully metabolized, to go from superficial adoption of a new state of affairs to deep internalization.

Before attempting a staged focal event—often a make-or-break endeavor in the change process—company executives must wrestle with the delicate question of leadership for change. This issue is particularly difficult if questions are raised about the capability of the CEO to drive the change effort. If we look at organizations that have experienced successful dramatic change, we see that an outsider has generally been brought in to make the process happen (Tushman, Newman, & Romanelli, 1986). Insiders have to overcome much more in the way of conscious and unconscious resistances than outsiders do in getting the change process on its way.

Changing the Corporate Mind-Set

As I have reiterated, letting go of the old ways of doing things is not only (or primarily) a cognitive process; it is, first and foremost, an emotional process. For that reason, to be successful at organizational transformation we must see the similarities between the individual and organizational change processes and learn what lessons we can from the emotional challenges of personal change.

I outlined earlier the mourning process that individuals go through when confronted by change. The same stages of mourning are applicable to change that takes place in a group setting. People who are asked to change themselves to accommodate a changing organization need time to digest what faces them and to mourn what no longer can be.

As in the case of individual change, corporate change, when first proposed, often engenders a state of turmoil. With the anxiety level rising, sometimes to the point of panic (among those who fear for their jobs, for example), normal organizational processes generally come to a halt or become ritualistic. People fall back on familiar routines, going through motions they know well as they try to deal with the announced change. This early in the game, few people are ready to accept that a new way of doing things has become necessary.

Due to the shock of what is happening to and around them, people in the organization may regress into a dependency or a fight-or-flight mode. Those in the dependency mode may wish for (and imagine that they have) an omnipotent leader who will set things right. Their dependency may also manifest itself in passivity, in a lack of initiative. Fight behavior, on the other hand, may be symptomized by a displacement of anger, by blaming or scapegoating others for what is happening. People regressing to fight behavior often exhibit a great deal of irritability and bitterness. However, those emotions are often directed not toward the corporation itself, or to the people and practices within it, but toward "others" who might be to blame. Customers, suppliers, the government, and competitors typically fall into that category. People turning to fight behavior are not yet ready to look at themselves in this difficult equation. Instead, they waste their energy on internal politics, engaging in turf fights rather than facing their real problems. Still other people regress not to dependency or anger but to flight behavior. Some actually leave the organization at the first signs of stress. Others simply withdraw; no longer participating in the activities of the office, they place their interests elsewhere.

These three modes of behavior cannot go on for long without dangerous corporate consequences. If people in the company refuse to look at their own role in the declining spiral, the organization will soon find itself in receivership. In organizations that are fortunate—and whose change drivers have been astute and skillful—employees reach that realization themselves in time to act on it. They understand that no miracle waits around the corner, that positive things happen to people who help themselves, that the steps needed to reverse the situation must be taken not by others but by themselves, that fighting change is of little use. As an increasing number of people in the organization share such thoughts, the corporate mind-set begins to change. Resistances are worn down, and the first tentative explorations of the new reality take place, even as, during the period of adjustment, people mourn what they have to leave behind.

In the final phase of organizational transformation, with that adjustment complete, people in the organization have redefined themselves. They have accepted the new way of doing things, recognizing its advantages, and they now collaborate. New values, beliefs, and thoughts have been internalized. People have a positive attitude toward the future.

As was touched on in the earlier discussion of engendering hope, the role of astute leadership is essential in an organization hoping to effectively navigate the transformation process. Leaders must recognize that it takes time to give up the old and embark on the new; that people facing organizational change, like those in personal change situations, need time to mourn the past. Effective leadership is a balancing act, especially during periods of change. Leadership that acknowledges the importance of the roles of envisioning, empowering, and energizing, and that also takes on an architectural role in setting up the appropriate structures and control systems, will go a long way toward revitalizing the organization.

Primary Factors Facilitating Change

Now that we have looked at the psychodynamics of the change process, a few observations are in order concerning factors that facilitate change. Studies of successful personal change efforts indicate that there two primary factors that help the change process and that may even, in certain cases, determine whether the transformation effort succeeds or fails: the presence of some kind of social support system to ease the process of change and transformation, and a personality style described in the literature as "hardy" (meaning that one's locus of control is more internal than external). Let us look at each of these factors in turn.

Social Support

Individuals who feel alone in their efforts to change behavior patterns have a difficult time changing. Without the support of their environment, their resistance to change is harder to overcome. Moreover, there is a link between the existence of social support and health maintenance (Bjorksten & Stewart, 1985; McCubbin & Thompson, 1989; Sperry, 1995). Given the stresses and strains associated with change, social support takes on a crucial buffering function. Indeed, social support is often the single most important factor in helping an individual overcome the barriers to change. People seem to sense this intuitively: those who decide to embark on a journey of transformation often seek out people who can give them the support they need, whether instrumental or emotional.

Instrumental support is task-directed. It involves such things as assigning another pair of hands for a job that needs to be done, obtaining specialized outside assistance for a challenging project, and providing authority along with responsibility—in short, handing over whatever resources are needed to make the change effort a success. *Emotional support,* on the other hand, is tied to self-esteem. This kind of support refers to ways of maintaining and bolstering a person's feelings about him- or herself. This support can be given by the spouse, other family members, friends, or colleagues at work—a network of people who offer reassurance, guidance, and an opportunity to share interests.

Sometimes both forms of support issue from the same source. Researchers have found that people in the process of change often seek out others who have been in a similar situation, partly to obtain practical help that seems to have worked for the other and partly to derive some consolation from not being alone in the situation (Vaughan, 1986). In addition, the person in pursuit of change often derives justification for his or her efforts to alter the situation by seeing others who have done the same.

Hardiness and Locus of Control

Some researchers divide the population into *internals* and *externals* (e.g., Rotter, 1966). That distinction implies that some people possess a more internal, others a more external, locus of control. People with an internal locus of control feel that they are in charge of their own lives; they perceive their destiny as affected by their own decisions, not by outside factors. They see a strong relationship between their own actions and what happens around them. This secure belief in themselves, this independence and self-confidence, makes such people less anxious; more active, striving, and achieving; more future and long-term oriented. They are also more proactive and innovative, though less prone to engage in risky behavior. So-called internals also possess a considerable amount of self-control. They tend to be more motivated and successful in life than their external counterparts, both academically and in their work. Their strong belief in their own capabilities makes these people difficult to influence, invulnerable to manipulation, and resistant to coercion.

Individuals with an internal locus of control find it easier than externals to take charge of and carry through major personal change. Their belief in their control of their own destiny prevents them from doubting the outcome of a self-initiated change process. Because they feel responsible for their own actions, they are aware that it is only they themselves who can orchestrate their own transformation. Once they have realized the necessity for change, they go ahead rather than wait for some outside sign or push to initiate the change. People with an external locus of control, on the other hand, often see change as a threat. Because they do not feel in control of the forces that affect their lives, they take a rather passive stand toward change, unable to take decisive steps in a new direction. Such an outlook makes them prone to depressive reactions.

The term *hardy personality* has been coined to describe people characterized by an internal locus of control (e.g., Kobasa, 1979). There is more to hardiness, however, than the feeling of control over the events of one's life. Hardy individuals feel a deep commitment to the activities of their lives. Deeply curious and eager to initiate new experiences, they perceive change as a positive challenge to further development. Hardy individuals have a strong commitment to self, an attitude of vigor toward the environment, and a sense of meaningfulness. In contrast, nonhardy people feel victimized by events and have a tendency to look at change as something undesirable.

The hardy personality style has affective, cognitive, and behavioral components that make people better survivors in stressful situations. Hardy individuals' feeling of control over what is happening to them and their lower need for security enable them to tolerate ambiguity better than others. They are said to possess an adaptive cognitive appraisal process that helps them to anticipate and internalize the changes they face. These people take charge; they make decisions; they feel that they are not at the mercy of events. They have a positive outlook toward life and face its challenges with resilience, flexibility, and adaptiveness; consequently, they show greater job involvement than others and put themselves easily into the role of catalyst.

It is that same positive outlook that makes hardy individuals more stress-resistant than others. Furthermore, hardy types are less prone to helplessness, depression, and physical illness (Seligman, 1989). Their commitment to self helps them preserve their mental health under strong pressure. With an outlook characterized by a sense of control, commitment, and challenge, and therefore buffered against stress and illness, they are effective at dealing with all of life's tasks. In particular, they have the skills to cope both psychologically and somatically with the stress caused by the change process.

The origin of a person's general attitude toward the environment whether hardy or nonhardy can be traced back to the kind of childrearing patterns he or she was subjected to. We can assume that the primary caretakers of hardy individuals exposed them to age-appropriate frustration and encouraged them in their childhood activities, thereby helping them to acquire a sense of control over their environment and to develop a positive sense of self-esteem.

Creating Regenerative Organizations

Given the importance of these two facilitating factors, leaders would do well to create an environment that fosters both social support and hardiness. It is in that sort of environment that change can flourish.

Making social support part of the corporate culture is a task that has to start at the top. The more effective leaders seem to have a considerable amount of emotional intelligence; they often possess what I describe in chapter 3 as a ''teddy bear'' quality, the ability to create a holding environment that ''contains'' the emotions of others. Leaders who have emotional intelligence provide a sense of security for followers; they inspire trust and confidence. Leaders who reveal the teddy bear quality in their dealings with others let employees know that genuine attention is being paid to them, that they are being listened to. Such leaders create a facilitating environment for change.

Hardiness is a tougher nut to crack. While research indicates that innovative, proactive companies have a larger percentage of people with an internal locus of control (a crucial component of hardiness) than other companies (Miller, Kets de Vries, & Toulouse, 1982), confirming the desirability of that orientation, internal or external locus of control can be deeply ingrained. To change the mind-set of an external into an internal is a major undertaking. Consequently, in most instances a company of externals cannot be cultivated, without changes in personnel, into a company of internals. However, companies subjected to a turbulent environment, those for which change is the norm rather than the exception, can promote hardiness by selecting, rewarding, and promoting people who have an internal locus of control. Employees with this outlook will be less resistant and more receptive than others to change efforts.

Organizational Transformation: A Practical Illustration

On October 29, 1993, the chairman of the board of Bang & Olufsen (B&O) could for the first time after years of losses predict a profit of 126 million Danish kroner (DKK) for the financial year 1993 to 1994. The company's share price had risen spectacularly, from DKK325 in 1990 to 1991 to DKK1,450 in 1994 to 1995. These figures indicated a dramatic turnaround of a long-tottering company (Balazs & Kets de Vries, 1997).

B&O was the crown jewel of Danish industry, the exclusive producer of high-tech, high-fidelity audiovisual systems and other related products. Since its beginning, the company had been at the forefront of design innovation, a philosophy promoted by the two founders of the company. However, that original philosophy stressing product design, which had earned the company much acclaim, carried within it the seeds of failure. The "holiness" of the design function came to reign over everything else, particularly cost and customer considerations. Saying no to a new product from the design department was taboo, something that would not be suggested by anyone hoping to stay long in the organization. Unfortunately, while the company won one design prize after the other, financially it was anything but a winner. The balance sheet had tottered around the red line for 22 years, an unheard-of period of time. As the present CEO, Anders Knutsen, said, recalling the situation during a presentation to a group of his key people, "Bang & Olufsen was not interested in making money; it was interested only in winning prizes."

In spite of the dismal financial figures, few people at B&O seemed to be seriously worried. Most employees were used to the fact that the company did not make a profit, but they had no serious concerns about its survival. Employment security had always been an implicit part of their contract. Whenever fledging doubts about the company's future hatched, top management's strong and confident statements reassured worriers. In the words of the present CEO, "Every year when we had some problems, it was not our fault. It was the outer world that was so evil to poor Bang & Olufsen."

Finally, when it became clear that the accounting period of 1990 to 1991 would bring a deficit of DKK135.5 million, the company's dismal situation could not be ignored any longer. The Supervisory Board decided to pull the plug, replacing the CEO who for 10 years had been allowed to run the company at his own discretion, with Anders Knutsen. Knutsen had learned B&O by starting out as a brand manager and working his way through different positions in production and product development, finally ending up as technical director.

Knutsen became CEO on July 1, 1992, facing strong opposition from both inside and outside the company. When the former CEO left, both the Supervisory Board and the Board of Directors underwent a reorganization at Knutsen's behest. Knutsen understood that to change the company he needed all the power he could get; thus one of his preconditions for taking on the role of CEO was that he would also become chairman of the Supervisory Board of a number of B&O's spin-off companies. With that precondition, the appointment was an obstacle. However, after rallying people inside and outside the company for a number of weeks, he managed to push it through: in September of 1992, he got his way. He finally had the power to act.

Outside opposition to changing the organization came primarily from the banks with which B&O was affiliated. From the moment of Knutsen's appointment, the banks opposed his new ideas. Most of them refused to give him the benefit of the doubt, canceling B&O's accounts or raising interest rates. These actions increased the crisis atmosphere that prevailed in the company.

Knutsen immediately demonstrated that he had what had been missing at B&O: leadership skills. He started by pronouncing a clear vision for the company, along with a mission statement that stated clearly how the vision could be achieved. Then he, together with the Board of Directors, elaborated a plan for the rationalization and restructuring of the organization. He called it Break Point '93.

The first step was an analysis of the company's cultural values, prepared by B&O's top executives, which centered around an intensive evaluation of the company's critical situation. In particular, the sacrosanctity of the process of new-product acceptance was placed under the microscope. Having overseen that analysis, and anticipating the difficulty of inculcating new values, the Board of Directors decided to turn to outside support. I was asked to present a seminar centered on leadership, organizational culture, and corporate transformation. The seminar was intended as a staged focal event of the sort discussed earlier; its implicit goal was to shake people up. Knutsen opened the seminar explosively, announcing that a considerable number of people in the factories had to be dismissed because of the poor order portfolio.

What followed was, as one B&O employee described it, "an atmosphere of chaos and upheaval." People were shocked and disoriented, uncertain how the future—their own and the company's—would look. The shock therapy seemed to achieve the desired effect, however. Participants, trying to impose order onto the prevailing chaos, threw themselves wholeheartedly into the activities of the seminar. Despite the risks, they experienced for the first time the power to do something about their own company. The final (but most critical) part of the seminar was a strategic dialogue with top management to help restructure and refocus the company. In the previous days they had been exposed to discussions about vanguard companies, effective leadership practices, and their own corporate culture and strategy. Participating in the design for the future made for motivation, commitment, and a sense of ownership. Soon hope started to replace chaos. The participants had discovered a pathway out of the mess they were in. They recognized the company's weaknesses, but they also saw a way of building on the company's strengths. The seminar also set the stage for a rewrite of the existing psychological contract in the organization. No longer was job security the main pillar of the contract. Instead, that pillar had become accountability and performance.

The goal of Break Point '93 was radical: it included a complete rationalization and reorganization of the company's every function. Organizationally, the changes had an important impact as well. The distance between top management and the shop floor was cut by reducing the overall number of executives and by slashing two management layers entirely; a total of 712 people were dismissed, although many were later rehired. As accountability was pushed deep down the lines, employees were expected to develop a sense of ownership and personal responsibility for the company.

Product acceptance, the old Achilles' heel of the company, since traditionally almost everything submitted by product design had been accepted, became much more selective. The most disturbing "culture shock" experienced during the transformation, this clearly signaled management's intent to change the company. Over a two-year period, B&O moved from a deficit that threatened its very existence to a surplus that exceeded all expectations. The first part of the change process had come to a successful end.

Concluding Comments

The changing competitive environment, with its increasingly frequent discontinuities, requires that organizations and their people be able to learn to change their behavior to sustain a competitive advantage. If an organization is unable to continuously *un*learn behavior which, having contributed to past success, is now ineffective, it is doomed to failure. The paradox of success—that it creates complacency and arrogance—is a great challenge to organizational leaders. Heraclitus' statement that "there is nothing permanent except change" is more true now than ever. For that reason, executives who have a poor understanding of change processes will be at a competitive disadvantage.

It is not an easy proposition to create a mind-set that welcomes change, to create an organization in which people's exploratory dispositions are fully deployed. As the mussel metaphor presented in the Introduction suggests, people get stuck in their ways. To prevent employees from settling down too firmly at their desks, to avoid turning the organization into a psychic prison characterized by rigidity and routine, leaders need to cultivate a culture of trust, a prevailing organizational attitude that encourages people to challenge established ways of doing things.

People in organizations with that sort of corporate mind-set will never take the recommendations of their powerholders for granted; they will question what their leaders have to say. Organizations that foster an atmosphere of constructive conflict, encourage contrarian thinking and a healthy disrespect for the boss, and make strategic dialogue the rule, not the exception, will be in the best position to remain aligned with the environment, however much or often it changes. Organizations characterized by this sort of culture of constructive dialogue will kill ill-conceived projects, unearth missed opportunities, and inform top executives of the concerns of their people. When such a mind-set prevails, it serves as an early-warning system of the need for change. The questioning attitude of this mind-set makes organizational preventive maintenance possible and creates an atmosphere of continuous learning.

Making such an organizational culture a viable proposition takes continuous effort, since change runs counter to the built-in conservatism of human behavior. Even while old resistances are breaking down, new ones are emerging. The danger of rigidification is ever present. We would do well to heed the words of W. H. Auden, who once wrote,

We would rather be ruined than changed
We would rather die in our dread
Than climb the cross of the moment
And let our illusions die. (1948/1976)

People who understand the dynamics of change, who realize that the tremendous opportunities inherent in a proactive stance far outweigh the temporary sense of discomfort that accompanies proaction, will be the winners in this world of discontinuities.

References

Auden, W. H. (1976). The age of anxiety. In E. Mendelson (Ed.), *W. H. Auden: Collected Poems.* New York: Random House. (Original work published 1948)

Balazs, K., & Kets de Vries, M. F. R. (1997). Bang & Olufsen: A company in transition. *INSEAD Case Study.* Cranfield University, U.K.: Case Clearing House.

Baumeister, R. F. (1994). The crystallization of discontent in the process of major life change. In T. Heatherton & J. L. Weinberger (Eds.), *Can personality change?* Washington, DC: American Psychological Association.

Bjorksten, O., & Stewart, T. (1985). Marital status and health. In O. Bjorksten (Ed.), *New clinical concepts in marital therapy* (pp. 121–145). Washington, DC: American Psychiatric Press.

Bowlby, J. (1980). *Attachment and Loss: Vol. 3, Loss.* New York: Basic Books.

Heatherton, T. F., & Nichols, P. A. (1994). Personal accounts of successful versus failed attempts at life change. *Personality and Social Psychology Bulletin, 29,* 664–675.

Johnson, J. G. (1990). Managing strategic change: The role of symbolic action. *British Journal of Management, 1,* 183–200.

Kets de Vries, M. F. R., & Miller, D. (1984). *The neurotic organization: Diagnosing and changing counterproductive styles of management.* San Francisco: Jossey-Bass.

Kobasa, S. C. (1979). Stressful events, personality, and health: An inquiry into hardiness. *Journal of Personality and Social Psychology, 37,* 1–11.

Lewin, K. (1951). *Field theory in social sciences.* New York: Harper & Row.

Maxwell, M. (1984). *The Alcoholics Anonymous experience.* New York: McGraw-Hill.

McCubbin, H., & Thompson, A. (1989). *Balancing work and family life on Wall Street.* Edina, MN: Burgess International.

Miller, D., Kets de Vries, M. F. R. & Toulouse, J. M. (1982). Top executive locus of control and its relationship to strategy making, structure, and environment. *Academy of Management Journal, 25,* 237–253.

Rotter, J. B. (1966). Generalized expectancies for internal versus external control of reinforcement. *Psychological Monographs, 80/1,* whole no. 609.

Seligman, M. (1989). Explanatory style: Predicting depression, achievement, and health. In M. Yapko (Ed.), *Brief therapy approaches to treating anxiety and depression*. New York: Brunner/Mazel.

Sperry, L. (1995). *Handbook of diagnosis and treatment of the DSM-IV personality disorders*. New York: Brunner/Mazel.

Stall, R., & Biernacki, P. (1986). Spontaneous remission from the problematic use of substances: An inductive model derived from a comparative analysis of the alcohol, tobacco, and food/obesity literatures. *International Journal of the Addictions, 21,* 1–23.

Tushman, M., Newman, W. H., & Romanelli, E. (1986). Convergence and upheaval: Managing the unsteady pace of organizational evolution. *California Management Review, 29,* 29–44.

Vaughan, D. (1986). *Uncoupling*. New York: Basic Books.

8

The Downside of Downsizing

"Hallo!" said Piglet, "what are you doing?"
"Hunting," said Pooh.
"Hunting what?"
"Tracking something," said Winnie-the-Pooh very mysteriously.
"Tracking what?" said Piglet, coming closer.
"That's just what I ask myself. I ask myself, What?"
"What do you think you'll answer?"
"I shall have to wait until I catch up with it," said Winnie-the-Pooh.
(A. A. Milne, *Winnie-the-Pooh*)

I have striven not to laugh at human actions, not to weep at them,
nor to hate them, but to understand them. (Spinoza)

An eye for an eye leads only to more blindness.
(Margaret Atwood, *Cat's Eye*)

This final chapter explores individual reaction patterns to the process of downsizing in the victims, the survivors (those staying with a company after layoffs), and the "executioners" (those responsible for the implementation of downsizing). I give the latter group special focus, examining coping behaviors that range from compulsive-ritualistic, to abrasive, to dissociative, to alexithymic-anhedonic, to depressive. The chapter then concludes with a number of practical recommendations about how to facilitate the downsizing process.

This chapter is based on an article published under the same title in *Human Relations* co-authored with Katharina Balazs (*Human Relations*, 1997, Volume 50, Number 1, pages 11–50).

Introduction

Downsizing, the planned elimination of positions or jobs, is a relatively recent phenomenon that has become a favorite business practice for a large number of troubled corporations. Starting with factory closures in sunset industries during the recession of the early eighties and continuing as an aftereffect of merger and acquisition mania, downsizing has become one of the inevitable outcomes of living in a global world where continual adjustments to products, services, and the price of labor are needed to remain competitive.

Since the late 1980s, nearly all of the Fortune 1000 firms have engaged in downsizing, and this trend seems to be continuing. Various developments in management indicate that the end of downsizing is nowhere in sight. One major contributing factor is the increasing popularity of global benchmarking. Finding one's overhead costs wanting compared to not only domestic but also international competitors is now seen as a convincing argument for taking large numbers of employees off the payroll. Another reason for the continued use of downsizing is the administrative impact of the revolution in information and communication technologies. Changes in these technologies have led to a growing redundancy of the traditional, go-between role of middle management, a group of people previously preoccupied with collecting, analyzing, and transmitting information up and down the hierarchy. Last, but certainly not least, downsizing is sometimes the price paid for strategic errors made by top management, the erroneous interpretation of market trends, for example.

Among the expected benefits of downsizing are such factors as lower overhead, decreased bureaucracy, faster decision making, smoother communication, greater "intrapreneurial" behavior, increased productivity, and better earnings. Its major raison d'être, however, is to make a company more efficient compared to its competitors. But whether these benefits materialize is another question. The effectiveness of downsizing as a way to bring a company back to organizational health and increased competitiveness has been seriously challenged. The actual gains may be much less than originally thought. According to a survey by the Society for Human Resource Management, more than 50% of the 1468 restructured firms surveyed reported that productivity either remained stagnant or deteriorated after downsizing (Henkoff, 1990).

A study by an outplacement firm noted that 74% of the senior executives in downsized companies that were surveyed experienced problems with morale, trust, and productivity (Henkoff, 1990). Another survey, profiled in the *Wall Street Journal,* found that of the 1005 downsized firms questioned, only 46% had actually cut expenses, 32% had increased profits, 22% had increased productivity, and 22% had reduced bureaucracy. According to a director of the Wyatt Company, layoffs and restructuring have a "severe adverse impact" on the morale of the survivors. Indeed, 58% of the surveyed companies reported that employee morale was seriously affected (Bennett, 1991). Research results have indicated that many organizations enjoy an initial upsurge in productivity immediately after downsizing but then become depressed and lethargic (Appelbaum, Simpson, & Shapiro, 1987; Custer, 1994). One consulting firm reported that stock prices of firms that downsized during the 1980s (after a temporary movement upward) actually lagged behind the industry average in the 1990s (Baumohl, 1993).

Dictated by tough economic principles, following the call of the stock market, downsizing was seen as solely positive in its early days, though it was unclear to what extent its effects would alter the rules of the corporate world. It was expected that, once a company had gone through downsizing, everything would "return to normal."

While nobody was willing or able to anticipate the detrimental social consequences this new practice might have, those consequences soon appeared on the horizon. The most prevalent one can be seen in the situation of white-collar workers. In the past (in cases of cyclical downturns, for example) it was blue-collar workers who had to bear the brunt of reductions in personnel. Now, downsizing having brought "cutback democracy" to the workplace, people in all job positions are included. Hourly blue-collar workers are affected, to be sure, but an increasing number of white-collar employees are now on the receiving end of cost-cutting programs. Blue-collar workers have always been used to, and have sometimes even anticipated, fluctuations in the job market. White-collar workers, on the other hand, were taken by surprise by downsizing's initial impact on job security. In the past decade, the protected middle class has had to learn to live with the shattered illusion of prosperity. They can no longer take it for granted that their children will have a better life than they did, for example; instead, downward mobility has become more common. And these are just some of the first, rippling effects of the new downsizing way of life, frightening indicators for the future.

The Illusion of the Quick Fix

Some management scholars have argued that one of the reasons for the failure of many downsizing efforts is an overly simplistic approach. Too many executives implement downsizing through an across-the-board reduction of headcount. This is generally an excessively short-sighted business strategy. Executives who take this approach, focusing on perceived internal efficiency rather than challenging the overall way the company does business, limit themselves to the implementation of superficial changes. Paradoxically, in situations of attrition, hiring freezes, or forced early retirement, the star performers are often the first ones to leave the company. Consequently, crucial skills in human capital disappear, and organizational memory is disrupted or completely lost. Furthermore, those who remain are often stuck with an increased workload. The result is a group of unhappy, over-worked employees, some of whom have to do tasks for which they have not been trained. To ease the disruption, patch-up solutions have to be found, sometimes with the help of costly consultants (an irony, given the initial drive to cut expenses and save money). Furthermore, due to the prevailing malaise in the company, downsizing may eventually beget more downsizing, causing "change fatigue" in executives and employees. It is because of consequences such as these that the effectiveness of downsizing has been called into question.

Granted, slashing people from the payroll generally has a temporary beneficial effect in the form of reduced overhead (as would holding back on capital investments and R&D), but mere cost-cutting is inadequate to prepare a corporation for the "global business Olympics." More is needed to ensure increased market share and profitability. Companies that take the downsizing route seem to be preoccupied with their past rather than focused on their future. As a consequence, they delay long-term investments for short-term gains, in part to elicit a positive reaction (often temporary) from the stock market.

The fact that future success depends on such employee-centered factors as constant innovation, exceptional customer satisfaction, and good corporate citizenship (i.e., teamwork rather than turf defending) implies that substantial investments have to be made in employees. Therefore, merely cutting people from the payroll is not the way to go. Wholesale cuts create resentment and resistance and thus affect employee loyalty and commitment. In fact, firms that engage repeatedly in downsizing have difficulty attracting the best and the brightest due to bad publicity (regardless of whether that publicity is issued officially or by word of mouth). As one wit very appropriately noted: downsizing, rightsizing, dumbsizing, capsizing! Symptomatic of downsizing's darker side is the fact that most firms do not succeed in their original effort and end up downsizing again a year later (Pearlstein, 1994).

From Downsizing to Reinventing

It is clear from this discussion that downsizing can take many forms, all of which attempt to improve organizational effectiveness, efficiency, productivity, and competitiveness. Despite this commonality, there is a progressive differentiation in people's perceptions of the downsizing phenomenon: from merely restructuring (getting smaller), to reengineering (getting better), to reinventing the corporation (getting smarter). In its broadest sense, downsizing is part of a continuous corporate renewal process.

A number of students of organizations have argued that this broader approach to downsizing, as opposed to across-the-board reductions, leads to a more positive long-term impact. These theorists see downsizing as affecting all the work processes in the organization. With the enlarged definition offered by this viewpoint, the goal of a downsizing effort becomes to reassess and alter the company's fundamental business practices. Thus the company's organizational design, work processes, corporate culture, and mission may face an overhaul. Not only functions but also hierarchical levels and even complete business units may need to be eliminated. In its widest sense, then, the term *downsizing* describes a complete strategic transformation effort that changes the values and attitudes of the company's corporate culture. In this definition, downsizing is not a stand-alone shortcut; rather, it is part of a company's continuous improvement scheme. As such, it takes on a long-term perspective, its objective being to look for ways to improve productivity, cut costs, and increase earnings.

Its mixed press notwithstanding, corporate downsizing is likely to remain an attractive option for many organizations. Even if the long-term benefits are questionable, downsizing shows that decisions are being made and actions taken. In addition, many consulting firms, recognizing a new and profitable niche, have thrown themselves into the downsizing arena. Yet, as mentioned before, there is a high social cost attached to this newest rage in management. Indeed, it appears that continuous downsizing and a motivated workforce are mutually exclusive.

Downsizing: Salient Issues

In spite of being a relatively new phenomenon in organizational life, corporate downsizing has inspired a great deal of research concentrating on different issues pertaining to the subject—research that has resulted in a number of important findings. The most extensive and systematic survey of corporate downsizing is a four-year study done by Kim Cameron, Sarah Freeman, and Aneil Mishra (Cameron, 1994; Cameron, Freeman, & Mishra, 1991, 1993; Freeman & Cameron, 1993). This study offers a theoretical framework of the process, focusing on possible implementation strategies, the organizational effects of downsizing, and best practices. A significant negative correlation between organizational effectiveness and downsizing through layoffs is one of the major findings of this research project. Although the study points to the effective management of the human resource system as one of the most critical factors in successful downsizing, it does not examine the downsizing process from the perspective of the individual.

Unfortunately, much of the subsequent literature follows this line of investigation. All too often employees, in the typical approach to downsizing, whether in corporate offices or in the research arena, are still treated in an abstract fashion. In the human-engineering approach to downsizing, people are seen more as liabilities than as assets, the emotional experience of the individual getting short shrift. It is exactly this changing nature of the relationship between individual and organization, however, that warrants further attention. It is difficult to be successful as an organization with a group of demotivated employees. Fortunately, some students of the downsizing phenomenon have taken on this problem from a more individual perspective.

The Breaking of the Psychological Contract

The major issue for those on the receiving end of downsizing, the survivors and the victims, concerns the *psychological contract*. This term was coined by the psychologist Harry Levinson to describe the unspoken agreement that exists between every organization and its employees, an agreement in which the organization promises lifetime employment in return for hard work and loyalty, a supportive response to employees' psychological needs and defenses in return for employees meeting the organization's unstated needs (Levinson, 1962). Downsizing breaks this implicit psychological contract between employer and employee. As a result, the feeling of employee dependency that may have evolved, over many years with an organization, into a sense of entitlement is twisted into a sense of betrayal.

The Concept of Employability

It is becoming increasingly clear that lasting, beneficial changes in the corporate world require the painful adaptation of those concerned to a radically different way of life, one without job security in the traditional meaning of the term. In response to that reality, many vanguard organizations are espousing the notion that fostering an "intrapreneurial" environment, one that allows employees to approach their jobs as individual entrepreneurs, moving in and out of the organization as their and the organization's needs dictate, requires a new relationship between the employee and the organization.

Career self-management, that is, taking control of one's job and career as opposed to letting the company take care of them (as in the old employment contract), is viewed as one possible solution to the problem of diminished job security. Toward that end, the term *employability* is replacing the concept of *job tenure*. The organization of the future is described as taking on a guiding role to help employees toward a self-employed attitude. In order to provide at least a modicum of security, organizations encourage employees to keep their work experience as up-to-date as possible so that they are better able to get a new job if laid off. A new, shorter-term employment contract is proposed as part of this solution which gives limited security for a defined period of time.

Helpful as these new ideas may sound on paper, this way of operating goes against the basic need for connectedness and affiliation and necessitates a great shift in thinking and expertise on the part of both employees and executives. For many people, particularly the ones having trouble dealing with ambiguity, employability comes with a considerable amount of stress.

Stress Reactions in the Workplace

Researchers sharing this perspective on the individual consider stress to be the crucial theoretical construct underlying the psychological dynamics pertaining to job loss. In Joel Brockner's (1988) study of the effects of work layoffs on survivors, for example, he shows clearly that organizational downsizing is a significant stress-inducing factor that has a profound influence on the work behaviors and attitudes of the remaining workforce. The continued threat of job loss, stimulating feelings of loss of control over one's environment and threatening one's internalized concept of self, is regarded as the primary cause of deteriorating psychological well-being in the workplace and accounts for many stress-related illnesses, such as heart disease and ulcers. These findings underline the importance of managing interpersonal relations to help employees deal with the stress caused by the downsizing process.

Researchers assessing how employees differ in their reactions to downsizing have identified financial distress and previous attachment to the job as the major factors contributing to employees' sense of despair (Leana & Feldman, 1988, 1990). In those employees who are devastated by downsizing, losing the job often evokes reactions comparable to those experienced at the death of someone close (Greenhalgh & Rosenblatt, 1984; Henkoff, 1994). Feelings of desperation over job loss may even culminate in violence or self-destruction, as illustrated by statistics that denote murder in the workplace as the fastest-growing form of homicide in the United States, with about 40% of those homicides followed by suicide (Thornburg, 1992).

Some researchers have explored possible defensive reactions aroused by the downsizing process. One common reaction seems to be denial, a coping mechanism common to both management and employees in the downsizing process (though the higher the organizational level, the stronger the denial tends to be) (Noer, 1993). Other researchers have identified various cognitive coping strategies leading to one of two different reactions to downsizing: denial-detachment (through which people distance themselves psychologically from the perceived threat) and hypersensitivity (through which they closely monitor for danger signs) (Greenhalgh & Jick, 1989).

The View from the Top

In most of these studies, little attention has been paid to the role of those in charge of the downsizing process. Yet a 1991 survey of 1005 companies conducted by the Wyatt Company indicates that the behavior of top executives, especially their treatment of surviving employees, is one of the main determinants of the success or failure of the downsizing process (Bennett, 1991; Lalli, 1992). The way top executives handle layoffs has been shown to have a significant impact on the degree of dysfunctionality in survivors' work behavior and attitudes (Brockner, 1988). The competence, knowledge, dynamism, and accessibility of leaders, along with their ability to clearly articulate a vision that provides motivation for the future, are crucial to a positive outcome (Cameron, Freeman, & Mishra, 1991). What makes downsizing so difficult for the executives involved is that they often have to discard the values that furthered their own advancement up the organizational career ladder. Many executives, to escape dealing with that conflict, become psychologically detached, focusing not on their employees but on projected organizational outcomes. This way of coping proves ineffective, however, as they attempt to deal with hostility, depression, absenteeism, and substance abuse among the workforce (Leana & Feldman, 1988; Noer, 1993; Smith, 1994).

Adding to the stress of the process for executives is the likely scapegoating of leaders and the loss of leader credibility (Cameron, Kim, & Whetten, 1987). This scapegoating (and the politicized environment that fosters it) causes many top executives to distance themselves from their employees to avoid criticism and antagonism (Cameron et al., 1993). They frequently react to layoffs by withdrawing from the remaining workforce. Already lonely top executives thus become even more isolated during downsizing and layoffs. Moreover, many of these executives are not prepared for the strong reactions of the survivors.

Many senior executives do not recognize the extent to which the productivity of the remaining employees depends on apparently trivial details of the implementation of the downsizing process. These implementation details, such as spelling out what milestones have to be achieved to arrive at the desired end-state and involving the remaining executives in the process, have a positive effect. By ignoring these details and the surviving subordinates' emotional state, however, executives become prone to grave mistakes that may lead to self-destructive behavior in survivors. Executives should expect their surviving subordinates to experience a wide variety of psychological emotional reactions, including anxiety, anger, guilt, envy, relief, and denial (Brockner, 1988; Henkoff, 1994), and they should help employees work through those reactions. In addition, they should work to avoid another common executive mistake: telling the survivors (in hopes that guilt will make them work harder) to be grateful that they still have jobs, a response that creates resentment and results in oppositional behavior (Noer, 1993).

Downsizing from a Different Perspective

Most authors in the existing literature on downsizing focus on the costs, emotional and professional, to those individuals who are at the receiving end of the process: the victims and the survivors. They deal, usually in a very descriptive way (listing various stress symptoms, for example), with the question of how the people whose jobs have been terminated cope with sudden unemployment. They also address the consequences for the survivors.

To get a better grasp of the psychology of the downsizing process, we have to go beyond what happens with victims and survivors. While the consequences to those individuals are important, we also need to address how the people who actually do the downsizing are psychologically affected. Interviews with executives involved in the process show quite clearly that this unpleasant task can have considerable emotional impact. For many executives, as was noted earlier, downsizing contradicts long-held attitudes toward business life. Those leaders, then, have to cope with the double burden of their own emotional reactions and those of the other survivors. They have to deal with major change while experiencing it themselves. These are very important considerations, especially given that the executives' psychological state is likely to have a serious effect on corporate culture, strategy, and structure.

In the discussion that follows, I will first focus on the victims and survivors, reviewing their reaction patterns. Then I will address the reactions of the ''executioners.''

Ways of Coping

Doing open-ended interviews with 60 ''victims,'' 60 ''survivors,'' and 80 ''executioners'' (the population mainly drawn from my INSEAD leadership seminar), I asked questions based on psychiatric, clinical psychological, and organizational diagnostic interviewing techniques. The questions elicited biographical and attitudinal information on employment, job situation, job loss, the downsizing process, and physical and mental health.

As a result of the interviews, victims were assigned to one of four reaction classifications (adaptable, depressed, Gauguin-emulating, or antagonistic) and "executioners" to one of six reaction classifications (adjusted, compulsive/ritualistic, depressed, alexithymic/anhedonic, abrasive, and dissociative). I made no attempt to classify survivors, limiting myself to a general description of how downsizing was experienced by that group of people.

Among the victims, the largest group turned out to be the adaptable (43.3%), followed by the depressed (30%), those "doing a Gauguin" (16.7%), and finally the antagonistic (10%). For the "executioners," the largest group was the one without any obvious symptoms (37.5%), followed by the compulsive/ritualistic (17.5%), the depressed (17.5%), the alexithymic/anhedonic (11.25%), the abrasive (8.75%), and the dissociative (7.5 %).

The Victims

Coping can be seen as a person's cognitive, emotional, and behavioral efforts to manage specific external and internal demands that are experienced as taxing. All of us have our own characteristic ways of dealing with stressful situations. Some people respond by taking a proactive stand, trying to take firm control over their lives, while others cope more reactively, attempting to escape or avoid stress. From our discussions with downsized individuals, we were able to distinguish a number of recurrent patterns. Bear in mind, however, that these descriptions are not exhaustive; rather, they are attempts at categorization in order to clarify how the process of downsizing affects the individual. Many different permutations and combinations are possible.

The Adaptable Victim

For some individuals in our study, the downsizing process engendered comparatively little drama. These people, who generally had a high skill level, succeeded in finding another job with relative ease, usually in a field similar to the one they had been working in. They tended to join smaller companies so as to feel less like a cog in a machine. Being in a new workplace generally had a positive effect, although the experience of downsizing gave some of these people a rather cynical outlook toward their new organization. After all, in spite of all the rational arguments given for their termination, their belief in the psychological contract had been shaken. When the transition between jobs was over, these adaptable individuals often discovered that in the new, smaller company, the daily challenges (and also the rewards) were greater and more immediate. Their position often encompassed a wider or somewhat different spectrum of responsibilities than in the former organization. This gave them the opportunity to learn new things and offered the chance for renewal. As one executive told us, "My dismissal was the best thing that's ever happened to me. I was literally dying on the job. Being forced to find a new job and prove myself once more has given me a greater feeling of vitality."

Those Who "Did a Gauguin"

One group of executives turned termination into a completely new opportunity. For this group, those who opted to "do a Gauguin" (see chapter 3), the experience of downsizing offered a new lease on life through career change as well as job change. After all too many working years, these executives were like the walking dead before downsizing struck. As one person described it, "Over the last decade, until just recently, I sleepwalked through life. The only times I felt *alive* were when I was with friends playing golf or tennis. This has changed tremendously since I shifted fields. I thoroughly enjoy coming to work now. I really like what I'm doing.''

Prior to their termination, these people faithfully and competently went through the motions of work, but they no longer got any pleasure out of it. Because their life was too comfortable to contemplate a change, however, they endured the status quo, but without being really productive and certainly without being creative. Finding themselves suddenly out of work was exactly the stimulus they needed to come back to life. Unemployment opened up the opportunity to pursue something they had always dreamed of doing but had never dared do. Those who were at midlife when faced with downsizing were forced to stop and reconsider their priorities. For the first time, they asked themselves what *they* wanted to do as opposed to what others expected from them.

Most of the Gauguin emulators were at middle age or beyond, old enough to have the sense that time was running out. They felt that if they failed to take action at this moment of opportunity, change would *never* happen. After years on the job, they had also acquired adequate financial security to provide them with a safety net. These underlying factors, combined with sudden unemployment, pushed them over the edge: they finally dared to take the leap they had always dreamed of.

People in this group often pursued what we might call a Protean career (after the Greek god Proteus, who was able to continually change shape). Many went for a major career (and often life) change—for example, from senior vice president of a bank to real estate developer, from CEO to public school educator, from computer analyst to art gallery manager. Some were even more adventurous, following Gauguin's example quite literally. In many instances, these apparently dramatic changes came as no great surprise to close friends and family. Those who made major career changes had generally already been involved in some capacity in their new field.

The Depressed Victim

Some people who were victims of downsizing ended up with depressive reactions. These were the people who had the most difficult time adjusting to the new situation they found themselves in. Generally, they felt betrayed by the organization to which they had devoted a considerable part of their lives. Because their sense of self-esteem was closely tied to organizational identity, the loss of familiar surroundings caused them to fall apart. Unable to move on, they became stuck in the mourning process. They avoided dealing with the new reality; they seemed to have no energy left to go out and find a new job; they were unable to concentrate on whatever they were doing; they procrastinated and were irritable. They also experienced a host of emotional and physiological problems: they often neglected their appearance; they had a tendency to suffer from insomnia and loss of appetite; and they were preoccupied with negative thoughts. Because of their depressive outlook, their fear of not being able to find another job often became a self-fulfilling prophecy; some of these victims ended up becoming part of the permanently unemployed. Alcoholism and other forms of substance abuse were common consequences. Marital problems, often resulting in divorce, led to a further deterioration of self-esteem and the fighting spirit, and suicidal thoughts were not uncommon.

Among the people with depressive reactions, one group initially took a proactive stand, making an effort to look for another job. When their efforts were stymied by repeated setbacks in the job market, however, they were forced to the realization that their skills were no longer wanted. Some of them eventually found another job, but one well below their former position. *Under*employment became a way of life for these individuals, creating serious problems centered around self-esteem and replacing their original proactivity with a depressive outlook on life.

The Antagonistic Victim

One natural reaction of people who are hurt is anger; we all experience that reaction on occasion. We manage our anger or aggression by turning it either inward or outward, depending on our basic personality. Those victims who experienced depressive reactions to downsizing tended toward inwardly directed aggression. Another group in this study of the psychological impact of downsizing turned their aggression outward, however. In some of these individuals, outwardly expressed aggression was the norm; in others, it was a heretofore repressed behavior pattern triggered by the trauma of being "rejected." For both subsets of this latter group, verbal and physical violence was the pattern of choice. The most common victims of their aggression were the members of their family. Sometimes, though, the anger extended outside the family circle. Among those who found other employment, some carried the aggression with them in the form of abrasive behavior on the new job, which led again to dismissal. In extreme circumstances, those who directed their aggression outwardly became quite dysfunctional, deciding to "get even" with those whom they saw as having caused their misery: they directed their violent impulses toward former employers, superiors, or colleagues, sometimes in the form of harassment or sabotage.

The Survivors

One finding that many researchers of the downsizing phenomenon agree upon is a cluster of reactions among those remaining in the organization which has become known as *survivor sickness* or *survivor syndrome* (Cascio, 1993; Noer, 1993). These terms refer to the way survivors react when many of their friends and colleagues are forced to terminate their relationship with the company.

The issue of survivor guilt was originally dealt with in the context of the survival of the Holocaust. In contrast, "survivor *sickness*" describes a set of attitudes, feelings, and perceptions that occur in employees who remain in organizational systems following involuntary employee reductions. These include anger, depression, fear, guilt, risk aversion, distrust, vulnerability or powerlessness, and loss of morale and motivation (Brockner, 1988; Cascio, 1993; Navran, 1994; Noer, 1993). The greater the survivors' perception of violation, the greater their susceptibility to survivor sickness seems to be.

The feeling of loss of control over the situation and the uncertainty caused by the possible loss of their own jobs can cause severe stress reactions in the survivors of downsizing. A sharp increase in the size of survivors' workload, longer working hours, and a reduction in vacation days, natural consequences of a smaller workforce, can reinforce this effect, leading to inefficiency and burnout (Brockner, 1988, 1992; Brockner, Davy, & Carter, 1985; Brockner et al., 1987; Mone, 1994).

By breaking up a complex set of interconnections, downsizing creates dramatic changes in the organizational environment. In an all-too-typical scenario, the downsizing process tears the organization's whole value system apart. Consequently, the corporate culture that used to serve as the glue that kept the organization together loses its amalgamating function, and feelings of rudderlessness and anxiety emerge.

The study on downsizing showed that job insecurity had an enormous impact on organizational effectiveness: many of the surviving executives asked themselves if they would be next in line; the dismissal of long-term employees and head-office staffers with a strategic overview resulted in the loss of institutional memory; specialists on whom one could rely for certain types of decisions were no longer there; and decision making had a short-term emphasis with serious repercussions for R&D, capital investments, and training and development. All these changes contributed to a sense of disorientation that had permanent consequences: the survivors perceived a significant and lasting change in their relationship to the organization. After an initial upsurge in productivity, they often settled into an attitude of fearful expectancy.

The survivors I spoke with reported that in companies narrowly defining downsizing as a simple cutback in personnel, commitment and loyalty to the employer disappeared. The survivors felt that they were getting very little in return for the additional roles they had been asked to take on. After the psychological contract between employee and employer had been broken, distrust toward top management caused survivors to believe that management was guilty until proven innocent. This blaming phenomenon in those who remained was often a defense mechanism, a form of projection that helped individuals confront their own survivor guilt. Fairness on the part of the organization when implementing layoffs was of crucial importance in minimizing this phenomenon.

The downsizing study also showed that survivors either (1) distanced themselves from the layoff victims (the response favored when survivors did not substantially identify with the victims) or (2) distanced themselves from the organization (when they *did* identify with the victims). In addition, to reduce feelings of guilt over their coworkers' dismissal, some employees increased their level of output. Because job insecurity fostered a negative attitude among remaining employees, they felt the need to outperform their coworkers. Furthermore, the remaining workers needed to redress the feeling of inequity elicited by their survival by convincing themselves that those who had been laid off deserved it. In some instances, then, a moderate level of job insecurity actually led to temporarily heightened productivity, but it had the opposite effect on morale.

The Executioners

From the interviews, it became clear that downsizing left an indelible imprint on executives who had implemented the process. We turn now to some of the factors that influence the

behavior and reactions of executives as they experience downsizing.

Most of us assume an unconscious "equation" in human
interaction: the belief that what we do to others will be done to
us. This *talion law*, the law of retaliation, often expressed as
"an eye for an eye, a tooth for a tooth" was first recorded
in Babylonian law, which states that criminals should receive
punishment equaling the injuries they inflicted on their victims.
This exacting retaliation has been the law of many societies
throughout history. Although modern Western society has found
other systems and forms of justice to compensate for injury,
talion law still operates in the collective and individual unconscious in the form of subliminal fear of reprisal. Feelings of
guilt, a general fear of retribution, and stress symptoms are the
manifestations of this subconscious belief.

In those responsible for implementation, downsizing brings
a fear of the talion law to the fore. Knowing that they are causing
people hurt and grief, the "executioners" may fantasize about
a reversal of the situation. That fear that someone might try to
"get even," if taken to the extreme, results in paranoid reactions.
Some executives, caught up in an escalation of aggression fueled
by paranoia, resort to preemptive action, crushing those they
perceive as threats.

The belief in talion law offers a partial explanation for the
fact that most of the executives I spoke with were reluctant to
do unpleasant things to others. Even those "executioners" who
had no fear of reprisals suffered considerable distress, however.
Having to fire old friends and acquaintances, people with whom
they had worked for years, was very painful. It is not surprising,
then, that so many of the participants in the study used euphe-
misms to disguise what they were doing, terms such as *dehiring,
disengaging,* and *recruiting,* with their Orwellian overtones.

The executives in the study reacted to the stress associated
with downsizing in various ways. Some coped comfortably,

while others regressed to troubling behavior patterns. Let us look now at some of the variations in response.

The Adjusted Executive

One group of executives handled the downsizing operation in a relatively well-adjusted way. From the interviews, no obvious dysfunctional reaction patterns could be discerned in these individuals; residual scarring was minimal. (I realized in making this classification that the appearance of normality could have been a veneer, the result of a properly executed defensive process. Because of a lack of corroborative evidence, however, I let this reaction pattern stand.)

The Compulsive–Ritualistic Executive

According to the extensive literature on the subject (elaborated in chapter 4), the compulsive personality is characterized by a preoccupation with order, parsimony, obstinacy, and perfection and by a need for mental and interpersonal control. This orientation is motivated by the aim to reduce anxiety and distress by maintaining a strong sense of control over oneself and one's environment and is achieved through self-imposed high standards. The compulsive's need for control is fulfilled by rigid attention to rules, procedures, and schedules.

The people in the study who belonged to this group were detail oriented (hearing all the notes but none of the music), excessively careful, inflexible, and prone to repetition. Characterized by interpersonal aloofness and restrained affectivity, they kept their emotions, "positive" as well as "negative," under tight control. They believed in complete deference to authority, bowing to the wishes of those above them. When they were in charge, they demanded deference from subordinates, giving rigid orders and insisting that those orders be followed to the letter.

Their need for control, whether conscious or not, and their self-imposed high standards often caused these personalities great distress. When the excessiveness of these traits was pointed out to them, they did not change their compulsive behavior, however, because that behavior served to maintain their psychic equilibrium.

The compulsive personalities in executive positions in the study devoted themselves almost exclusively to work and productivity. They hardly ever participated in leisure activities; and when they did, they felt uncomfortable about neglecting work. They were not apt to delegate tasks, and they did not easily work with other people. Meticulous and detailed planners, they were unwilling to consider changes even when the situation itself changed. They controlled both spending and employee conduct as tightly as they controlled their day planner.

One of the main defensive patterns found in this compulsive group of executives was that of isolation, which (see chapter 5) refers to the separation of an idea from the affect that accompanies it, but that remains repressed. While isolation can take on very primitive characteristics, in organizational life it is usually employed in a rather mature form: it generally takes the form of affect separated from cognition and manifests itself in such patterns as rationalization, moralization, compartmentalization, and intellectualization. As an example, by focusing on all the details of an issue, compulsive executives manage to avoid the affect-laden whole.

Given these tendencies, it is no surprise that compulsive executives reported conducting their downsizing operation in a precise and specific manner. They planned the complete downsizing procedure in great detail and then adhered to the plan exactly, without tolerance for even the smallest deviation. They reduced uncertainty as far as was humanly possible by meticulous planning, ritualistic follow-up, tight control, and a complete centralization of power.

Because one of the major impetuses of their behavior was an underlying fear of disapproval and punishment, the compulsive executives did everything to make others regard their behavior as "proper" and "correct." Priding themselves on their (perceived) fairness and sense of duty toward others, they followed rigid, mechanical procedures that reinforced their own and others' perception of the adequacy of such procedures. They hired consulting firms to activate certain functions in an effort to depersonalize layoffs, for example, and called outplacement firms into action to provide those "rightfully" laid off with a "fair chance" at reemployment through training in the job-search process. At the same time, they found in the downsizing process a legitimate outlet for their repressed hostility. By doing their utmost to present downsizing as a perfectly implemented process necessary for the good of everyone involved, they were thus able simultaneously to cater to the needs of their personality structure and to appease their sense of guilt.

One of the executives, a man typical of the compulsive–ritualistic type, responded to a question about how he felt when deciding to lay off 300 people with a speech about the company's need to attain a certain return on investment, the cost of the newly installed information system, and the dangers of the global situation. When prompted again about his feelings, he resumed his monologue, going into great detail about the criteria used in selecting both a consulting firm to assist in the restructuring process and an outplacement outfit to assist in helping those laid off. Then he launched into a commentary on the termination benefits that were given to the laid-off employees. In all of these comments, he never once referred to his feelings. When pressed yet again to discuss his feelings with respect to downsizing, he finally said that he felt it had been a job well done.

The Abrasive Executive

Research has shown that people with abrasive personalities share certain characteristics with compulsive–ritualistic individuals (Levinson, 1978). They too are driven, above all, by a strong need for perfection. They push themselves to achieve self-set, unrealistic expectations, attempting to match their current self-image to the person they would like to be. Despite all their efforts, however, they are unable to live up to those expectations and experience a mounting sense of frustration, which in turn evokes aggressive feelings. The strength of these aggressive feelings is determined by the extent of the discrepancy between where they perceive themselves to be and where they would like to be, a discrepancy that remains despite their best efforts. Because abrasive types have such exaggerated standards for themselves that most likely originated with their first caregivers, they are never able to completely close the perceived gap. Eventually, their anger and aggression can no longer be contained. Like water surging over a broken dam, their hostility and aggression spill over, directed toward colleagues and subordinates, family and friends.

The abrasive personality is usually highly intelligent, possesses excellent problem-solving skills, is quick at grasping situations, and is adept at finding workable solutions. Because of these qualities, people with this personality can frequently be found in senior executive positions. Their intelligence and quick wit, however, are often accompanied by impatience, arrogance, and a lack of interpersonal skills. These executives are intensely rivalrous; they know their own abilities and do not trust others to be equally capable. By showing open contempt for their subordinates, abrasive people create in their coworkers feelings of inadequacy that destroy self-confidence and suppress initiative and creativity. Like compulsive executives, they also feel a strong need for control of both self and others, which results in a tendency to dominate.

Abrasive personalities often show signs of "reactive narcissism," signs such as emotional coldness, grandiosity, vindictiveness, and a sense of entitlement. Because age-appropriate development did not occur when these individuals were growing up (probably due to a poor holding environment for frustrating experiences), many acquired a defective, poorly integrated sense of identity, leading to an unstable sense of self-esteem. Those early experiences may have left a legacy of bitterness and vindictiveness. Thus, apart from being forever frustrated in what they set out to do, some of them also experience an urge to get even for the wrongs they feel they have experienced.

Abrasive people use aggressive tactics in dealing with others which they have learned from their parents or other caretakers who used severe disciplinary measures to "tame" their offspring. They know from experience that coercion is the way to get other people to do what they want. They view others as extensions of themselves, as devices for their own self-aggrandizement, to be freely and legitimately used for their own purposes. Furthermore, they see themselves as special and feel that they deserve to be treated differently than others. Likewise, they believe that the boundaries of proper behavior do not apply to them.

The abrasive executives in the downsizing study, when put in charge of downsizing, generally adopted reaction patterns that corresponded to their personality traits. When laying people off, they resorted to the primitive defense mechanisms of splitting (as noted earlier, the division of objects into "good" and "bad") and devaluation in order to appease their strong feelings of guilt. Through splitting, they created an us-versus-them mentality in the organization, putting the blame for the problems the company found itself in on the employees who were about to be dismissed. In addition, they tended to rationalize the process by devaluing those subjected to it, that is, by belittling the people they had downsized, calling them "deadwood" or "rotten apples."

For example, one executive I interviewed kept harping about the people he had laid off. According to him, "It was those SOBs in my organization who were responsible for the company's decline in sales and profitability. Firing them was the best thing I've done in a long time. Good riddance. Actually, I've probably been too soft all along. I should have done it much sooner and fired more! Unfortunately, I was given free rein only recently, after the retirement of my predecessor." He also contrasted other corporate cultures with his own global corporation, making the splitting even more pronounced. It became clear from his conversation that these corporate cultures had been devalued and had carried the brunt of his downsizing effort. This executive's actions are reminiscent of the behavior of "Chainsaw Al" or "Rambo in Pinstripes" (alias Albert Dunlop), who is now celebrated as America's premier turnaround artist (Dunlop & Andelman, 1997). After directing a downsizing process at Scott Paper, he repeated this performance at Sunbeam Corporation where he got fired because of "creative accounting." Although he seems to be able to obtain short-term results (the shareholders at Scott have not done badly, nor has he), one can question the long-term effects of his brutal practices on the people in corporations that have had him at the helm.

This scapegoating of the victims, extreme as it may seem to most people, found strong resonance among some of the survivors in the organization. These survivors, who also needed defense mechanisms, in their case in order to cope with feelings of uncertainty and threat, turned to the previously described identification with the aggressor syndrome (A. Freud, 1966). In other words, they coped with their feelings of impotence by identifying with the executive who was in charge of their fate. This identification enhanced their self-esteem by creating the illusion of a merger with the powerful figure. Such alliances with the aggressor reinforced the survivors' often prevailing us-versus-them attitude, making them feel part of the "winning camp" and reinforcing the mental distance felt toward the victims. The result was a feeling of legitimacy in the scapegoating of the "losers" (Kets de Vries, 1980, 1993).

The dangers of having an abrasive executive in charge of the downsizing process seem obvious. Even in the best case, such a leader is likely to engender a negative, counterproductive attitude among employees. In the worst case, he or she can trigger a series of destructive processes among members of the organization that result in a disastrous outcome for the company's attempted renewal process.

The Dissociative Executive

One of the reaction patterns I found among executives who implemented downsizing was dissociation (see chapter 3). Allied to the denial defense, dissociation, the separation and exclusion of mental processes that are normally integrated, is a primitive way of dealing with stressful situations, an emergency measure in times of extreme stress. Typically, what sets this defense in motion is a situation charged with painful emotions and psychological conflict. Dissociation, which serves as a shut-off mechanism, an alteration in the perception of reality, is a way of protecting oneself against what are perceived to be unbearable experiences. As mentioned earlier, a person who resorts to this way of coping removes from conscious awareness and control a complex of associated mental elements such as thoughts, images, feelings, sensations, and desires. Dissociation is a distorted experience of the self associated with a sense of unreality (or strangeness) and profound detachment. In the words of one of the top executives who experienced dissociation:

> I wasn't really there when I had to fire a few hundred people. Granted, I was there physically, but certainly not emotionally. I remember distinctly being in a daze, standing in one of the company's meeting halls, trying to explain to the employees why they were going to be laid off. It was as if I were looking at myself from the outside, watching myself in a play. This sensation became even worse when I had to lay off people a second time. It was like I was acting in a dream!

Many of the executives in the downsizing study described themselves as being completely detached from what they were doing while engaged in downsizing, firing literally hundreds or even thousands of people. They felt like spectators in the process, going through the motions but not really feeling part of them. Although inner mental processes and external events went on exactly as before, these things lacked personal relation or meaning to the individual concerned. This feeling of unreality was experienced, as the above quote illustrates, as detachment from one's own mental processes or body. The person became an outside observer, feeling like an automaton or someone moving through a dream. Associated features were dizziness, anxiety, hypochondriacal concerns, fears of going insane, and disturbances in the sense of time and space.

A loss of the capacity to *experience* emotions occurred in dissociated executives, even though they sometimes appeared to *express* emotions. Some people experiencing dissociation were driven to vigorous activity to induce sensations intense enough to break through the wall of unreality. In the study, as in general, people prone to this disorder had a keen and unfailing awareness of the disturbance in their sense of reality. As a matter of fact, their self-observation capacities were heightened. Although they complained about feelings of estrangement and absence of emotions and often manifested considerable anxiety, they showed no evidence of either a major disturbance of affect or disorganized thought processes. As an occasional isolated experience, dissociation was rather common among the subjects of the downsizing study. In some people, however, it was a recurrent phenomenon, often accompanying depression.

The Alexithymic–Anhedonic Executive

While dissociation does not cause a major disturbance of affect, alexithymic manifestations can. Executives who suffered from alexithymiclike symptoms, especially people who repeatedly engaged in the process of downsizing, began to have problems with a diminishing ability to feel. In some instances, this developed into alexithymic reactions.

As we saw in chapter 2, alexithymics are emotionally color-blind. In the case of serious alexithymic reactions, individuals have an extreme reality-based cognitive style, an impoverished fantasy life, a paucity of inner emotional experience, a tendency to engage in stereotypical interpersonal behavior, and a speech pattern characterized by endless, trivial, repetitive details.

Some of the executives I spoke with had entered the work-force with a mildly alexithymic disposition; that is, they had difficulty experiencing and recognizing emotions from the outset. Others developed such tendencies after a specific stressful event or series of events. Those who worked in organizations in which control of emotions was the norm had these tendencies rein-forced; and certainly the traumatic experience of being the main actor in a downsizing process exacerbated them. Some of the people I talked with, veterans of downsizing, had become com-pletely numb after repeated downsizing. Executives susceptible to this disorder increasingly experienced difficulty feeling, yet they often ignored the distress signals given by their minds and bodies. Frequently, these people were somatizers, that is, they complained about vague medical problems while the real issue was emotional distress. As one executive said, when asked how he felt during the downsizing process, ''I really don't *know* how I feel; my wife tells me how I feel. To be honest, I'm quite confused about feelings. It's difficult for me to talk about emo-tional differentiations. I have no strong positive or negative feel-ings. But the process of having to engage in downsizing gives me a literal pain in the gut.''

After repeated downsizing efforts, some of these people acquired a sense of deadness; their behavior took on a robotlike quality. Because external details brought some life to their inner deadness, they often ended up using work as a kind of drug. They took flight into *doing* to prevent *experiencing*. The uncon-scious aim behind their detail-focused work orientation was to avoid painful reflection on the effects of downsizing.

As we saw in chapter 3, anhedonia, the loss of interest in and withdrawal from all activities that ordinarily provide plea-sure, is closely associated with alexithymia. This pattern mani-fests itself through difficulty in maintaining concentration and interest in the activities that previously occupied attention. A frequent complaint among the anhedonic executives in the down-sizing study was boredom. As their original enthusiasm about work faded, these executives became increasingly disinclined to engage in normal workplace activities. (This loss of pleasure was applicable to private life as well.) A number of the executives interviewed complained about their lack of work enjoyment, noting that their original enthusiasm for the job had dissipated. With both interest and concentration diminished, they tended toward procrastination, postponing decisions and becoming increasingly ineffective. Most felt that the continuous process of downsizing had contributed to their dissatisfaction with organizational life and life in general.

The Depressed Executive

It is only a small step from anhedonia to depression. I have already commented on the depressive reactions among the *victims* of the downsizing process. The experiences of the *implementers* were similar. In fact, depression was a regular occurrence among *most* of the downsizing interviewees, though it varied from simply a depressed mood and feelings of guilt to serious thoughts of and even attempts at suicide.

The depressed executives in the study generally experienced a flattening of affect, an inability to respond to the appropriate mood of the occasion. They were able to see only the darker side of things, preoccupied as they were with gloomy thoughts. Many perceived life as a burden, not worth living. In addition, they occasionally had inappropriate emotional reactions, bursting into tears at the workplace, for example. They also experienced a noticeable loss of energy: their activity level dropped, and they, like depressive victims, sometimes neglected their personal appearance. They tended to suffer from insomnia as well; and even if they slept, they often felt tired (or even exhausted) in the morning. They complained that food had lost its appeal, with weight loss a common result. Sexual interest also diminished: that special feeling of intimate enjoyment was no longer there, and in some instances impotence occurred.

Often executives who became depressed turned to self-accusation. In many, a remarkable switch occurred: after directing aggression outward in the process of downsizing, these executives now directed it inward. Due to this new sense of culpability, they were ready to believe the worst about themselves. And as the main executioners in a downsizing drama, they did not find it difficult to identify sins. Increasingly, they blamed themselves for the harm they had caused others.

Working Through Loss

Victims and survivors of the downsizing process were at opposite ends of the change spectrum. In comparing their situations, however, I noted some similarities in their reactions and in their cognitive and emotional approaches to events. Both groups had to endure extremely stressful events, both had to cope with the loss of colleagues and friends, and both had to "start a new life"—one that was bereft of the perceived security that had earlier governed their working identities.

The Process of Mourning

Most people work for more than just money; they have *intrinsic* motivators as well, one of which is the need for belonging. A sense of belonging to a larger unit is important in the establishment of a person's identity. To be part of an organization, to pursue a lasting career, offers that opportunity. For many people in the study, organizational and career identity were important in the construction of overall identity and thus constituted a major source of self-esteem.

Given the amount of time people spend at work, companies can be regarded as symbolic families. The people one interacts with on the job often become part of one's inner world and are therefore important for one's overall well-being. In the case of the subjects of the study, separation from members of this "family," whether through one's own layoff or that of colleagues, came with a sense of separation and loss. Such a loss, for most people, created a need to "mourn" and resulted in the sequence of four mourning reactions described in chapter 7 (Bowlby, 1980; Kets de Vries & Miller, 1984); (1) state of shock, (2) a state of disbelief, (3) discarding of the old way of doing things, and (4) realization of a new identity.

As people work through the three initial stages of the mourning process, they begin to discard past patterns of thinking, feeling, and acting. A gradual acceptance of the new situation develops, both personally and organizationally, along with a willingness to go through a process of self-examination. That self-examination results in a redefinition and even reinvention of the self. As the mourner tentatively explores new opportunities and seeks to establish a new equilibrium, he or she feels a growing sense of hope; new choices seem possible. A more proactive attitude and an orientation toward the future emerge. Arrival at this phase indicates that the person has come to grips with the new reality.

The downsizing study indicated that quite a few executives were unable to finish mourning what had happened to them. Unable to proceed beyond the early stages of the mourning process, they held on to primitive defense mechanisms, denying reality and clinging to the past. People caught in this situation continued to function as if nothing had happened, trying to uphold their illusions. Some people responded to the perceived withdrawal of status and respect with aggression and destruction. Others used displacement (redirection of anger away from the responsible party toward someone else), cognitive dissociation, and splitting as defense mechanisms.

Burnout

Recent research has pinpointed a relationship between the phenomenon of downsizing and both the increase in disability claims for mental disorders and the incidence of stress-induced illness

(Smith, 1994). For a number of people, downsizing is generally accompanied by emotional, cognitive, and physiological manifestations that can be grouped under the label *burnout*. Burnout is an amalgamation of stress reactions. The main symptoms are feelings of emotional exhaustion, lack of energy, and emptiness. Depersonalization and a cynical, dehumanizing, and negative attitude toward people combine in a stress syndrome that often accompanies cases of severe burnout (Cordes & Dougherty, 1993).

Burnout implies a deterioration of mental health symptomized by self-esteem problems, irritability, depression, helplessness, and free-floating anxiety. In addition to the emotional exhaustion, lack of energy, and emptiness mentioned earlier, symptoms include insomnia, headaches, nausea, chest pains, gastrointestinal disturbances (such as ulcers and colitis), and allergic reactions. The consequences of burnout include an increase in substance abuse, employee turnover, and absenteeism, and sometimes even suicide. Downsizing, because of its chronic stress and the disruption it brings to interpersonal contacts, may accelerate and amplify the manifestations of burnout (although there is no one-to-one correlation).

The downsizing study indicated that many of the victims of the downsizing process showed signs of burnout as a reaction to their layoff. Survivors and "executioners" also showed signs of burnout, especially after repeated layoffs. Coping patterns for all three groups were colored by these burnout symptoms.

Among the "executioners," the conflict surrounding role ambiguity was an important factor in the development of burnout. Executives tended to perceive themselves as the "builders" of the organization and the guardians of the well-being of their employees. Downsizing forced them to fire people, thus violating what they saw as their proper role. The guilt that this inner conflict created, coupled with the fact that downsizing layoffs were generally not a one-time occurrence but had to be implemented repeatedly, contributed to a sense of failure in executives. Blaming themselves for lacking the necessary skills to solve the problems of the organization, executives saw themselves as no longer competent; they lost their sense of achievement. The result was a diminished sense of self-esteem. Eventually, these conflicting feelings gave rise to burnout.

The Tactics of Downsizing

We have seen the great variety in reaction patterns typical among individuals affected by the downsizing process. That process, narrowly defined (that is, as stand-alone across-the-board cuts rather than layoffs that are part of a continuous corporate transformation), *however carefully it is done,* will leave wounds. However humane one tries to be, individuals will be hurt; and in the process, the company itself will be negatively affected. Successfully implementing a narrow downsizing effort is difficult if not impossible. Indeed, downsizing as a measure of expediency *inevitably* causes more harm than good. Only if downsizing is applied in its broader sense is the outlook more positive.

Moreover, even if an organization survives a narrowly construed downsizing, such a process is no guarantee of the company's future success. The most important dilemma remains: people need to believe in the new organization to make it work, but they need to see that it works in order to believe in it!

Many executives first face others' and their own unexpected emotional reactions when they are already deeply involved in downsizing activities. Even executives who have a detailed strategic plan generally stumble when they set out to realize that plan, because they fail to take into account one of the most significant determinants of the success or failure of their efforts: the behavior of the people involved. However, by acknowledging from the beginning that downsizing is an emotionally fraught process for all concerned and by actively preparing themselves and their subordinates for the various psychological reactions that are likely to emerge during the process, executives can significantly limit the likelihood of disaster.

To Downsize or Not to Downsize?

As we have seen, downsizing demands a considerable price in human suffering. And as the previous descriptions have shown, no party to the process is excluded from pain. Although downsizing in its narrowest sense has proven to be an operation whose costs generally exceed the benefits, the somber statistics that buttress that view do not seem to have deterred many companies from choosing downsizing, sometimes repeatedly. The key questions, then, are these: Taking into consideration the human factor, if an organization decides, in spite of the obvious risks, to go ahead with a narrowly construed downsizing effort, what is the best way to do it? And what can be done to avoid falling into the classic downsizing traps?

First of all, it must be remembered that every effort at downsizing is an attempt to change both the individual and the organization, a fact that has ramifications. As we saw in the previous chapter, some form of pain is necessary in effecting change. A stimulus to seek a new order of things, pain is a primary motivator. But students of human behavior also know that pain *alone* is not enough. Without pleasure somewhere in the equation, pain simply makes people depressed. Thus an additional necessary ingredient in the change process is hope. It is the hope of a new, exciting future that drives the people affected by the change process forward.

One of the common mistakes in early downsizing efforts, as I have noted, was seeking to remedy excessive costs, often the sole perceived reason for organizational ineffectiveness, through sharply reduced headcount alone. Selectivity in the process, grounded in an exciting vision for a new future, was conspicuously absent in these early efforts and remains elusive today. As I have emphasized repeatedly, however, mere headcount strategies, if not accompanied by adjustments in other components of the organization, are more often than not doomed to fail. Indiscriminate downsizing is reminiscent of surgery with an extremely dull scalpel. As I have indicated, layoffs, if considered necessary, have to be part of a comprehensive change process in the organization. This often includes a complete, systemic change in the company's culture, a "reengineering" process, achieved partly by the departure of employees lacking the necessary skills and flexibility and partly by an influx of new, enthusiastic people with the creativity and energy to reinvent the organization. Making investments in people in the form of training and education, and in new equipment and machines, sends a strong signal about management's belief in the organization's future. Such practices therefore lessen survivor guilt and limit dysfunctional coping patterns.

An important consideration in any downsizing effort is work redesign. A frequent complaint of survivors in the downsized organization is that the dismissal of employees results in an increased workload, putting an additional burden on already anxious and disoriented individuals. In order to avoid this unnecessary strain, it is essential for management to clarify each person's new role, responsibility, and workload.

The Dynamics of Layoffs

One of the most essential preimplementation tasks of executives involved in a downsizing operation is the development of a coherent strategic rationale for layoffs. In the early days of downsizing, employees were often laid off *en masse* or encouraged to leave through early retirement offers or "golden handshakes." Having made no deliberate personnel selection, management was content to see as many people as possible leave the organization. I have already indicated that such across-the-board cuts usually lead to the loss of organizational muscle, in the form of essential knowledge and memory. The departure of key employees may, in the worst case, result in the complete demise of the organization. By first picturing in detail the future organization and carefully choosing the key employees necessary to run it, and then constructing a new organizational chart around these key people (offering them better positions or an augmentation in salary, even if only a small amount), organizations can avoid expensive mistakes that result in the costly retraining of survivors, the rehiring of already fired employees (for a price!), and the need to resort to outside consultants.

An important consideration when layoffs are deemed unavoidable for the company's survival is the speed with which dismissals are implemented. Even though downsizing should be part of a gradual, continuous corporate renewal process, a way of life rather than a one-shot move, management must remember that a stable working environment is crucial to the psychological well-being of both victims and survivors. Human beings generally have a low level of tolerance for uncertainty. As a matter of fact, the work of worrying about what *might* happen can be more stressful than the feared event itself. When faced with the threat of uncertainty, people appease their anxiety by acting impulsively and destructively as they attempt to steady their disturbed psychological equilibrium. Keeping the possibility of layoffs dangling above the survivors' heads for weeks or even months results in an atmosphere of fear and paranoia that leads to diminished productivity and can trigger organizational paralysis.

The Importance of Communication

Communication is one of the most significant aspects of the downsizing process, yet, as mentioned earlier, executives often reduce communication while downsizing. There are numerous reasons for this. Time constraints head the list: executives face increased pressure, too much to do in too little time, when involved in radical corporate transformation. Furthermore, they are reluctant to confront people face to face with bad news, not realizing that giving false hope to employees might have dire consequences. Employees who try to cope by denying the situation will, if not given clear warning signals, make no serious attempt to look for other work. As a result, they will be caught unprepared when the ax falls.

As I have noted, downsizing executives often withdraw from the rest of the workforce, concentrating on the technical aspects of the process out of fear for their own and their employees' emotional reactions. These executives see communication as "idle chatting," a waste of time, and do not realize that a lack of accessibility results in growing distrust on the part of employees. They fail to see that being open about the dilemma and showing that they are not indifferent to it are likely to trigger sympathy and thus a greater willingness on the part of the employees to cooperate and pull the company through.

A further reason for insufficient communication may be executives' reluctance to share disturbing information for fear of causing damage to morale and productivity. Yet, as has been mentioned, it is precisely the lack of realistic information that is apt to cause the greatest damage. Employees usually know more than management is aware of; and what they do not know, they try to piece together from information obtained from various sources. This gives rise to rumors, often wildly exaggerating reality, that distract employees and mortally wound morale. One of the most effective ways for executives to maintain credibility and trust is to communicate everything, constantly, and in detail. By being accessible and interacting frequently with employees, management is in the position to provide reassurance to those in need of it by clarifying the situation and being honest and open about its consequences.

Managing the Victims

One of the most crucial factors in the success of a downsizing process is the executives' behavior toward the victims. Careful handling of those who are laid off benefits the organization as well as the victims. As we have seen, survivors react strongly to what they perceive as unfair treatment of those who have been laid off. Clearly, survivors' behavior, morale, and productivity are directly affected by the way layoffs are managed. By providing the victims with tangible caretaking services (such as outplacement consulting and psychological and career counseling), actively trying to help them find new jobs, and assisting them in bridging the transition, management can make the best of a precarious situation.

Conclusion

While I hope that this chapter will contribute to a better understanding of the impact of downsizing on the individual, this exploratory study makes it clear that much more work has to be done before the key parameters of downsizing are fully understood. As I have demonstrated, downsizing is a process that brings out a myriad of poorly understood emotional reactions. We have seen that downsizing, when not done properly, particularly if interpreted in its narrowest sense, can be a very blunt instrument, one that wounds people's deepest value and belief systems and thereby causes a great deal of stress. Monitoring the stress level of the different parties in the process is therefore essential, as is the facilitation of constructive coping strategies.

At the center of the downsizing process is the way people deal with change, the subject of the previous chapter. Only those who are knowledgeable about the process of individual change and corporate transformation can get a solid handle on downsizing. Indeed, we would do well to abandon the word *downsizing* altogether and replace it with the term *corporate transformation*, the process of continuously aligning the organization with its environment and shaping an organizational culture in which the enduring encouragement of new challenges stands central. Reframing the term in this wider sense offers a much more constructive way of looking at the process. Those who are ready to join in this process of continuous challenge and learning can take encouragement from the words of the French philosopher Montaigne: "It is the journey, not the arrival, that matters."

References

Appelbaum, S. H., Simpson, R., & Shapiro, B. T. (1987). The tough tests of downsizing. *Organizational Dynamics, 16,* 68–79.

Baumohl, B. (1993, March 15). When downsizing becomes dumbsizing. *Time, 55,* 55.

Bennett, A. (1991, June 6). Management: Downsizing does not necessarily bring an upswing in corporate profitability. *Wall Street Journal,* B-1.

Bowlby, J. (1980). *Attachment and loss: Vol. 3. Loss.* New York: Basic Books.

Brockner, J. (1988). The effect of work layoffs on survivors: Research, theory, and practice. In B. M. Shaw & L. L. Cummings (Eds.), *Research in organizational behavior* (Vol. 10, pp. 212–255). Greenwich, CT: JAI Press.

Brockner, J. (1992). Managing the effects of layoffs on survivors. *California Management Review, 34,* 9–28.

Brockner, J., Davy, J., & Carter, C. (1985). Layoffs, self-esteem, and survivor guilt: Motivational, affective, and attitudinal consequences. *Organizational Behavior and Human Decision Processes, 36,* 229–244.

Brockner, J. et al. (1987). Survivors' reactions to layoffs: We get by with a little help from our friends. *Administrative Science Quarterly, 32,* 526–541.

Cameron, K. S. (1994). Strategies for successful organizational downsizing. *Human Resource Management, 33,* 189–211.

Cameron, K. S., Freeman, S. J., & Mishra, A. K. (1991). Best practices in white-collar downsizing: Managing contradictions. *Academy of Management Executive, 5,* 57–73.

Cameron, K. S., Freeman, S. J., & Mishra, A. K. (1993). Organizational downsizing and redesign. In G. P. Huber & W. H. Glick (Eds.), *Organizational change and redesign* (pp. 19–63). Oxford: Oxford University Press.

Cameron, K. S., Kim, M. U., & Whetten, D. A. (1987). Organizational effects of decline and turbulence. *Administrative Science Quarterly, 32,* 222–240.

Cascio, W. F. (1993). Downsizing: What do we know? What have we learned? *Academy of Management Executive, 7,* 95–104.

Cordes, C. L., & Dougherty, J. T. W. (1993). A review and an integration of research on job burnout. *Academy of Management Review, 18,* 621–656.

Custer, G. (1994, October). Downsizing's fallout may be widespread. *APA Monitor,* 49–50.

Dunlop, A., & Andelman, B. (1997). *Mean business.* New York: Fireside.

Freeman, S. J., & Cameron, K. S. (1993). Organizational downsizing: A convergence and reorientation framework. *Organization Science, 4,* 10–28.

Freud, A. (1966). *The ego and the mechanisms of defense* (rev. ed.). New York: International Universities Press. (Original work published 1936)

Greenhalgh, L., & Jick, T. (1989). Survivor sense making and reactions to organizational decline: Effects of individual differences. *Management Communication Quarterly, 2,* 305–328.

Greenhalgh, L., & Rosenblatt, Z. (1984). Job insecurity: Toward conceptual clarity. *Academy of Management Review, 9,* 438–448.

Henkoff, R. (1990). Cost cutting: How to do it right. *Fortune, 121,* 40–49.

Henkoff, R. (1994). Getting beyond downsizing. *Fortune, 129,* 30–34.

Kets de Vries, M. F. R. (1980). *Organizational procedures: Clinical approaches to management.* London: Routledge.

Kets de Vries, M. F. R. (1993). Doing a Maxwell: Or why not to identify with the aggressor. *European Management Journal, 11,* 169–174.

Kets de Vries, M. F. R., & Miller, D. (1984). *The neurotic organization: Diagnosing and changing counterproductive styles of management.* San Francisco: Jossey-Bass.

Lalli, F. (1992, February). Learn from my mistakes. *Money,* 5.

Leana, C., & Feldman, D. C. (1988). Individual responses to job loss: Perceptions, reactions, and coping behaviors. *Journal of Management, 14,* 375–389.

Leana, C., & Feldman, D. C. (1990). Individual responses to job loss: Empirical findings from two field studies. *Human Relations, 43,* 1155–1181.

Levinson, H. (1962). *Men, management, and mental health.* Cambridge, MA: Harvard University Press.

Levinson, H. (1978, May, June). The abrasive personality. *Harvard Business Review,* 86–94.

Mone, M. (1994). Relationships between self-concepts, aspirations, emotional responses, and intent to leave a downsizing organization. *Human Resource Management, 33,* 281–298.

Navran, F. (1994). Surviving a downsizing. *Executive Excellence, 11,* 12–13.

Noer, D. M. (1993). *Healing the wounds: Overcoming the trauma of layoffs and revitalizing downsized organizations.* San Francisco: Jossey-Bass.

Pearlstein, S. (1994, January 4). Corporate cutbacks yet to pay off. *Washington Post,* B-6.

Smith, L. (1994). Burned-out bosses. *Fortune, 130,* 100–105.

Thornburg, L. (1992). Practical ways to cope with suicide. *HR Magazine, 37,* 62–66.

Conclusion

You know life . . . it's rather like opening a tin of sardines. We are all of us looking for the key. (Alan Bennett, *Beyond the Fringe*)

Only the insane take themselves quite seriously. (Sir Max Beerbohm)

I make myself laugh at everything, for fear of having to cry.
(Pierre-Augustin Beaumarchais, *Le Barbier de Seville*)

If you live long enough, you'll find that every victory turns into defeat.
(Simone de Beauvoir, *Tout les hommes sont mortels*)

So little done. So much to do. (Alexander Bell, last words)

Recently, I visited an exhibition at the Museum of Modern Art in Stockholm. Among the various objects featured, all of which mirrored the absurdity of present-day society, I was struck by two items in particular. One was a display called "The State Hospital" by the American artist Edward Kienholz. This display leaves no visitor untouched; it has a devastating emotional impact. Looking through a barred window, one is faced with an extraordinarily depressing scene: a cell in a ward for senile patients with a naked old man strapped to the lower bunk, his body like a skeleton covered with a leathery skin. To round off this disagreeable scene, a chamber pot has been placed on the floor. The old man's head is a fishbowl with a few live goldfish in it, of whom one occasionally can catch a glimpse as they swim by. Like comic-strip figures who have bubbles above their heads holding text describing their thoughts, this person has a bubble made of plexiglass illuminated by neon. This bubble, though, encircles an unusual form of "text": an exact copy of

291

the person. A double of the old man is strapped to the upper bunk, his head also made up of a fishbowl with live goldfish.

The reason this scene is so devastating, creating a sense of horror and pity, is that we realize that the complete mental life of the patient is contained in this bubble. He lives in a world without hope, fantasy, or play. He is like the fish in the fishbowl—senseless, going around in circles. For this person, there is only the immediate present. There is no past, no memories; there is no future. He is engaged in total operational thinking. Oblivious to what is happening in the world around him, he has withdrawn into a narcissistic cocoon. Relationships with other people are almost nonexistent, perfunctory at best. He evokes the horror of being dead (in effect) while appearing alive. His is a life without purpose or meaning.

As part of the same exhibition that housed the Kienholz piece, the museum had another display that concerned an old man. But in this case there was lots of life. This old man was a person who knew how to play, how to stay alive and remain mentally alert, how to connect with people. The display showed a number of pictures taken in Iceland of what can best be described as the "inside outside house." What got this project started was a story in a book titled *Islenzkur Adall* (Icelandic Aristocracy). This book by Thobergur Thordarson (1984) recounted the life of a number of unusual people in Iceland. One of the "aristocrats" mentioned in the book was Solon Gudmundson, who lived in a small fishing village in northwest Iceland. Solon seemed to have been a man of many talents, poetry and carpentry being among them. At times he would make very special and personal objects that served no practical purpose except to help develop his and other people's consciousness. Although (because of his bizarre behavior) some people might have called him mad, his madness was accepted because he didn't bother anybody. He was able to take care of himself and others. Furthermore, his art enriched the village; it was a welcome topic of conversation.

When he was an old man, Gudmundson sold his house and decided to build a new one using mostly wood and corrugated iron, building materials that are widely employed in Iceland. He planned, however, to build the new house differently. He wanted to construct the building in reverse order. His idea was to put corrugated iron on the inside and finish the outside with wallpaper. When asked why he planned to build the house in such a way, he answered with a faint smile: "Wallpaper is to please the eye, love, so it is reasonable to have it on the outside where more people can enjoy it." He did not get very far with the project, however. Some very concerned friends managed (with considerable difficulty) to persuade him to retire to an old people's home. There he was well cared for until he died in 1931. In the summer of 1974, a small house was built in the same fashion as Gudmundson intended to construct it nearly half a century earlier.

Compare the man in the state hospital, one of the walking dead, with Gudmundson, who seemed to be very much alive, animating other people with his topsy-turvy ideas. He was a person who turned the world upside down, and in doing so helped people see things in a different way. In fact, he is *still* having a positive effect: he puts us in touch with our irrational side; he stimulates the exploratory part of us; he makes us laugh. He is a person who creates meaning by presenting paradoxes.

Transcending the Irrational

Our journey through the various essays of this book was a search for meaning, an effort to make sense out of human behavior in organizations that is apparently irrational. My objective in this book was to help readers look beyond the obvious, help them realize (though maybe not in such a stark way as Kienholz or the artist who depicted Gudmundson) that there is another world out there beyond the directly observable. It is my hope that the texts presented will help readers decipher the absurd, the irratio-nal, and the incomprehensible in their own organization, will help them see that superficially strange behavior is not in the realm of mystery. Decoding organizational scripts through an understanding of executives' inner theaters and connecting these scripts with espoused rational actions may help readers become more effective organizational detectives and may result in better decision making.

As a means of establishing identity and maintaining self-esteem, work has always been an anchor of psychic well-being. Freud's primary criteria of mental health—*Liebe und Arbeit* (love and work)—still have the ring of truth. It is because work is so essential to human existence that becoming more adept at organizational sense making is important. Dysfunctional work-place behavior, particularly when acted out by senior executives, can have a ripple effect, not only causing organizational disequi-librium but also seriously affecting all the players who make up the organization. Those with the ability to make sense out of the surrounding chaos will be best able to maintain their mental equi-librium.

As the various essays in this book have indicated, irrational behavior in organizations is not a rarity; on the contrary, it is ever present. In fact, as psychoanalyst and sociologist Eliott Jaques has pointed out, organizations actually contribute to de-pressive and persecutory anxiety, thereby exacerbating worker irrationality (Jaques, 1955). There are many undercurrents in organizational life that cause executives to deviate from the tasks to be accomplished, creating an irrational dimension (Bion, 1959). Much as we hate to admit it, these organizational under-currents are an inevitable part of the human condition.

The Importance of Real Work

Because organizations are invested with a considerable amount of psychological meaning, affiliation with an organization is one of the ways individuals cope with economic and social upheaval; that affiliation contributes to a measure of stability. Organizations serve as orientation points in a sea of change, as outlets that help their members cope with the stresses and strains of daily life. To prevent irrational undercurrents from derailing the real work that has to be accomplished, dependable, trust-inspiring leadership has to "contain" and constructively direct these undercurrents to a common purpose.

Unfortunately, many organizations once assumed responsibility for the role of providing a "holding environment" to contain the anxiety and other emotions of their workers, through the agency of senior management, are now unwilling to take on this function. Other times it is not a matter of willingness: managers who do not possess what I have called the "teddy bear" quality, who are emotionally "illiterate," are simply unable to provide this containment function. When the unspoken psychological contract described in chapter 8, that provides for emotional containment, is broken, people become distrustful and anxious and the undercurrents come to the fore. Some people respond with fight-or-flight behavior, as expressed in political games and turf fights. Others choose withdrawal from the organization or isolation from their colleagues. As people become increasingly anxious and distrustful, their dependency needs surge, hampering effective decision making, and their social defenses detract from the real work people in organizations have to undertake. All these developments augur ill for the future of the organization, contributing to an increasing sense of meaninglessness about work and prompting employees to devote their attention and energy elsewhere.

Humankind's Search for Meaning

The man in the cell in the state hospital symbolizes the death of meaning. In contrast, Gudmundson celebrated life; he realized that without meaning we are dead. *Meaning* is that arena where the soma (the body), the ego, and the polis (the social side of the person) meet. Unlike animals, which are guided by their instincts rather than by lengthy developmental processes, people need to see meaning in their activities, relationships, and lives.

According to the psychiatrist Victor Frankl, "Life can be made meaningful in a threefold way: first through what we give to life (in terms of our creative work); second in what we take from the world (in terms of our experiencing values); and third, through the stand we take toward a fate we can no longer change (an incurable disease, an inoperable cancer; or the like) (1963, 1967). Meaning is revealed through a sense of illumination that arises from these three elements. It implies acquiring a sense of balance between inner and outer reality. It is the affirmation of the person within a sea of social forces, the experience of being part of something, of feeling effective.

In short, individuals need to commit themselves to issues and actions that are valuable, that have a positive impact. Naturally, such commitments are experienced in a highly subjective manner. True meaning, however, is derived only from commitments to certain emotionally invested objectives and causes that drive a person to transcend his or her own abilities. For most of us, the search for meaning is the search for continuity in a life of discontinuity, the acquisition of a finality that goes beyond the individual.

Although we all have our own subjective interpretations of this search for meaning, the motivational need systems described in the Introduction (attachment and exploration, for example, which are means of self-affirmation) are important guides in the search. These need systems create a subjective reality that serves as a marker in an individual's life course. To attain a sense of balance between inner and outer reality, experiences of meaning have to relate to the kinds of activities that reverberate with the basic motivational need systems. This "match" between subjective and social world makes for a sense of authenticity, constancy, and hope.

In this search for meaning, for continuity, leaving some kind of legacy is an important component. Work, particularly creative work, can offer such a legacy. The investment of energy through meaningful activity at work transcends personal concerns and is of particular value in creating a sense of continuity. It makes for a sense of significance and orientation. The creation of a "heroic self-image" through work is an affirmation of the person's sense of self and identity; as such, it can be an important form of narcissistic gratification.

Any student interested in humane and effective organizations should ask him- or herself how these motivational needs centered around work that drives humankind's search for meaning can be integrated into organizational life. What can organizational leaders do to make people's existence in their organizations more meaningful? In this age of discontinuity, what can be done to minimize the negative side effects of organizational life? What can be done to give employees the kind of purpose that encourages them to "stretch" themselves?

Values of Effective Organizations

The question of attaining stretch is not new. Organizational leadership has always been on the outlook for better ways to create a greater sense of purpose among employees. From mission statements in annual reports to celebrations at company picnics, senior executives have tried to find the answer to this question. In their own search for meaning, senior executives have created visions, presented descriptions of the organization's purpose, and made statements about the values and beliefs that make up the organization's corporate culture.

Unfortunately, in most instances, the bulk of managerial attention is usually devoted to quantitative objectives—such factors as profit maximization, return on investment, and shareholder value. Such criteria are important, to be sure, but they are insufficient in creating the kinds of organizations that get the best out of people. Although specific quantitative criteria can be viewed as milestones that have to be reached for satisfactory performance, they are not enough to create a sense of "flow"—that feeling of exhilaration and total involvement that makes individuals lose a sense of time—and inspire people to make an extraordinary effort (Csikszentmihalyi, 1997). To achieve those loftier goals, we need to go beyond purely quantitative criteria to specific values and beliefs that determine the norms of appropriate organizational behavior. It is these values and beliefs that determine whether organizational members can subsume their own sense of meaning under that of the larger organizational entity.

My observations of high-performance organizations have shown me a number of values that are salient. As my discussion of teamwork among the pygmies (chapter 6) indicated, one of the most important organizational values is a team orientation, a willingness to subdue one's own personal objectives to those of the team. Candor, the willingness to communicate frankly and openly, is also on this list, and because candor cannot exist in the absence of trust, that too must be included. A feeling of trust is based on concepts of fairness, credibility, consistency, competence, honesty, mutual support and respect, and integrity. In organizations grounded in those elements, empowerment is not an empty slogan; decision-making authority truly is driven deep down. People have a sense that they can affect organizational performance; they have a voice and are being listened to. Furthermore, those elements stifle paranoid thinking.

Another value high on this list is respect for the individual, which results in tolerance for differences. Although many companies subscribe to this value on paper, few behave accordingly. In many organizations, or so we can conclude from corporate behavior, only lip service is given to this value. The incredible success of the Dilbert cartoons highlights the discrepancy between organizational rhetoric and reality.

Other values should also be included on this list. For example, high-performance organizations are market driven; they have a customer focus that sends them out of their way to satisfy their customers, be they external or internal. Another prevailing value is competitiveness; employees that drive great companies are characterized by a strong achievement orientation. Management of such companies hold innovation as a core value. They seek to attract and foster people with an entrepreneurial attitude, and they create a corporate culture in which people are not afraid to take risks because failure is accepted. But work is not all fun and games in high-performance organizations; accountability is also emphasized. People in these organizations are aware that, as the saying goes, what doesn't get measured doesn't get done.

Continuous learning is also among the key values in high-performance companies. To prevent a sense of stagnation, people need continuous growth and development. Speed of action, starting at the top, is another important characteristic of these companies. A sense of fair play is crucial as well; employees must feel that they are treated equitably. Furthermore, successful organizations have a commitment to constructive feedback; employees are given suggestions on how to do things better, and successes are recognized and celebrated.

But all of the preceding values are worthless in the absence of a compelling, connecting vision shared by all. Everyone in the organization, from the CEO to the mail clerk, needs to sense that they are a necessary part of that vision. And they must all be strongly committed to making that vision reality. In the process of carrying out the corporate vision, senior executives must "walk the talk"; that is, practice what they preach.

Meta values That Make for "Flow"

Although the values and practices described above go a long way toward explaining the success of many high-performance companies, are these values *sufficient* to explain exceptional performance? Need other values be espoused by organizations that hope to get the best out of their people? Given humankind's deep desire for meaning, are there other steps that can be taken to make life more meaningful in organizations, that can help create a sense of transcendence?

I have found at least a partial answer to these questions by talking with executives in the field. Time after time I have asked executives about those experiences that they most valued in their organizations, about those circumstances under which they felt at their best, about those times when they experienced a sense of flow, about incidents that made them feel as excited as they had as kids. The responses generally include the following: being involved in a start-up activity, being involved in a turnaround process, being part of a high-performance team, being engaged in successful mentoring. When we take a closer look at these responses, we discover that they dovetail with the basic motivational needs mentioned earlier.

Apparently, engaging in a start-up or turnaround activity provides a sense of meaning. Participating in such activities gratifies people's sense of exploration; it allows the opportunity to do something new and to grow; it permits individuals to assert themselves. It also implies the act of creating something that can be left as a kind of legacy. The affiliative motivational system comes to the fore through the sense of community created by being part of a high-performance team and through the sense of generativity implied in engaging in successful mentoring. Getting pleasure out of seeing the next generation grow and develop offers a meaningful form of continuity.

One conclusion that can be drawn from this kind of feedback from executives is that the best companies possess a set of metavalues that closely echo the earlier described motivational need systems. Because attachment and affiliation make for a powerful underlying motive in humankind's search for meaning, the first important meta value contributing to exceptional performance is the organizational version of *love:* a family feeling, a sense of community. Attachment and affiliation are the basis for trust, mutual respect, and a holding environment where people feel safe. High-quality interpersonal relationships within the organization serve as a way of dealing with existential loneliness, which is a basic form of anxiety. This sense of community—the preparedness to help others—goes a long way toward creating a cohesive culture and a sense of goal-directedness. It also helps foster distributed leadership (as described in chapter 6). In organizations that encourage healthy ways of relating, senior executives obtain vicarious pleasure from seeing their younger executives grow. This sense of generativity, this willingness to take on the role of coach and mentor, sets "loving" organizations apart.

Furthermore, employees in successful companies seem to enjoy themselves; they seem to have *fun*. In too many companies this second metavalue is completely ignored. When working becomes a chore, employees may feel like the mental patient depicted by Kienholz. In organizations that do not value fun, executives behave like zombies at the office; they sleepwalk through their day living depersonalized lives in depersonalized organizations. Insightful executives in high-performance organizations have realized, however, that taking people on an exciting adventure can make all the difference in inspiring them to make an exceptional effort. That is because having fun at work gratifies another essential motivational need: humankind's need for exploration and assertion.

If organizations, by addressing these basic motivational need systems underlying humankind's search for meaning, help employees transcend their own personal needs, help them contribute something to society, the impact can be extremely powerful. Naturally, companies operating in certain industries have a competitive advantage. (Consider, for example, companies in the biotechnology industry working to preserve and improve human life, or the field of education.) Companies that lack a specific humanitarian focus can also assist employees in their search for meaning, however, for example, by encouraging them to engage in community projects at company expense. (Timberland, Fannie Mae, and Samhout are good examples of this sort of organization.)

A Summing Up

The antidote to humankind's fear of death is the embracing of life, the acceptance of our human condition, the creation of meaning. The meaning we all seek is related to a sense of accomplishment and personal competence, the creation of something of value. It has to do with the desire to affirm our existence, the wish to transcend our personal death and to leave something behind. The challenge to organizational leaders is to recognize humankind's search for meaning and create circumstances that allow people in organizations to go beyond narrowly defined organizational vision and mission statements. Organizational leaders have the responsibility to institute collective systems of meaning, to stimulate the collective imagination of their people. They have to create a congruence between personal and collective objectives so that the work done in their organizations makes sense to their people, a feeling that develops only when people's individual motivational need systems and the organization's values are aligned. When that alignment exists, organizations are embued with meaning, allowing employees to make the exceptional effort that characterizes great companies.

Leaders who take such initiatives create what can be described as *authentizotic* organizations. This term is derived from two Greek words: *authenteekos* and *zoteekos*. The first conveys the idea that the organization is *authentic*. In its broadest sense, the word *authentic* describes something that conforms to fact and is therefore worthy of trust and reliance. As a workplace label, *authenticity* implies that the organization has a compelling connective quality for its employees in its vision, mission, culture, and structure. The organization's leadership has communicated clearly and convincingly not only the *how* but also the *why,* revealing meaning in each person's role. These are the kinds of organizations where people find a sense of flow; where they feel complete and alive.

The term *zoteekos* means "vital to life." In the organizational context, it describes the way in which people are invigorated by their work. People in organizations to which the *zoteekos* label can be applied feel a sense of balance and completeness. In such organizations, the human need for exploration, closely associated with cognition and learning, is met. The *zoteekos* element of this type of organization allows for self-assertion in the workplace and produces a sense of effectiveness and competency, of autonomy, initiative, creativity, entrepreneurship, and industry.

With the entry into the twenty-first century, it becomes the challenge of organizational leadership to create corporations that possess these authentizotic qualities. Working in such organizations will be an antidote to stress, provide a healthier existence, increase the imagination, and contribute to a more fulfilling life. These will be the kinds of organizations that help their employees maintain an effective balance between personal and organizational life.

Creating authentizotic organizations, however, is not a simple assignment as the rise and fall of many organizations indicates. The leadership equation contains numerous traps. As the saying goes, nothing kills like success. Hubris is a common trait among organizational leaders. As many of the anecdotes in these chapters have shown, being in a position of leadership invites reality distortion and dysfunctional action. When leaders are exposed to the projective processes of subordinates who want to please people in positions of power and authority, many lose the ability to distinguish between reality and fantasy. They become like the famously obese Ottoman Sultan Abdulaziz, who inspected his 350-pound bulk in a special slimming mirror every morning. He wanted to see only what he hoped to see. That sort of self-deception is as unhealthy for the organization as it is for the individual. Such distorted mirroring does not contribute to the creation of authentizotic organizations. On the contrary, the absence of reflection in action, the lack of self-awareness about the effects of one's behavior, may have organizational pathology as a consequence. In the final analysis it is only congruence between the inner and the outer worlds that will foster both individual *and* organizational health. As the American humorist

James Thurber allegedly said, ''All men should strive to learn, before they die, what they are running from, and to, and why.''

References

Bion, W. R. (1959). *Experiences in groups, and other papers.* London: Tavistock.

Csikszentmihalyi, M. (1997). *Finding flow.* New York: Basic Books.

Frankl, V. E. (1963). *Man's search for meaning: An introduction to logotherapy.* Boston: Beacon Press.

Frankl, V. E. (1967). *Psychotherapy and existentialism: Selected papers on logotherapy.* New York: Washington Square Press.

Jaques, E. (1955). Social systems as a defense against persecutory and depressive anxiety. In M. Klein, P. Heimann, & R. Money-Kyrle (Eds.), *New directions in psychoanalysis* (pp. 478–499). London: Tavistock.

Thordarson, T. (1984). *Islenzkur Adall.* Reykjavik: Malog Menning.

About the Author

MANFRED F. R. KETS DE VRIES brings a different view to the much studied subjects of leadership and the dynamics of individual and organizational change. Applying his eclectic training as an economist (Econ. Drs., University of Amsterdam), student of management (ITP, MBA, and DBA, Harvard Business School), and psychoanalyst (Canadian Psychoanalytic Society and the International Psychoanalytic Association), he probes the interface between international management, psychoanalysis, psychotherapy, and dynamic psychiatry. His specific areas of interest are leadership, career dynamics, executive stress, entrepreneurship, family business, succession planning, cross-cultural management, and the dynamics of corporate transformation and change. A clinical professor of leadership development, he holds the Raoul de Vitry d'Avaucourt Chair of Human Resource Management at INSEAD, Fontainebleau, France (and has five times received INSEAD's distinguished teacher award). He is program director of INSEAD's top management program, "The Challenge of Leadership: Developing Your Emotional Intelligence" and co-program director of the joint master/diploma program "Coaching and Consulting for Change." He has also held professorships at McGill University, the Ecole des Hautes Etudes Commerciales, Montreal, and the Harvard Business School, and he has lectured at management institutions around the world. He is a member of numerous editorial boards and a founding member of the International Society for the Psychoanalytic Study of

Organizations. *The Financial Times, Le Capital, Wirtschafts-woche,* and *The Economist* have called Manfred Kets de Vries one of Europe's leading management thinkers.

Kets de Vries is the author, co-author, or editor of 17 books, including *Power and the Corporate Mind* (1975, new edition 1985, with Abraham Zaleznik), *Organizational Paradoxes: Clinical Approaches to Management* (1980, new edition 1994), *The Irrational Executive: Psychoanalytic Explorations in Management* (1984, editor), *The Neurotic Organization: Diagnosing and Changing Counter-Productive Styles of Management* (1984, new edition 1990, with Danny Miller), *Unstable at the Top* (1988, with Danny Miller), *Prisoners of Leadership* (1989), *Handbook of Character Studies* (1991, with Sidney Perzow), *Organizations on the Couch* (1991), *Leaders, Fools and Impostors* (1993), the prize-winning *Life and Death in the Executive Fast Lane: Essays on Organizations and Leadership* (1995) (the Critics' Choice Award 1995–1996), *Family Business: Human Dilemmas in the Family Firm* (1996), *The New Global Leaders: Percy Barnevik, Richard Branson, and David Simon* (1999, with Elizabeth Florent), *Struggling with the Demon: Perspectives on Individual and Organizational Irrationality* (2000), *Meditations on Happiness* (forthcoming), and *The Leadership Mystique* (forthcoming).

In addition, Kets de Vries has published over 150 scientific papers as chapters in books and as articles in such journals as *Behavioral Science, Journal of Management Studies, Human Relations, Administration & Society, Organizational Dynamics, Strategic Management Journal, Academy of Management Journal, Academy of Management Review, Journal of Forecasting, California Management Review, Harvard Business Review, Sloan Management Review, Academy of Management Executive, Psychoanalytic Review, Bulletin of the Menninger Clinic, Journal of Applied Behavioral Science, European Management Journal, Harper's* and *Psychology Today.* Furthermore, he has written numerous case studies, including six that received the best case of the year award. He is a regular columnist for a number of magazines. His work has been featured in such publications as *The New York Times, The Wall Street Journal, The Los Angeles Times, Fortune, Business Week, The Economist, The Financial Times,* and *The Herald Tribune.* His books and articles have been translated into fourteen languages.

Kets de Vries is a consultant on organizational design/transformation and strategic human resource management to leading U.S., Canadian, European, African, and Asian companies. He has done executive development, consulting, and coaching work in over thirty countries with companies such as Volvo Car Corporation, NovoNordisk, KPMG, Novartis, Heineken, Air Liquide, Alcan, Alcatel, Shell, BP, Unilever, ABB, Aegon, Hypo Vereinsbank, L.M. Ericsson, Lufthansa, Nokia, Bonnier, Rank Xerox, BZW, Investec, SHV, Andersen Consulting, GE Capital, Bain Consulting, Bang & Olufsen, Goldman Sachs, and Lego. The Dutch government has made him an Officer in the Order of Oranje Nassau. He was also the first fly fisherman in Outer Mongolia and is a member of New York's Explorers Club.

Name Index

Subject Index